The Modern

Spanish Stage

The Modern Spanish Stage

FOUR PLAYS

Edited by Marion Holt

A MERMAID DRAMABOOK

Hill & Wang
New York

Contents

Introduction   vii
Chronologies of Plays   xxiii

THE CONCERT AT SAINT OVIDE   1
(*El concierto de San Ovidio*)
   By Antonio Buero Vallejo
   Translated by Farris Anderson

CONDEMNED SQUAD   139
(*Escuadra hacia la muerte*)
   By Alfonso Sastre
   Translated by Leonard C. Pronko

THE BLINDFOLD   211
(*La venda en los ojos*)
   By José López Rubio
   Translated by Marion Holt

THE BOAT WITHOUT A FISHERMAN   315
(*La barca sin pescador*)
   By Alejandro Casona
   Translated by Richard Damar

Introduction

THEATRE has been a vital part of Spain's cultural tradition since the middle of the sixteenth century when an actor-writer named Lope de Rueda began to present his simple plays (or *pasos*) in the streets of Seville and Madrid. Within a few decades theatres replaced the improvised stages of touring groups in the major cities, and all elements of society could be found at the performances of *comedias*. In the seventeenth century, Europe's most truly national drama reached its zenith in the Spanish capital with the works of Lope de Vega, Tirso de Molina, and Calderón. Even Cervantes had been an aspiring playwright before he became the creator of the modern novel. His concern in *Don Quixote* with the conflicts between reality and illusion and the frequent examples of play-acting in his masterpiece suggest the fascination that the theatre held for him.

In the nineteenth century, the theatre of Romanticism flourished in Spain; audiences relished the poetic despair of tragic heroes such as Don Alvaro or the troubadour Manrique—and, particularly, the flamboyance of Zorrilla's romanticized and not-so-tragic version of *Don Juan Tenorio*.[1] The

1. Tirso de Molina's Golden Age play *El burlador de Sevilla* first introduced Don Juan Tenorio to Spain, and

romantic tradition continued into the second half of the century in the melodramas of José Echegaray, a clever craftsman who transferred the extravagant passion from the castle to the drawing room. Echegaray's plays seem artificial and contrived today, but during his lifetime he was honored and acclaimed as a major dramatist.[2]

In spite of periods of repression and political instability, there have been notable examples of theatrical and literary creativeness in Spain in the twentieth century. The most exciting developments in modern Spanish literature began at the turn of the century when the nation had reached a state of total defeat in the war with the United States. The writers of this "Generation of '98" were deeply concerned with the varied problems of Spanish intellectual, political, and social life and were not primarily devoted to the theatre. However, both Miguel de Unamuno and Azorín, who were better known as essayists and novelists, attempted works for the stage; and thirty years after the novelist-playwright Ramón del Valle-Inclán died, his harsh and grotesque plays—considered virtually unproducible in his lifetime—began to be recognized as works of extraordinary power and to

---

ultimately to the entire Western world. However, it is José Zorrilla's nineteenth-century drama that is still performed yearly in Spanish-speaking countries the week of November 1.

2. There seems little doubt that Echegaray's work—as well as Spanish literature of the Golden Age—influenced Pirandello's development as a playwright. For a detailed presentation of the Italian dramatist's debt to Spain, see Wilma Newberry's "Echegaray and Pirandello," *PMLA*, March 1966.

attract the attention of the more imaginative directors of Spain.

The dominant figure of the Spanish theatre in the early twentieth century was Jacinto Benavente, who succeeded in putting to rest the excessive histrionics of past decades and in bringing a new naturalness to the stage. Although not a dramatist of the highest order, Benavente did achieve an international reputation. He was awarded the Nobel Prize for literature in 1922 and enjoyed a career that spanned more than fifty years.

On the eve of the Spanish Republic, Spain appeared to be entering a new and productive theatrical era. Members of a young, enthusiastic generation of dramatists were making their first experiments in playwriting. The most outstanding of these was, of course, Federico García Lorca; but he was not an isolated figure. This new theatrical life, however, was disrupted and fragmented by the Civil War. Before the conflict was over, Lorca had been tragically killed and his talent lost to the Spanish theatre. Of the young playwrights who went into exile, only Alejandro Casona, from a base in Buenos Aires, achieved a degree of success and recognition.

In the early 1940's the odds against significant theatre in Spain were formidable. The unfortunate state of the economy, strict censorship,[3] and

3. Censorship of plays has existed in Spain since the end of the Civil War in 1939. No dialogue or plot situations were permitted that were interpreted as giving offense to the "fundamental principles of the State." Until 1963 the readers employed—they were frequently priests—had no established norms to follow, and approval or rejection could be per-

the cautiousness of producers were serious obstacles
to experimentation in form or the presentation of
provocative themes. The aging Benavente continued to produce new works of no exceptional
interest, and several dramatists who had begun to
write for the stage just before or during the period
of the Republic resumed their careers. Perhaps the
best of these was the erratic but highly gifted
humorist Enrique Jardiel Poncela.[4] The single new

---

sonal and unpredictable. Certainly Spanish censorship has
been erratic. Works denied performance one year have
gained approval at another time with insignificant changes;
and plays have been approved for publication when stage
performances were prohibited. A comparison by Patricia
W. O'Connor ("Censorship in the Contemporary Spanish
Theater and Antonio Buero Vallejo," *Hispania,* May 1969)
of the original mimeographed copies of Buero's plays sub-
mitted to the censors with the versions actually performed
reveals that some of this playwright's strongest plays have
suffered only minor changes, and that a controversial early
work, *Aventura en lo gris* (*Adventure in Greyness*), was
granted approval after a number of years and performed
in a version that was somewhat stronger than the original.
On the other hand, Buero's *La doble historia del doctor
Valmy* (*The Double Case History of Doctor Valmy*) is
still forbidden production several years after its submission.
In 1963 censorship was relaxed to a degree. Official norms
were established and a regular censorship committee, mostly
lay, was appointed. The basic restrictions are against any
expressions that would give offense to the Catholic Church
or to the person of the Chief of State, or that would
threaten the security of the State. In recent years, blunter
dialogue and bolder treatment of sexual themes and political matters have been in evidence.

4. Spanish names frequently prove puzzling in the English-
speaking world. Officially, a person uses both paternal and
maternal family names, in that sequence (e.g., E. Jardiel
Poncela). The names are sometimes joined by *y* (and). If
one name is dropped, it is the mother's family name. However, literary figures are not always consistent, especially if
the paternal name is a very common one. The two best-

figure of consequence to appear was a sensitive young writer named Víctor Ruiz Iriarte, whose talent was to develop more fully in subsequent years.

It was not until 1949 that signs of revitalization could be discerned. In October of that year, the première of *Historia de una escalera* (*The Story of a Stairway*) introduced Antonio Buero Vallejo, an unknown playwright whose work had been awarded the Lope de Vega Prize and a professional production. It was the first time since the Civil War that a new drama had been deemed worthy of the award. The promise of Buero's first produced play was confirmed the following year with the production of an earlier work, *En la ardiente oscuridad* (*In the Burning Darkness*), and he was quickly established as the finest dramatic talent of the postwar period.

In April of 1949, José López Rubio, a member of the prewar group of dramatists, resumed his career after a period of writing and directing for motion pictures both in Spain and in America. López Rubio's *Alberto,* which had its first performance on April 29, 1949, represents a renewal of the intellectual comedy in Spain, just as Buero's *The Story of a Stairway* marks the rebirth of serious drama.

---

known examples of famous writers who are referred to by the maternal name are Benito Pérez Galdós and Federico García Lorca, who are generally called Galdós and Lorca—though catalogued in libraries under Pérez and García. Of the playwrights represented in this book, Antonio Buero Vallejo retains both names but is frequently called Buero (never Vallejo); Alfonso Sastre Salvador has always been Sastre. José López Rubio retains his double name. Alejandro Casona was the pseudonym of Alejandro Rodríguez Alvarez.

The next few years saw progressive improvement in the quality of productions and also an increase in imaginative works of light satire and poetized realism. Not all critics were pleased by what they considered an excess of plays that evaded some of the harsher realities of contemporary life, and they dubbed them *"teatro de evasión."* But works of the order of Miguel Mihura's *Tres sombreros de copa (Three Top Hats)*, Ruiz Iriarte's *El landó de seis caballos (The Six-Horse Landau)*, and López Rubio's *La venda en los ojos (The Blindfold)* need no apology. They rank well above the level of escapist comedy and reveal superior talents.

A date of particular significance for the postwar Spanish stage is March 18, 1953, when a group of student actors called the T.P.U. (Teatro Popular Universitario) performed Alfonso Sastre's *Escuadra hacia la muerte (Condemned Squad)* in the national Teatro María Guerrero by special dispensation of the authorities. Already known as an outspoken critic of the existing theatre and an active worker for experimental groups, Sastre now received public recognition as a playwright committed to drama of social consequence. Both in theme and form *Condemned Squad* was strikingly different from the customary theatrical fare. The play had only three performances but its point had been made and would not be forgotten by the enthusiastic groups that saw the production.

In the early 1960's new dramatists such as Carlos Muñiz, Lauro Olmo, and Antonio Gala began to attract favorable critical attention; and in 1963, Alejandro Casona returned to Spain after the highly successful Madrid première of *La dama del alba*

(*The Lady of the Dawn*). Several of the works he had written during his long exile became major box-office successes, but he was to complete only one new play before his death in 1965.

When Spanish drama of the postwar period is surveyed in its entirety, it becomes evident that the offerings of the Madrid stage, particularly since 1949, have been far more varied and inventive than is generally supposed. In spite of censorship and the conservative tastes of a large segment of the theatre public, a substantial number of plays of enduring interest have been written.

Four writers who can be considered representative of the various trends and aspects of the modern Spanish stage are Antonio Buero Vallejo, Alfonso Sastre, José López Rubio, and Alejandro Casona. Their works reveal talents that are individual and distinct, but each playwright has contributed significantly to a continuation of Spain's theatrical tradition.

Antonio Buero Vallejo (b. 1916) is the acknowledged leader in the field of serious drama. At the outbreak of the Spanish Civil War in 1936 he was a young art student at the Escuela de Bellas Artes in Madrid. Not yet twenty, he enlisted in the Republican medical corps, and at the end of the war was imprisoned for six years. When released in 1945, he temporarily resumed his painting career before turning to the theatre. Between 1945 and 1949 he wrote three full-length plays and a one-act piece.

The major works that Buero completed during the first decade of his career were, with two exceptions, approximately contemporary in setting. In

1958 he turned to historical drama, using historical personages and events as the subjects of three
successive plays. Each presented a visionary at odds
with a society that refuted its own dreamers—political and artistic. The best of the three is *El
concierto de San Ovidio* (*The Concert at Saint
Ovide*), which was inspired by an eighteenth-cen-
tury engraving of an actual concert of blind men
at the fair of Saint Ovide in Paris shortly before
the French Revolution. Buero re-creates in the mas-
terful final scene of the second act the action de-
picted in the engraving, just as he had ended his
play on Velázquez, *Las Meninas*, with a tableau
which shows the painter with the subjects of the
painting known throughout the world as "Las
Meninas." In *The Concert at Saint Ovide*, Valentin
Haüy, who witnessed the "atrocity" of the actual
concert in 1771 when the blind musicians were
mocked and ridiculed, is a historical character who
became the teacher of the more famous Louis
Braille. In the play he is only an observer, unin-
volved in the tragic story of David, the blind violinist, and his pitiful disciple and betrayer Donatien.
But it is this outsider who is moved to bring to
reality the vision that David had of blind men
reading, performing, and reaching artistic fulfill-
ment.

Buero's first play, *In the Burning Darkness*, also
deals with the blind. The setting is a school where
the life of an optimistic group of self-deluding
blind students is suddenly disturbed by the appearance of a rebellious young man attired in black
(Ignacio) who refuses to conform to a training pro-
gram he abhors. He proclaims his burning desire

to see the stars—and even more: to reach them if he had his sight. This almost messianic youth is destroyed, and his inner torment is transferred to the very boy who murders him. *In the Burning Darkness* and *The Concert at Saint Ovide* are parables of man's struggle against the darkness, and Buero has called his more recent play just that: "*una parábola.*" Both works also illustrate the playwright's fondness for musical motifs and his concern with visual symbols to achieve a more complete theatrical effect.

El tragaluz (*The Window*), performed in 1967, has been Buero Vallejo's most successful play at the box office. The drama opens in the distant future, when technology has provided a method for replaying events of the past to re-evaluate their importance, but the principal action takes place in the present and deals with a conflict within a contemporary Spanish family who suffered a traumatic separation during the chaotic period of the Civil War.

Mito (*Myth*), described as a "book for an opera," was published in 1968. Written in verse, it is a complex treatment of the Quixote–Sancho Panza theme, with the modern Quixote a decrepit actor who sees visions of superior beings from Mars. Just as the famous knight of Cervantes is deceived by an ordinary man dressed in armor, the actor Eloy is mocked by other actors performing their own depraved version of his illusion.

Buero's reputation has grown steadily since he first gained recognition—if not financial security—with the production of *The Story of a Stairway*, and his plays show greater originality and depth than those of any other dramatist of the postwar period.

Although Alfonso Sastre (b. 1926) has had fewer plays performed in Spain than Buero Vallejo, his agitation for theatre of social consequence and his frequent critical essays on drama and its purposes have made him a major force in the modern Spanish theatre. As a student at the University of Madrid in the late 1940's he began a vigorous criticism of the theatrical establishment. During this period he wrote numerous articles and collaborated on several experimental plays. He was also instrumental in the founding of the Teatro Popular Universitario, the theatrical group which staged his *Condemned Squad* in 1953.

In spite of the recognition which came with *Condemned Squad,* Sastre's subsequent works have not found a large audience and some of his better plays have been denied performance by the censors. It is not surprising that the Sastre plays that have been performed professionally have been those which do not deal directly with political conflict. However, the playwright himself does not advocate an ideological theatre, and even in those dramas which incorporate to some degree the theme of revolution—such as *Guillermo Tell tiene los ojos tristes* (*Sad Are the Eyes of William Tell*), *Tierra roja* (*Red Earth*), and *El pan de todos* (*Every Man's Bread*)—he does not present revolt as an absolute solution to society's injustices.

Outstanding among the plays which have not been staged in Spain is *Sad Are the Eyes of William Tell,* in which the dramatist treats the legend of the Swiss patriot in a highly original manner.

Sastre's version alters the familiar tale by having Tell actually kill his son and then destroy the tyrant. Soldiers appear in modern uniform and carry twentieth-century weapons to emphasize the timelessness of the dramatic situation. Divided into seven scenes and employing songs to comment directly to the audience, it is a play whose structure suggests the influence of Bertolt Brecht. However, Sastre's work as a whole is more often compared with that of Sartre and the American playwright Arthur Miller.

Condemned Squad, because of its setting in a future world war, has lost none of its immediacy and remains one of Sastre's most effective dramatic efforts. Although antimilitaristic in tone, it is less a statement against the misuse of human beings in wars they are unable to comprehend than a study of responsibility and guilt. In the first half of the drama, a sense of despair and frustration is created in the five scenes leading to the crucial sixth scene in which the leader of the squad is murdered by four of the soldiers on Christmas Eve. The second part of the play traces the effect of the violent act upon the guilty men as well as upon the innocent soldier Jack (called Luis in the original Spanish version).

Sastre has spoken out boldly on several occasions against censorship in Spain. In 1961 he prepared a strong statement in collaboration with the critic José María de Quinto demanding abolishment of pre-censorship. The opposition he has encountered both from the censors and from producers concerned with box-office returns has hampered his career, and only three of his original works (and two adaptations of foreign plays) have been produced for the Madrid stage since 1960.

Playwright, translator, film director and scenarist, José López Rubio (b. 1903) entered the Madrid literary world at an early age and published a book of short stories and a novel before he was twenty-five. In 1929 *De la noche a la mañana* (*Overnight*), a play written in collaboration with Eduardo Ugarte, received the first prize in a contest for new playwrights sponsored by the newspaper *ABC*. In 1930 López Rubio accepted a contract with Metro-Goldwyn-Mayer to write dialogue for Spanish versions of films made in the United States. Although busily engaged in cinematic activities, he did not lose interest in the stage. In 1935 he began work on *Celos del aire*,[5] a play that was to receive the Fastenrath Prize of the Real Academia Española when it was finally performed in Madrid in 1950.

On returning to Spain after the Civil War, López Rubio devoted himself principally to scriptwriting and directing; but by 1948 he had completed three new works for the theatre. The second period of his career begins in 1949 with the première of *Alberto*, a serious comedy about an imaginary man created by the residents of a Madrid pension to manage their affairs. The theme of the play, the unpredictable effect of created illusion on the lives

5. *Celos del aire* is a title that does not translate easily into English. It is derived from the name of a *comedia* of Calderón's, *Celos aún del aire matan*—loosely: "Even imaginary jealousy can kill." When the play was performed in Italian, the title was completely altered to *Due più due. sei* (*Two Plus Two Are Six*).

of individuals, appears in several of the play-wright's subsequent works.

The Blindfold belongs to an especially produc-tive period in López Rubio's career which followed the success of *Alberto,* and it is one of the best of his serious comedies. It is a play both satiric and poetic; there are passages of dialogue that come close to theatre of the absurd, and the opening scene, which to the unwary appears to be a cliché of conventional exposition, turns out to be com-pletely unrelated in actual substance to the basic plot of *The Blindfold.* Certainly the "madness" of the protagonist shows the dramatist's kinship with Pirandello, and the calculated play-acting by the aunt and uncle recalls certain works by Jean Anouilh; yet such dramatic characteristics are also a part of a long Spanish tradition that stems from Cervantes and Calderón.

In 1958 López Rubio produced a completely atypical work, *Las manos son inocentes (Our Hands Are Innocent).* A stark and uncompromising study of the moral decay of a contemporary couple beset by economic problems with which they cannot cope, the play came as a surprise to the devotees of the playwright's comedies and its merits were overlooked by some critics.

For several years López Rubio has been engaged in research for a history of the Spanish stage. Still awaiting production is his serious drama *La puerta del ángel (The Way of the Angel),* set in provin-cial Spain.

Alejandro Casona (1903–1965) spent a long pe-riod of his life outside Spain but his career began and ended in Madrid. Although some of his most important plays were first performed abroad during his period of exile, these works all reveal strongly the Spanish origin of the author and are essentially a part of the modern Spanish theatre.

Like Buero Vallejo and López Rubio, Casona first gained recognition by winning a literary award. In 1933 his *La sirena varada* (*The Stranded Mermaid*) received the Lope de Vega Prize, with the customary professional production. During the period of the Spanish Republic, Casona organized a theatrical troupe similar to García Lorca's La Barraca group to carry theatre to the remote areas of Spain, and for five years he worked with his "people's theatre." Before turning to drama, Casona had prepared himself for an academic career, and his *Nuestra Natacha* (*Our Natacha*), performed during the Civil War, argued for reform and liberalization in Spanish education.

In 1937 the playwright left Spain for Mexico and finally settled in Argentina. Three of his most admired plays—*The Lady of the Dawn, La barca sin pescador* (*The Boat Without a Fisherman*), and *Los árboles mueren de pie* (*Trees Die Standing*)—were first performed in Buenos Aires between 1944 and 1949. In 1962 Casona came to Spain for the Madrid première of *The Lady of the Dawn*. Moved by the warm reception of both critics and public, and encouraged by friends, he decided to return permanently to his homeland the following year. Unfortunately, he was unable to continue his career with vigor. Weakened by a heart condition, he underwent surgery in the summer of 1965 and died a few months later.

The fantastic and the supernatural are integral parts of much of Casona's work. Death, in the guise of a beautiful woman, is the "Lady of the Dawn" in the play by that name. Recognized only by the old and not feared by children, she is destined to wander the earth with the feelings of a woman of flesh and blood who must watch the creatures she touches perish. The Devil is a character in both *Otra vez el Diablo* (*The Devil Again*) and *The Boat Without a Fisherman.*

The story of the man who makes a bargain with the Devil to will the death of an aged and wealthy Chinese Mandarin and thus inherit a fortune is the subject of a novella by the nineteenth-century Portuguese writer Eça de Queiroz. It is Queiroz who invented the idea of tempting a man of the middle class with a middle-class devil. Richard Jordan, the stock manipulator of *The Boat Without a Fisherman,* and Teodoro, the insignificant civil servant of Queiroz's *O Mandarim,* are struck with remorse and drawn to the scenes of their "bloodless" crimes—but with quite different results. Teodoro's search ultimately proves futile; Casona's Richard Jordan outwits the Devil by destroying his former self and is redeemed by the love of the widow of the man whose death he had willed.

Casona's final original play was a historical drama based on the life of the Golden Age writer Quevedo. Like his earlier work it was colored by the fantastic and the poetical.

MARION HOLT

Chronologies of Plays

DRAMATIC WORKS OF ANTONIO BUERO VALLEJO
(With year of first performance in Spain)

Historia de una escalera (1949)
Las palabras en la arena (one act) (1949)
En la ardiente oscuridad (1950)
La tejedora de sueños (1952)
La señal que se espera (1952)
Casi un cuento de hadas (1953)
Madrugada (1953)
Irene o el tesoro (1954)
Hoy es fiesta (1956)
Las cartas boca abajo (1957)
Un soñador para un pueblo (1958)
Las Meninas (1960)
El concierto de San Ovidio (1962)
Aventura en lo gris (1963)
El tragaluz (1967)
Performed in England
La doble historia del doctor Valmy (The Double Case History of Doctor Valmy, translated by Farris Anderson) (1968)
Published but unperformed
Mito (libretto for an opera) (1968)

DRAMATIC WORKS OF ALFONSO SASTRE
(With year of first performance in Spain)

   Escuadra hacia la muerte (1953)
   La mordaza (1954)
   La sangre de Dios (1955)
   El pan de todos (1957)
   El cuervo (1957)
   Medea (based on Euripides) (1958)
   La cornada (1960)
   En la red (1961)
   Oficio de tinieblas (1967)
Performed by experimental groups
   Ha sonado la muerte (1946)
   Uranio 235 (1946)
   Cargamento de sueños (1948)
Published but never performed in Spain
   Ana Kleiber
   Muerte en el barrio
   Guillermo Tell tiene los ojos tristes
   Tierra roja
   Asalto nocturno
   Prólogo patético

DRAMATIC WORKS OF JOSÉ LÓPEZ RUBIO
(With year of first performance in Spain)

   De la noche a la mañana (1929)
   La casa de naipes (1930)

(NOTE: López Rubio has also translated and adapted more than twenty-five foreign works for the Madrid stage, including Miller's *Death of a Salesman* and *A View from the Bridge,* Wilde's *The Importance of Being Earnest,* Montherlant's *Le Cardinal d'Espagne,* and the Dale Wasserman book and lyrics for *Man of La Mancha.*)

Alberto (1949)
Celos del aire (1950)
Estoy pensando en ti (one act) (1950)
Veinte y cuarenta (1951)
Una madeja de lana azul celeste (1951)
Cena de Navidad (1951)
El remedio en la memoria (1952)
La venda en los ojos (1954)
Cuenta nueva (1954)
La otra orilla (1954)
El caballero de Barajas (musical comedy) (1955)
La novia del espacio (1956)
Un trono para Cristy (1956)
Las manos son inocentes (1958)
Diana está comunicando (1960)
Esta noche, tampoco (1961)
Nunca es tarde (1964)

DRAMATIC WORKS OF ALEJANDRO CASONA
(With year of first performance)

La sirena varada (1934)
Otra vez el Diablo (1935)
Nuestra Natacha (1935)
Prohibido suicidarse en primavera (1937)
El crimen de Lord Arturo (1938)
Romance de Dan y Elsa (1938)
Sinfonía inacabada (1940)

(NOTE: All of Casona's works between 1937 and 1957 were first performed in Buenos Aires or other Spanish American capitals. Since 1962 all the major plays he wrote while living outside Spain have been produced in Madrid. *The Boat Without a Fisherman* had its Madrid première in 1963. Ginastera's opera *Don Rodrigo*, with a libretto by Casona, was performed in Buenos Aires in 1964 and in New York City the following year.)

Las tres perfectas casadas (1941)
La dama del alba (1944)
La barca sin pescador (1945)
La molinera de Arcos (1947)
Los árboles mueren de pie (1949)
Retablo jovial (five one-act plays) (1949)
La llave en el desván (1951)
Siete gritos en el mar (1952)
La tercera palabra (1953)
Corona de amor y muerte (1955)
Carta de una desconocida (based on a novel by Stefan Zweig) (1957)
La casa de los siete balcones (1957)
El caballero de las espuelas de oro (1964)

The Concert at Saint Ovide

A PARABLE
IN THREE ACTS

By Antonio Buero Vallejo

El concierto
de San Ovidio
Translated by Farris Anderson

Characters

LOUIS-MARIE VALINDIN, *impresario*
PRIORESS *of the Asylum of the Quinze-Vingts*
SISTER LUCIE
SISTER ANDREA
GILBERT, *blind beggar*
LUKE, *blind beggar*
ELIJAH, *blind beggar*
NAZAIRE, *blind beggar*
DAVID, *blind beggar*
DONATIEN, *blind beggar*
ADRIENNE, *mistress of Valindin*
CATHERINE, *maid*
JEROME LEFRANC, *violinist*
IRÉNÉE BERNIER, *carpenter*
LATOUCHE, *police commissioner*
DUBOIS, *police officer*
VALENTIN HAÜY
BOURGEOIS COUPLE
FIRST LADY
SECOND LADY
DANDY

Prologue

The action takes place in Paris, from summer to autumn in the year 1771. In the thirteenth century Saint Louis of France founded the Asylum of the Quinze-Vingts to give shelter to three hundred blind men of Paris. A legend states that the institution was founded by the king for the purpose of gathering there three hundred knights who had been blinded in the Crusades. This legend is false, for the Asylum was not created for noblemen, but rather for beggars. And as the centuries went by, begging continued to be the means of livelihood for almost all the destitute blind who sought and found shelter there. In more modern times, however, the institution came to know prosperity. The bulls and edicts issued in its favor by popes and kings, the accumulation of legacies, bequests, and alms—all these brought well-being to the Asylum, and its directors found it necessary to curb the luxury with which some of the inmates had begun to dress.

The worthy foundation has survived to the present, and today it is located in the former barracks of the Black Musketeers, near the Place de la Bastille, where it was moved in 1780. Our story takes place nine years before the Asylum of the Quinze-Vingts was moved. Still at its original location in

3

Champourri, it occupied at that time a parcel of land next to the Cloister of Saint Honoré which today has become part of the Place du Carrousel. By royal permission the rooms and utensils of that building—which has today disappeared—displayed the French fleur de lis, *as did the uniforms of the inmates. In spite of this royal consideration, in the year 1771 begging was still the primary means of support for the institution's blind inhabitants. Their route took them from the Asylum to the Fair of Saint Ovide, which, since that year, has taken place in what is today the Place de la Concorde and was then called the Place de Louis Quinze. A group of beggars, in their daily wanderings, unknowingly determined the fate of a great man and consequently gave birth to our story.*

The street scenes are played along the front of the stage. The set consists of an elevated platform which is reached by one or two steps. On this platform the Asylum, VALINDIN's *house, and the shack at the fair are to be suggested, as the situation may require.*

Before the curtain rises, a chorus of men and women is heard praying. The curtain rises on a reception room at the Asylum. Large blue curtains, sprinkled with fleurs de lis, *hang behind the steps of the platform. At right the* PRIORESS *stands motionless, facing the proscenium. She is old and drawn; her expression is cold and she appears thoughtful. Behind her two nuns—*SISTER ANDREA *and* SISTER LUCIE*—stand near the steps. At left Monsieur* VALINDIN *smilingly observes the* PRIORESS. *He is about fifty years old and appears harsh and resolute. His hair is unpowdered. He wears a black*

velvet cloak with silver buttons, half-length boots
with light-colored trim; under his right arm he
holds his black tricorn hat which is adorned with
a fine silvered stripe. With his left hand he fingers
the sword which hangs at his side.

Act One

VOICES *Pater noster qui es in coelis, sanctificetur*
nomen tuum, adveniat regnum tuum, fiat volun-
tas tua sicut in coelo et in terra. Panem nostrum
quotidianum da nobis hodie, et dimitte nobis
debita nostra sicut et nos dimittimus debitoribus
nostris. Et ne nos inducas in tentationem, sed
libera nos a malo. Amen.

VOICE An Ave Maria for our beloved king and
protector, Louis the Fifteenth, and for all the
princes and princesses of his line. *Ave Maria . . .*

VOICES *. . . gratia plena, Dominus tecum, bene-*
dicta tu in mulieribus et benedictus fructus ven-
tris tui, Iesus. Sancta Maria, Mater Dei, ora pro
nobis peccatoribus, nunc et in hora mortis nostrae.
Amen.

VOICE *Gloria Patri, et Filio, et Spiritui Sancto.*

VOICES *Sicut erat in principio, et nunc et semper,*
et in saecula saeculorum. Amen.

VALINDIN Well, Reverend Mother?

Without looking at him, the PRIORESS *raises her*
hand, ordering him to be silent.

VOICE *Benedic, Domine, nos et haec tua dona quae*

de tua largitate sumus sumpturi. Per Christum Dominum nostrum.

VOICES *Amen.*

PRIORESS *(after a pause.)* Have they been seated yet?

SISTER LUCIE *(peeking through the curtain.)* They're kissing the bread, Reverend Mother.

PRIORESS *(turns toward* VALINDIN.*)* Monsieur Valindin. . . . Your name is Valindin, isn't it?

VALINDIN *(bowing.)* Louis-Marie Valindin, at the service of Your Reverence.

PRIORESS Monsieur Valindin, you have come at a very early hour. As you see, our poor inmates have not yet had their breakfast.

VALINDIN I trust you will forgive that particular aspect of my character, Reverend Mother. When I am involved in something beneficial, I prefer to tend to it right away.

PRIORESS *(nodding.)* The Baron of Tournelle has vouched for that. In his letter he describes you as an enterprising and competent man.

VALINDIN Perhaps not really, Mother. Even after all these years I cannot say that I am wealthy.

PRIORESS Do not let that trouble you. This house is not wealthy either, and it has been alive for five centuries.

VALINDIN If Your Reverence and the men approve the idea, we could go ahead and arrange everything today.

PRIORESS In this house we do not move quite so rapidly, Monsieur Valindin.

VALINDIN Perhaps you would give me permission to talk with them. . . .

PRIORESS It's better that I speak to them first.

(*Silence. She paces, then stops.*) Are you a musician, Monsieur Valindin?

VALINDIN   No, Mother. But I have musicians ready to help me. The songs are already written.

PRIORESS   What you propose is extremely unusual. Those six men would have to rehearse a great deal, and even then I fear that all your efforts would be in vain. You do not know how clumsy the poor things are.

VALINDIN   If Your Reverence would consent to let me try them out. . . . We can even do it here if you prefer.

PRIORESS   By no means. It would not be well for the other brothers and sisters to hear them. This undertaking seems too strange to be wholesome. I trust there is some other place where you can rehearse?

VALINDIN   In my own house, Mother. I live at number fifteen, Rue Mazarin. (*He laughs.*) Even though I travel greatly, I thought it best to keep my headquarters here. In France the only way to get anything done is to do it in Paris.

PRIORESS   Or in Versailles.

VALINDIN   (*agreeing.*)   Or in Versailles. (*Smoothly.*) So then, Your Reverence agrees?

PRIORESS   (*startled.*)   I did not say that. (*She paces, then stops.*) . Worldly songs.

VALINDIN   (*sighs.*)   Your Reverence must realize that this is for a fair. That's the kind of song the public wants. And these songs are no more worldly than many of those your men sing on the streets. . . .

PRIORESS   (*dryly.*)   If one can really call that singing. . . . We are poor, Monsieur. All France is hungry and the Asylum is no exception. We are obliged to tolerate those excesses, against our desires. God does not permit the blindness of these three hundred unfortunate creatures just so that they will lose their souls. He wants them to offer prayers in the streets, just as they do in the churches and at wakes. This is a house of prayer and work. Ever since Saint Louis founded it, the Asylum of the Quinze-Vingts has lived in the eternity of prayer and in the simple tasks which give us our bread and our clothing. Anything else is vanity. A blind man may show an unusual skill, but he, like all his blind brothers, was born to pray morning and night, since that is all their misfortune permits them to do consistently well. But the Asylum is no longer what it used to be. . . . The legacies and bequests hardly cover our needs. . . . And our poor inmates must be fed.

VALINDIN (*his eyes dampen and he takes a few steps toward her; he appears genuinely moved.*) Very beautiful words indeed, Mother. And very true. . . . (*He wipes away a tear.*) Please forgive me. . . . I fear I'm a bit too sensitive at times. What you have said moves me deeply. You know that the idea I have explained to you has its spiritual side—which, I assure you, I do not consider its least important aspect. If we can reach an agreement you will not only furnish me with the opportunity of contributing financially toward the maintenance of this holy house, but also with the consolation of the prayers which your poor blind inmates will offer each year for my sinful soul.

PRIORESS (*she has listened to him impassively.*)
Nevertheless, your proposal leads me to assume
that you sympathize with the new ideas.

VALINDIN   But Reverend Mother, in our age, who
does not? This is 1771! The world is shrinking
and men are opening up new areas of knowledge
and wealth. But I know my limits! I shall never
admit the nonsense of men like Rousseau or Vol-
taire, and I am fully aware of my debt to the
saintly virtues of our elders. The Baron of Tournelle, who has always honored me with his protection, can assure you of that.

PRIORESS   The Baron is one of our most generous
patrons and his word has strength in this house.
But your idea disturbs me, Monsieur.

VALINDIN   Perhaps you could postpone your decision. I am not an educated man and I express
myself clumsily, but . . .

PRIORESS   I have not said I was rejecting your proposal. (*Troubled.*) In all good conscience, I do
not know that I *can* reject it. (*With a look of
displeasure.*) When we have an opportunity to
do something for the good of these unfortunate
ones, we must accept it. . . .

VALINDIN (*moving a step nearer.*) Mother, I truly
wish it were possible for me to make the reward
even greater, but I fear I must insist on my
original offer. My means permit me to go no
higher: one hundred francs now and another
hundred when the fair closes. Unless, of course,
you would prefer to take your chances on a per-
centage of the profits.

PRIORESS (*looks at him suddenly and sharply.*)
What are you saying? This house does not do

business. Those two hundred francs represent a donation in return for prayers. Nothing more.

VALINDIN (*he bows, contritely.*) Prayers, which, I repeat, I most humbly require.

A silence, which is broken by VOICES *behind the curtains.*

VOICE *Deus det nobis suam pacem.*

VOICES *Et vitam aeternam. Amen.*

PRIORESS There is nothing more I can say to you until I have spoken with them. I must not decide against their will. Sister Lucie, show Monsieur Valindin to the door. (SISTER LUCIE *moves downstage left.*) Come back tomorrow, Monsieur. (*She smiles coldly and holds out the rosary to him.*) Even if you must come early.

VALINDIN (*kisses the rosary.*) Thank you, Reverend Mother. God be with you.

SISTER LUCIE Follow me, Monsieur.

VALINDIN *bows and exits left behind the nun, under the gaze of the* PRIORESS. SISTER ANDREA *peeks through the curtains.*

SISTER ANDREA They are putting on their collection boxes, Reverend Mother.

PRIORESS Bring me the six whom that gentleman named, and then leave us alone.

SISTER ANDREA *bows and exits through the center of the curtains. The* PRIORESS *paces thoughtfully. She is briefly distracted from her meditations by two hand-claps by* SISTER ANDREA, *offstage; then she resumes her pacing.*

SISTER ANDREA (*voice.*) Attention! The Mother Prioress orders the presence of brothers Elijah, Donatien, Nazaire, David, Luke, and Gilbert. Brothers Elijah, Donatien, Nazaire, David, Luke, and Gilbert, by order of the Mother Prioress! (*Sound of approaching tapping canes.*) For the third time, brother Gilbert! Come, now! The Mother Prioress is waiting!

SISTER ANDREA *reappears and holds open the curtain as the six* BLIND MEN *enter. She occasionally helps one of them down the steps.*

PRIORESS   Come, my sons. (*She holds out her hand to* LUKE, *who is an old man.*) Careful. Remember the steps.

The BLIND MEN *all come down. The last one down is* GILBERT, *who smiles innocently and naively.*

GILBERT   Good morning, Mother Prioress!

LUKE, ELIJAH, *and* NAZAIRE   Good morning, Mother. We hope you are well.

Touching each other in such a way as to form a human chain, they line up in front of the PRIORESS.

PRIORESS   Thank you, my sons. (*With a gesture she dismisses* SISTER ANDREA, *who exits through the curtains.*) What was detaining you, Little Bird?

GILBERT (*laughs.*)   I didn't remember my name!

PRIORESS   Silly! Now, try to understand well what I am going to say to all of you.

GILBERT   I understand everything!

PRIORESS (*smiles and pats him on the shoulder.*) Of course. (*To the others.*) How did the soup taste today?

NAZAIRE (*laughs.*)   It tasted like there wasn't very much of it.

PRIORESS (*seriously.*)   It's true that it is not abundant. (*She paces. The* BLIND MEN *whisper among themselves. She stops.*) What are you whispering about?

NAZAIRE That's the first time we've ever heard
you say that, Mother.

The PRIORESS *smiles without enthusiasm, replies
with a grunt, and continues to pace. The six* BLIND
MEN *continue to wait in a row. Suddenly it is
difficult to distinguish one from the other. Many
elements tend to make them resemble each other to
the point of losing their individual identities: their
lifeless eyes, the jerkiness of their movements, the
cane which each one carries, their secular clothes
which are alike in their simplicity and raggedness,
and the identical rectangular patch of blue cloth
on each chest, on which is mounted a saffron-colored*
fleur de lis. *All are bareheaded. Except for* LUKE,
*they all wear around their necks a tin alms box
which rests against their chests below the* fleur de lis.
*Upon closer observation, the differences among the
men become apparent.* LUKE *is old, grey-haired, and
tired.* DONATIEN *is a boy not yet seventeen years of
age; he tries to be carefree and casual in his gestures and expressions, but their awkwardness reveals the insecurity of adolescence. His face would
not be bad-looking if it had not been hideously
pock-marked by the smallpox which left him blind.*
NAZAIRE *is mature, heavy, strong. His face, also, is
slightly marred by smallpox scars; it is mischievous
and generally smiling, like that of a carnival rogue.*
ELIJAH *is thin. His eyelids are closed and he never
smiles.* GILBERT *is approximately forty years old.
His sharp, angular features possess a certain painful,
virile beauty; his eyes, slightly crossed, sometimes
appear actually to see. These qualities contrast
sharply with his imbecile laugh, his infantile speech,
and his childish naiveté. He is a victim of meningitis.*

Finally, DAVID *is about thirty-five years old. He is pale and thin. His beautifully manly hands are, at the moment, still, in contrast to those of his companions, who reveal the nervousness with which they await the words of the* PRIORESS.

PRIORESS (*stopping in front of them.*) Where are your violins?

ELIJAH   We pick them up on the way out.

PRIORESS   Gilbert, do you still go out with brother Elijah?

GILBERT   Yes, Mother. I sing and he plays.

PRIORESS   Who brought in the most yesterday?

NAZAIRE   I believe I did. Twenty-two sous.

PRIORESS   And the least?

DAVID   I did, Mother. Twelve sous.

PRIORESS   You, again? Why is that?

DAVID   I just let the time slip away from me. . . .

PRIORESS (*reproachfully.*) Without playing.

DAVID   Forgive me.

PRIORESS   Your brothers are the ones who must forgive you. You should be bringing in more than they, but instead you often bring in less.

ELIJAH   Now you've hit his sore spot!

PRIORESS   All right. You see we are not bringing in very much. The poor can give very little to the poor. But in September the Fair of Saint Ovide will open. This year it promises to be especially good because it will be held in the biggest plaza in all Paris: the Place de Louis Quinze.

NAZAIRE   The fairs are like bread from heaven for us poor people! At Saint Laurent a few years ago I made a fortune!

ELIJAH   Don't worry, Mother. We always take advantage of the fairs.

PRIORESS   Listen well to what I am going to say to you. We were visited this morning by a certain Monsieur Valindin. He plans to open a café with an orchestra at the fair, and he wants to feature something which I cannot even imagine, but which I must tell you about: a little orchestra of blind musicians. You.

ELIJAH *(startled.)*   Us?

PRIORESS   It seems that he has been observing you for some time. He says that he would teach you several songs and that you, Gilbert, would be the singer for the group. I told him that you could only learn them by ear, that you cannot harmonize, and that in our chapel we do not even attempt it. But he says he has musicians who could teach you. What do you say? *(A long silence.)* Speak!

ELIJAH   Let brother Luke speak.

LUKE *(stammering.)*   Did that gentleman want me, too? I don't even go out with the others to beg.

PRIORESS   Somehow he found out that you used to play the cello before you lost your sight and that you still play it sometimes in chapel. He included you because he wants some variety in the instruments. Luke, you have played with orchestras.

LUKE *(sadly.)*   Music is easily forgotten.

PRIORESS   At any rate, tell us if you think Monsieur Valindin's project is feasible.

LUKE *(thinks about it.)*   No. *(He sighs.)* Blind men could never do that. They can't read the music.

PRIORESS   What do the rest of you think? *(She looks at them, one by one. DAVID steps forward nervously but says nothing.)* Yes, David?

DAVID   I would like to know . . . what Your Reverence thinks.

PRIORESS   I have already told you. I think as Luke does.

DAVID   It seems to me . . . (*He stops.*)

PRIORESS   Go on.

DAVID   It seems to me that Your Reverence has not said all she thinks.

PRIORESS   (*she looks at him steadily, then moves away a few steps.*) True. I think the man cares nothing about music and does not know what he wants. I think he will dismiss you the day after the fair opens—that is, if he does not change his mind during the rehearsals. I think your mission is to pray, not to play licentious songs. But I am not convinced that I can refuse you the benefits that he offers. He would give you forty sous per day, plus your meals—which would undoubtedly be a bit more appetizing than what you get at our poor table. . . . (*Pause.*) Besides, he has offered to leave the Asylum a bequest for prayers. If you agree to do it, your brothers and sisters in misfortune would also benefit. And regardless of what he decides to do with you, your salary would begin with the first rehearsal and would continue as long as you work for him, even if he does dismiss you before the fair opens. . . . I do not know what to advise you. (*A silence.*) And I see that you yourselves do not know what to think, either. All right. You have my permission to stay right here and discuss it as long as you wish. You will give me your answer at noon. (*She moves right, then turns before reaching the exit.*) But you must keep in mind two things.

First: If he does not dismiss you, you cannot back out. The contract would oblige you to work for him for the duration of the fair, and if you please the public, to travel with him for a year, performing at other carnivals in the province.

DONATIEN (*frightened.*) Travel with him for a year?

PRIORESS   Yes. That would mean your withdrawal from the Asylum. You could not even wear that emblem which today is your protection . . . and which must not become involved in dealings which are liable to be misinterpreted.

DAVID   And the second thing?

PRIORESS (*seriously.*) The second thing is a plea. If you accept, never forget that you are brothers before God, and that you must always behave as brothers. May God guide your decision. (*She exits. There is a deep silence.*)

GILBERT   Aren't we going out to beg?

ELIJAH   Quiet, Little Bird.

NAZAIRE (*strikes the step with his stick.*) Let's sit down. (*He does so.*)

DONATIEN   Yes, let's. (*He feels with his cane, then sits.* GILBERT, LUKE, *and* ELIJAH *follow suit.* DAVID *remains standing, motionless.*)

NAZAIRE   The sly old bitch! I'm tempted to turn down the offer, just to get back at her. She'd love us to accept!

LUKE   That isn't true.

NAZAIRE   Don't make me laugh! (*Mockingly.*) "Think of our poor table, my sons! You will eat better and so will we!" Ha! I'd exchange my plate for hers any time!

LUKE   You aren't being fair.

NAZAIRE   Has she ever invited you to sit at her
table? That's where all the Asylum's gifts and
bequests end up.

ELIJAH   So you're turning down the offer?

NAZAIRE   We'll have to think about it. It's true
that we would get our bellies full, for a change.
And boys, a show like ours would attract women
like flies at every fair in France. . . . (*He licks
his lips.*)

DONATIEN   (*laughs excitedly and sings softly.*)
"When Colasa reveals her shapely knees"——

ELIJAH   Quiet! The Mother might hear you!

NAZAIRE   Oh, leave the little one alone! Let him
have his fun! Brothers, what have we been doing
here for the past few centuries? I'll tell you what:
We've been rotting away, little by little.

ELIJAH   Some get married.

NAZAIRE   Yes, with the sisters from the women's
section. That's just another way of rotting! That's
what the people with eyes have done to us!
They've made the world for themselves and left
us to rot! If you ask me, they all ought to be
hanged!

LUKE   And then what would become of us without
them?

NAZAIRE   You're not a blind man.

LUKE   What are you talking about?

NAZAIRE   You had eyes for the first twenty-five years
of your life! You're not one of us!

LUKE   (*sadly.*) I know better than you that all
we're doing here is sitting around, waiting to die.

NAZAIRE   Well, I'm going to do something about
it!

GILBERT   Oh, now I understand! I say let's do it! I can sing. It will be like a comedy!

ELIJAH   What do you know about comedies?

GILBERT   (*laughs.*)   That's the only thing I do know about! My parents sold me to a blind man and I went around to the fairs with him. I saw a beautiful comedy. . . . I'd like to do that. . . . I saw . . . (*Laughs.*) Then I got the fever and I don't remember much after that. But I did see! I did!

NAZAIRE   Be quiet, silly. The only thing worth fooling with is eating and screwing.

ELIJAH   We're not musicians. Gilbert and I make our money because people pay us to be quiet. I hate music! I was born blind. My parents bought me an old, beat-up violin that I could scratch around on——

DONATIEN   Can't you stop talking about parents?

DAVID *turns his head to listen.*

NAZAIRE   What's the matter? Did yours put one over on you, too?

DONATIEN   (*after a brief pause.*)   No. Go on, brother Elijah.

ELIJAH   I was going to say that I never had a teacher. In a year and a half I managed to pick out two songs. Now I only know fifteen, and I don't even know them very well. I play on two strings—I can't manage all four. There has never been any such thing as an orchestra of blind men!

LUKE   And there never will be!

ELIJAH   (*bows his head.*)   We're not good for anything.

DAVID *appears irritated; he silently shakes his head.*

LUKE   I guess we're good for praying. . . .

NAZAIRE (*bows his head.*) They all ought to be hanged!

DAVID *twists his hands indecisively. A silence.*

GILBERT (*who has listened smilingly to them all.*) I say we do it!

NAZAIRE And so do I, damn it all! (GILBERT *laughs happily.*) It doesn't make any difference how I ended up here or how I learned to saw a fiddle, but I'll tell you one thing: I've been around and I know what hunger is. And I happen to be hungry . . . and not just for food. No matter what happens to us, we can't get any worse off than we are now. Donatien, as soon as you get yourself one of those girls, you'll forget about your parents. It's hard to forget them, I know, but I managed to do it. Come on, Luke! Say you'll do it!

LUKE Sure, I'll do it. Nothing makes much difference to me any more.

NAZAIRE That makes three of us!

ELIJAH Make that four. This way, at least we'll get our bellies full.

DONATIEN (*he raises his head, intrigued.*) David hasn't said anything.

NAZAIRE He'll say yes! Won't you, David? (*Silence.*) Did he leave?

DAVID I'm here.

DONATIEN (*anxiously.*) Are you for it?

DAVID Yes, I am. But you're not.

ELIJAH What are you talking about?

DAVID You think you've said yes, but you've really said no! You've accepted his offer, but you're doing it for the food, for the women. What happens if you think about your violins? That terrifies you! You have to say yes to your violins, not to the food and women! (*He goes excitedly from one to the other.*) That man is no fool—he knows what he wants. I have a feeling he and I could become very good friends, because he has come up with an idea that I've had inside me for years without daring to express it. Although I have said something about it to one of you.

DONATIEN (*moved.*)   That's true.

DAVID   Now we can do it, brothers! Each of us can learn his part by ear, and we'll have an orchestra of blind musicians!

NAZAIRE   You're forgetting that man doesn't care about music.

DAVID   But he has musicians working for him who also think it's possible! Brothers, we must throw ourselves into this thing wholeheartedly! The people who have eyes must be convinced that we are men—just as much as they are—not sick little animals!

ELIJAH   Men can read.

DAVID (*he has become excited and obstinate.*)   So can we!

ELIJAH   You've lost your mind!

LUKE *clucks his tongue with pity.*

NAZAIRE (*after a moment.*)   He's crazy.

DONATIEN   No, he isn't. He means that we could get people to read books to us. . . .

DAVID   I mean that we can read them ourselves.

NAZAIRE (*laughs.*)   He's worse than Gilbert.

DAVID   Go ahead and laugh! I've always thought what none of you dared to think, and I'll always learn things that you don't dare to learn!

LUKE   What sort of things?

DAVID (*after a brief pause.*)   Haven't you ever heard of Melanie de Salignac?

NAZAIRE (*mockingly.*)   And who might she be?

GILBERT (*smiling.*)   A beautiful lady!

DAVID (*seriously.*)   Yes, she's beautiful. I believe she is the most beautiful woman on earth.

ELIJAH   What about her?

DAVID   She knows about science, languages, music. . . . She can read and write. All by herself! I don't know how she does it, but she reads—in books!

ELIJAH   So what?

DAVID   She's blind.

NAZAIRE (*derisively.*)   Really now, David. . . .

ELIJAH *laughs.*

DAVID   Idiots! That's no fairy tale! She's here! In France!

ELIJAH   Where in France?

DAVID   I don't know—some place . . .

NAZAIRE   Have you ever met her?

DAVID   No. But maybe some day we can all meet her.

ELIJAH   Who told you about her?

DAVID (*hurt.*)   Some people I trust.

NAZAIRE (*laughs.*)   They were pulling your leg!

LUKE   I never heard of her.

DAVID   She exists, you fools!

ELIJAH (*needling him.*)   Maybe that's where you are when you ought to be bringing in some money —maybe you're off talking to those people you trust.

DAVID (*dryly.*)   Not always. Yesterday I was under the balcony of a palace, listening to a string quartet. It was a very long concert.

NAZAIRE (*laughs.*)   Melanie was probably playing.
Laughter from ELIJAH, *which* GILBERT *naively
seconds.*

DAVID   We could play the same kind of music I
was listening to yesterday!

ELIJAH   You think it would be easy because you
know how to play! You've heard Luke—you know
how he plays!

DAVID (*intensely.*)   You're all dead and don't even
know it! You're all cowards!

ELIJAH   Just a minute now . . .

DAVID   Elijah, if you weren't a coward you would
play on all four strings! It's easier than playing
on two! But you have to want to! You have to say
yes to your violin!

DONATIEN (*rises.*)   All right, I'll say it!

DAVID   Thank you, Donatien. (*He gropingly takes
his hand.*)

LUKE (*bitterly.*)   You're just a blind man swinging
wildly about with his cane!

DAVID (*he feverishly draws back his hand and strikes
the floor with his stick.*)   A blind man's blows
can be as deadly as anyone else's arrows! You
think I'm deluded because I talk to you about
Melanie! But Nazaire, you know that with my
stick I can hit you right on the back of the neck
whenever I want to! I've done it many times when
we were playing. And you know why? Because
when I was a boy, they laughed at me when I
tried to use my stick to defend myself against
bullies! I decided my stick was going to become
an eye, and that's just what it is. Brothers, if we
all decide that our violins are going to sing together, they will! It's just a matter of *wanting* it!

And if you don't want it, just resign yourselves
to this living death that has us trapped here. (*A
silence.*)

NAZAIRE (*rises.*)   All right . . . you tell the Mother
that we'll accept. I'm going out to beg. (*He goes
up the steps.*)

DAVID (*moved.*)   Then you'll all do it?

LUKE (*rises.*)   I'm going to my room.

DAVID   But do you say yes, with the rest of us?

LUKE   I said it at the very beginning.

LUKE *and* NAZAIRE *exit through the curtain.*

ELIJAH (*rising.*)   Let's get to the street, Little
Bird. (GILBERT *rises and takes him by the arm.*)

GILBERT   It will be a beautiful comedy! We'll
wear costumes! Elijah, my costume will be the
prettiest of all. . . . (*They exit through the
curtain. A pause.*)

DAVID   Donatien, they said yes! A tiny, timid little
yes, but they said it. (*He places his hand on*
DONATIEN'S *shoulder.* DONATIEN *squeezes it,
moved.*) We'll do it! I know we can do it!

*Music begins to play. It is the Allegro from Corelli's
"Concerto Grosso" in G minor. The lights fade
slowly. When they come back up, the curtains have
been opened and we see a room in* VALINDIN'S *house.
There is a door at the back, another in the alcove
left, and another down right. At right, a silver
jewelry box, some knitting, a pitcher of wine, and
glasses are on a small table. There are several
chairs, at the table and along the walls. In short, it is
the living room of a comfortable bourgeois. The
concerto continues for a few moments. When it
stops playing,* VALINDIN *enters through door up
center. He wears a satisfied expression.*

VALINDIN   Adrienne! (*He goes to the table and leaves some papers which he has brought in. He curiously examines the jewel box, then runs his hand across a chair. His expression is that of a pleased man.*) Adrienne! (*He goes to door right.*) Where are you, my little tramp?

ADRIENNE (*voice.*)   I'm fixing my hair!

VALINDIN   Why doesn't Catherine fix your hair?

ADRIENNE (*voice.*)   I prefer to do it myself.

VALINDIN   You're awfully late getting up this morning. (*He pours himself a glass of wine. After glancing at door right, he drinks it in one swallow. Then he moves the little table and taps one of its legs.*)

ADRIENNE (*meanwhile; voice.*)   I'd say *you* got up rather early.

VALINDIN (*still holding the glass, he turns to the door.*)   I had to go back to the Asylum. They've agreed to do it.

ADRIENNE (*voice.*)   I know.

VALINDIN   You already knew?

ADRIENNE (*voice.*)   A half hour ago they brought over a cello and some violins.

VALINDIN   It looks like I'm not the only one who gets up early. Where did you put the instruments?

ADRIENNE (*voice.*)   In the other room.

VALINDIN   Perfect. The contract is already signed. I got the notary right away.

ADRIENNE (*voice.*)   I should hope so.

VALINDIN (*he laughs and paces.*)   After I got through at the Asylum I took a walk over to the plaza. They've already assigned the sites for each booth, and we've got a good one. It's off at one end, but it's good.

ADRIENNE (*voice.*) You're already starting to get like you were last year!

VALINDIN And you're already nagging! May I ask how I was last year?

ADRIENNE (*voice.*) You spent twenty-four hours a day in the café.

VALINDIN (*sets down his empty glass.*) Why not? It's my café!

ADRIENNE (*voice.*) And this year you'll do the same thing all over again, won't you? You'll be there until all hours, carrying on by yourself.

VALINDIN Of course.

ADRIENNE (*voice.*) With a bottle.

VALINDIN What do you mean by that? You know I hardly ever drink any more! (*He smooths back his hair.* ADRIENNE *enters. She is wearing a pretty morning dress. She is in her thirties and is attractive, although not beautiful. It is still possible to detect in her some strains of the rustic peasant girl which have not been completely eradicated by city life. She has a black beauty spot on her cheek.*) Good Lord! My little tramp has gone and gotten herself all prettied up. (*He starts to put his arms around her, pointing to her beauty spot.*) She even looks like a lady!

ADRIENNE (*breaks away.*) Leave me alone.

VALINDIN (*moves away.*) Today we're certainly getting off to a bad start. (*Next to the table.*) You know, this table wobbles. (*He shakes it.*) I'll tell old Bernier to come fix it.

ADRIENNE (*dryly.*) Are they going to rehearse here?

VALINDIN Morning and evening. They'll eat in the tavern down the street. (*He shakes the table.*)

ADRIENNE And will they sleep here, too?

VALINDIN   No. As long as we're in Paris they will sleep at the Asylum.

ADRIENNE   Well, that's *something,* anyway.

VALINDIN   (*approaches her.*) Come, now. Why this bad mood? I really don't think you can complain. With me you have everything you want . . . and you get it without working. Surely that's a lot better than singing and dancing at carnivals.

ADRIENNE   You're lying! I'll end up being your waitress again!

VALINDIN   (*laughs.*) We all have to help out a bit. Besides, you won't just be a waitress; you'll be in charge of the waitresses.

ADRIENNE   I'll be in charge of one waitress—the only one.

VALINDIN   We certainly don't need any more than one. But for the moment she's your personal maid. You're living like a great lady, and all you do is complain.

ADRIENNE   I'm bored.

VALINDIN   Work on your knitting.

ADRIENNE   It bores me!

VALINDIN   You don't know what you want.

ADRIENNE   I felt better when I could sing and dance.

VALINDIN   (*violently.*) You felt better when you could tramp around! Because that's what you are: a playful little tramp. But Valindin knew how to tame you, didn't he? And now you've joined forces with Valindin, haven't you? (*He laughs.*) It cost me a pretty penny, I'll admit. How many times have you scared me?

ADRIENNE   (*smiles.*) I don't remember.

VALINDIN   (*comes up behind her and takes her by*

the shoulders.) Now my little tramp has finished running. . . . Now she has her own house and her own café at the fair.

ADRIENNE Mine?

VALINDIN (*he takes something from his pocket.*) Yours. Do you know what the café will be called?

ADRIENNE What?

VALINDIN Chez Adrienne. (*He starts to put around her neck a gold brooch which hangs from a velvet ribbon.*) My little wanderer . . . who finally stopped wandering. . . .

ADRIENNE What's this? (*She takes the brooch and looks at it.*)

VALINDIN To celebrate the signing of the contract.

ADRIENNE (*softened.*) It's very pretty. . . . Thank you. (*She starts to put it on.*)

VALINDIN Let me put it on you. (*He puts it on her, then kisses her on the neck.*)

ADRIENNE Have you been drinking already?

VALINDIN Just one glass.

ADRIENNE (*flirting.*) Since you're feeling so gener- ous this morning, why don't you reconsider . . . and let me sing and dance in "my" café?

VALINDIN (*furious.*) That again? (*He moves brusquely away and paces.*)

ADRIENNE (*goes toward him.*) That bunch of blind beggars is going to be a disaster!

VALINDIN We'll see.

ADRIENNE (*spitefully.*) You're an ass!

VALINDIN (*laughs.*) Yes, an ass. But a *golden* ass! When people are hungry, that's the time to do business with them.

ADRIENNE And the time for women.

VALINDIN (*he roughly seizes her arm.*) What do

you mean by that? (*She looks at him fearfully.*) You don't love me? All right, so what? I know better than you what's good for you! You'll thank me for it some day, after you give me a son and you see that everything I have is for him —for your son!

ADRIENNE   I don't want any children.

VALINDIN   But *I* want them. Understand? I'm no kid any more, but I'm still capable of showing you who Valindin is. I'll get what I want. And you know why? Because I know how to combine practicality with goodness. I'm goodhearted and philanthropic, but remember, my dear, that philanthropy is also profitable. Those blind men are going to bring in money for us, and I'll pay them by teaching them to live! At the Asylum they were rotting away, little by little. With me they're going to become famous, and they'll be able to earn a living for themselves. . . . (*His voice chokes.*) It's so elevating to do good for one's fellow man! (*He takes out a handkerchief and blows his nose while* ADRIENNE *watches him uneasily.*) I dare say they will be more grateful to me than you are. Everyone needs a protector, and I'll be theirs. I myself was fortunate enough to have one in the Baron of Tournelle, God bless him. If it had not been for him, I would never have been able to get started in anything when I came out of the Navy. He was kind enough to find me a position with the royal family, and thanks to that job I was able to survive for a few years until I got on my feet. . . . (*Laughs.*) As a matter of fact, I'm still collecting that salary. . . . It does come in handy. God bless our king!

ADRIENNE You never have told me what your job is with the royal family.

VALINDIN (*laughs and lowers his voice.*) I was employed as the personal barber for a prince who had not yet been born. I don't remember his name. It doesn't matter; the poor thing was born dead.

ADRIENNE (*laughs.*) I suppose you combed his hair for the funeral?

VALINDIN Of course. You learn to do a lot of things in the Navy. (ADRIENNE *laughs.*) You can laugh if you want to, but it's thanks to that position that I can wear this sword. (*He pats the pommel affectionately.*) It's a privilege accorded the royal barbers. (*He moves toward her.*) Our son will wear one, too, even if he is of humble birth. (*She avoids his gaze.*) Because by the time he's a man, money will be worth as much as noble birth. And he will have money!

ADRIENNE Isn't that someone at the door?

VALINDIN Probably Lefranc. I told him to come by.

ADRIENNE (*goes to the door.*) I hear a tapping noise.

VALINDIN Then it's they.

ADRIENNE (*annoyed.*) Already?

There is a timid knocking at the upstage door.

VALINDIN Of course. Come in!

The door is opened by CATHERINE, *a fairly attractive and rather stupid servant girl.*

ADRIENNE In that case, I'll leave you. (*She starts off right.*)

CATHERINE The blind men are here, sir.

VALINDIN Bring them in. (*To* ADRIENNE.) Don't go. I want you to meet them.

ADRIENNE *looks annoyed. She sits next to the table and picks up her knitting.* CATHERINE *brings in* NAZAIRE. *The other* BLIND MEN *follow, all holding on to each other. The emblem of the Quinze-Vingts has disappeared from their tunics.*

CATHERINE   Here's the door. . . . Right through here. . . .

VALINDIN   Welcome, my friends.

NAZAIRE   God's blessings on this house.

VALINDIN   And on all of you.

ADRIENNE   (*grudgingly.*)   God be with you.

NAZAIRE   Is that your wife?

VALINDIN   That's . . . Yes, that's my wife. You may leave, Catherine. (CATHERINE *exits and closes the door after her.*) Did you come alone?

ELIJAH   Oh yes. We know our way around the city.

VALINDIN   Very well, my friends. We have a great deal of work ahead of us. Are you ready for it?

BLIND MEN   (*happily.*)   Yes, sir.

VALINDIN   You will have to learn ten songs. The melodies are very simple. Which of you is the singer? (*Pause.*)

ELIJAH   (*elbows* GILBERT.)   That's you.

GILBERT   Me?

VALINDIN   Are you the singer?

ELIJAH   Yes, sir, he is. It's just that he's a bit . . . simple.

GILBERT   (*smiling.*)   My name is Little Bird.

ADRIENNE *muffles an exclamation of disgust.*

VALINDIN   (*after looking at* GILBERT, *perplexed.*) Well you, Little Bird, will have to memorize the songs. Do you think you can?

GILBERT   Oh! That's all I ever do!

VALINDIN Hmm. . . . Very well. The violinist
will be here soon to start teaching you the songs.
The rest of you will simply follow the melody
with your instruments. Everyone will play the
same melody, the same rhythm. There will be
many long hours of rehearsal. I hope you will
be patient.

DAVID Won't we play different parts?

VALINDIN (*smiles.*) Don't worry, I realize I
couldn't ask you to do that. You'll all play in
unison. Why the gloomy faces? Is something
wrong?

DAVID (*steps forward.*) Monsieur Valindin, we
. . . we were thinking that you *could* ask us to
do that. (VALINDIN *glances at* ADRIENNE *in amazement.*) We believe we can do it.

VALINDIN *looks at* ADRIENNE, *who shakes her head in
disgust. She points at her forehead, to indicate her
opinion that* DAVID *is slightly insane.*

VALINDIN But . . . different parts haven't even
been written.

DAVID They could be written.

VALINDIN That's a great deal of work. Besides, you
don't——

DAVID We could do it! With your permission, I
myself will take the responsibility of learning all
the parts and teaching them to the rest of the
men. I'm not afraid of work.

VALINDIN At any rate, you'll have to discuss all
that with the violinist. Come along now, I'll take
you to the room where you will have your rehearsals. You'll soon know your way around the
house without my help. (*He takes* NAZAIRE *by
the hand and leads him to the alcove.*) This way.

The BLIND MEN *gropingly seek each other, then feel their way along with their canes, accompanied by the dry tapping sound.*

DAVID   Monsieur Valindin, please listen to me. . . . It isn't so difficult. . . .

VALINDIN   (*he exits; his voice is heard offstage.*) Yes, yes, we'll talk about it later. . . . Careful, now. . . . Don't go breaking anything with those sticks of yours. . . . Watch out for the cabinet, now. . . .

The BLIND MEN *follow him out. The sound of their canes gradually fades away.* DAVID, *who is about to exit also, stops and slowly turns around, recalling vaguely that someone else is still in the room.* ADRIENNE *watches him steadily for a moment, then lays down her knitting and rises.*

ADRIENNE   Shall I take you? (DAVID's *face grows dark. Without replying, he exits through the alcove, leaving the door open behind him. The sound of his cane fades away.* ADRIENNE *utters a sound of disgust and begins to pace, nervously. There is a knock at the door upstage center.* ADRIENNE *stops.*) Come in.

Enter JEROME LEFRANC. *He is a thin man of sickly complexion and nervous smile. He is neatly dressed, but his clothing is old. His hair is unpowdered. His lace cuffs and shirt front are dingy.*

LEFRANC   (*he bows.*) Good morning, Adrienne. My congratulations.

ADRIENNE   (*ill-humoredly.*)   For what?

LEFRANC   I see that you have finally been promoted to lady of the house. That is no small accomplishment for a former carnival girl.

ADRIENNE   (*with a perverse smile.*)   Do you still

play the violin, Monsieur Lefranc? When will I
have the pleasure of congratulating you on your
promotion to Director of the Opéra-Comique?

LEFRANC (*laughs listlessly.*) Come now, Adrienne!
Can't you take a bit of a joke from an old friend?

ADRIENNE One joke for another. . . .

LEFRANC It would appear that our dear Valindin
has done something to annoy you. Where might
I find him?

ADRIENNE (*coldly.*) In there. With them.

LEFRANC Oh, is the circus here already? I suppose
I am a bit late. Ah, here he is now.

VALINDIN *enters through the alcove.*

VALINDIN I don't like to waste my time, Monsieur
Lefranc.

LEFRANC (*jeering slightly.*) That's what you think.

VALINDIN There are your songs. The lyrics are all
finished now. (LEFRANC *picks them up from the
table and leafs through them.*) What sort of
repertoire will you be bringing to the fair this
year?

LEFRANC (*looking over the songs.*) An excellent
repertoire, Monsieur Valindin! And the titles are
really quite elegant: "The Gardener and His
Master," "Cinderella"——

ADRIENNE Last year in the café I sang the arietta
from "Cinderella." Do you remember?

VALINDIN (*after a quick glance at* ADRIENNE.) What
about new numbers?

LEFRANC (*looks at him slyly.*) We are rehearsing
the opera which Monsieur Grétry was kind
enough to place in our hands. It will undoubtedly be the sensation of the fair!

VALINDIN (*annoyed.*) Monsieur Grétry?

LEFRANC Yes. (*He tosses the pile of music onto the table.*) Considerably better than these vulgar little ditties.

ADRIENNE As I recall, you are the composer of those "vulgar little ditties." . . .

LEFRANC Yes, as a matter of fact. Written especially for those poor blind devils . . . who would only mutilate whatever they were asked to play.

VALINDIN (*gruffly.*) I'm not afraid of your Grétry. Bring the music and let's go rehearse. (*He moves toward the alcove.*)

LEFRANC (*picking up the music.*) Assuming that's possible. I'm afraid you may have gotten yourself into a bit of a disaster.

VALINDIN However it turns out, remember that you promised not to say a word about this to your director.

In the distance, a violin begins to play the Adagio from the third movement of Corelli's "Concerto Grosso."

LEFRANC Of course, Monsieur Valindin. After all, you are paying for this. But I do hope you realize that these poor devils are going to be atrocious. (*He starts to accompany* VALINDIN, *then stops and listens attentively.*) What is that?

VALINDIN (*looks at him and listens.*) It's they.

ADRIENNE One of them is playing by himself.

LEFRANC Is this a joke?

VALINDIN What do you mean?

LEFRANC (*dryly.*) Why have you brought in another violinist? I don't like that.

VALINDIN (*takes him by the wrist and brings him downstage, lowering his voice.*) Good Lord.

man! Are you saying that blind fiddler is *good?*

LEFRANC That one who is playing now isn't blind.

ADRIENNE (*has moved to the door and stands listening.*) He does play well. . . .

VALINDIN *goes to the table, pours himself a glass of wine, and drinks.*

LEFRANC All right, the joke has gone far enough! Who is that?

There is a knock at door upstage.

ADRIENNE (*she sees that* VALINDIN *is not moving.*) Come in!

CATHERINE *enters.*

CATHERINE Old Bernier is here, Monsieur.

VALINDIN (*pays no attention to her.*) I wonder if the others play like that, too. . . .

LEFRANC (*realizes he is not being deceived.*) If he's blind, he hasn't been for long. . . . And he must have been a musician before. . . .

VALINDIN (*strikes the table with his fist; oddly, he seems annoyed.*) Let's go in there. (*He moves rapidly toward the alcove, followed by* LEFRANC.)

CATHERINE (*coughs.*) Monsieur . . . Old Bernier . . .

VALINDIN (*stops.*) What? Oh, yes. (*To* ADRIENNE.) Tell him about the table. I'll be right back.

He exits with LEFRANC. CATHERINE *exits.* ADRIENNE *continues to listen attentively, fascinated by the sound of the distant violin. Enter* IRÉNÉE BERNIER. *He wears the clothes of a workingman. He appears to be around fifty years old. His bearing is humble; his face reveals a peasant background.*

BERNIER With your permission, Madame Adrienne?

ADRIENNE Come in, Monsieur Bernier. Monsieur

Valindin will be back in a moment. How is your family?

BERNIER   I don't know, Madame. I won't go back to the village until winter.

ADRIENNE   (*she continues to listen to the music and therefore does not give him her full attention.*) Don't they write you? (*The music stops.* ADRIENNE *goes to the alcove, listens for a moment, and closes the door.*)

BERNIER   They don't know how to write. Sometimes they find someone to do it for them, but there's really no need for it. Anything they might want to tell me, I already know.

ADRIENNE   (*goes to his side.*)   And what would that be?

BERNIER   Well . . . just that I should be sure to bring home all I can. . . . Things like that.

ADRIENNE   (*nods understandingly.*)   Did he tell you to stop by here?

BERNIER   I was the one who wanted to talk with him, Madame.

ADRIENNE   He wants you to take a look at this table. It wobbles.

BERNIER   (*looks at the table.*)   That's nothing. Tomorrow I'll bring some glue.

ADRIENNE   (*sits and picks up her knitting.*)   Won't you sit down?

BERNIER   I'm all right, Madame Adrienne. . . . You see, I came to ask Monsieur Valindin— maybe you could ask him for me. . . .

ADRIENNE   What's wrong?

BERNIER   Well, I . . .

The alcove door opens and BERNIER *falls silent.* LEFRANC *enters, scowling. He stops downstage. Be-*

hind him enters DAVID, *who gropes his way quickly
to* LEFRANC's *side. Finally,* VALINDIN *enters and
stands near the alcove. He crosses his arms and
makes an effort to control his indignation.*

LEFRANC I simply do not understand!

DAVID You understand enough to know that I
could do it.

LEFRANC No, I tell you!

DAVID *stammers.*

BERNIER (*takes advantage of the break in the conversation.*) Good morning, Monsieur Valindin.

DAVID *raises his head at the sound of the new voice.*

VALINDIN Hello, Irénée. I'll be with you in a
minute.

Suddenly, DAVID *goes toward the table.* ADRIENNE
sees him coming; she stands. DAVID *senses her presence and changes his course slightly, running his
hand along the table's edge. As he approaches* BER-
NIER *he once again turns and, with his cane, begins
to feel his way along the wall.*

BERNIER The table can be easily fixed, Monsieur
Valindin.

DAVID *is now moving toward the door.*

VALINDIN (*motions* BERNIER *to be quiet.*) And
might I know where you think you are going?
(DAVID *stops.*) Yes, I'm talking to you! What is
your name?

DAVID David.

VALINDIN Well now, David, I suppose you realize
you've made your comrades angry with you.

DAVID They wanted to be angry with you, but
they didn't dare.

VALINDIN Are you making fun of me?

DAVID No.

LEFRANC   He's mad. We've already seen that.

DAVID   (*goes toward him.*)   Anyone with an ear can follow someone singing harmony. There's no reason why a violin cannot play that second part for the others to imitate. And even less reason why a cello couldn't do it!

ADRIENNE   That's true. . . .

VALINDIN   What do you know about it?

ADRIENNE   I used to be a singer! Remember?

VALINDIN   Shut up.

LEFRANC   Adrienne, with instruments it isn't that easy. But this man is the stubbornest human being I have ever encountered in my life. (*He pauses, upset.*)

VALINDIN   And he knows perfectly well that even if he does have a good ear, the others are not even musicians!

DAVID   If we are so bad, why do you want us at all?

VALINDIN   (*caught off guard.*)   Well . . . because in spite of everything, the show will be marvelous! Literally unheard of. If you will all simply cooperate and do what we ask of you, your group will be good. But you insist on dreaming about the impossible. Come on, now. Get back to rehearsal. (DAVID *suddenly goes upstage center. When he reaches the door, he stops and runs his hand over it.*) Where are you going? (DAVID *does not reply. His hand is on the latch.*) That's the way to the street! (DAVID *does not move.* VALINDIN, *surprised, approaches him. His face grows hard.*) Maybe you'd like to go to the street?

LEFRANC   Let me speak with him. Perhaps I can make him see how wrong he is. . . .

VALINDIN   (*harshly.*)   Not here. Do it in front of

the others. We shouldn't have brought him here.
(*He takes* DAVID *by the arm.*) Come on.

DAVID (*holding back.*) I'm not going back in
there.

VALINDIN You don't want to be criticized in front
of them, do you? Well, that's exactly what's going to happen. Let's go. (*He pulls at him, un-
successfully.*) I said let's go!

ADRIENNE Louis! Don't!

DAVID I won't go back in there! (*As he says this
he brings his cane down sharply on* VALINDIN'*s
foot.* VALINDIN *leaps back with an exclamation
of pain.* DAVID *moves back one step and stands
waiting, tense and alert.* VALINDIN *looks at him
steadily.*)

ADRIENNE (*frightened, she runs to hold him back.*)
Louis!

VALINDIN That . . . was an accident, wasn't it?
You intended to hit the floor . . . didn't you?

ADRIENNE Of course he did! He's blind, Louis!

VALINDIN Fortunately for him. (*He approaches*
BERNIER.) You see, Irénée? All I want to do is
provide work for the poor and needy, and some
of them are too stupid to take it. You tell this
donkey how Valindin treats the poor. You, the
father of six children! You, who have to leave
your town and come to Paris every autumn to
work as a tinker and carpenter! You tell him
what would have long ago happened to you and
your family if it hadn't been for Valindin. . . .

BERNIER (*coughs.*) Well . . . I . . .

VALINDIN Exactly, my friend, exactly. (*He paces.*)
But as you see, there are some people who refuse
to understand the beauty of philanthropy.

LEFRANC   David, you haven't been blind very long, have you?

DAVID   Since I was eight years old.

LEFRANC   Eight years old? Who taught you to play the violin?

DAVID   The man who taught my master's children showed me the positions. Then I figured out the rest by myself.

VALINDIN *looks at* LEFRANC, *who makes a gesture of disbelief.*

LEFRANC   My son, you have a good ear, but you know nothing about music. I have spent my life studying harmony, and I assure you it's a very difficult science. In order to do what you want, we would have to write two violin parts and one cello part for each song. That would be a great deal of work. And then, how would you learn your parts? You couldn't read them.

DAVID   If you play them, we can imitate you.

LEFRANC   And if we did it that way, how much time do you think we would spend just learning one song? (*Silence.*) A month?

DAVID   No!

LEFRANC   Yes, my friend! Yes!

DAVID   We have to do it . . . even if it does take a month to learn each song!

VALINDIN   You're forgetting that the fair opens in eleven days.

DAVID (*startled.*) Eleven days?

VALINDIN   Yes! And here we stand, wasting precious time!

LEFRANC   Frankly, I think you will play the songs miserably, even if you only play them in unison. I only hope Monsieur Valindin knows why he hired you, because I . . . (VALINDIN *is gesturing to him frantically, trying to tell him not to say anything that will discourage* DAVID.) I mean . . . he's a very generous man and he knows what he's doing. Only *he* would see that you are capable of doing something worthwhile. I'm sure that whatever you do will be admirable. . . .

VALINDIN Of course it will. And besides, boy, I want to lend dignity to your work. I want to make it possible for you to earn a living without having to beg. Come on, now; it's late and I have a lot to do! Take him back in there, Lefranc. (DAVID *hesitates.* VALINDIN, ADRIENNE, *and* BERNIER *watch him.* LEFRANC *takes* DAVID *by the arm.* VALINDIN *says paternally*) Go along, David.

DAVID *shakes off* LEFRANC's *arm and exits very slowly through the alcove.* LEFRANC *follows him.* VALINDIN *runs to the door and closes it softly.* BERNIER *coughs and looks at* ADRIENNE.

ADRIENNE Louis, Bernier wanted to ask you something.

VALINDIN (*looks apprehensively toward the alcove.*) Let's just hope this works out all right. I have a lot at stake here, and I will not let the whole operation be sabotaged by a . . . by a lunatic. (*Moves to the table. His tone is now calmer.*) How's the peacock coming, Irénée? Did you find some good sheet metal? (*Pours himself a drink.*)

ADRIENNE (*places her hand on his arm.*) Louis . . .

VALINDIN (*crossly.*) Adrienne, it's only one glass! (*He drinks.* ADRIENNE *sighs and sits down to renew her knitting.*)

BERNIER Well . . . as a matter of fact . . . that's

just what I wanted to talk with you about, Monsieur Valindin. . . . Sheet metal is very expensive now.

VALINDIN (*dryly.*)   What's that supposed to mean?

BERNIER   The money you gave me to buy it . . . well, it isn't enough.

VALINDIN (*abruptly sets his glass down on the table.*)   The amount of money I gave you was based on the cost of the materials.

BERNIER   Yes, but on last year's prices, Monsieur Valindin. This year everything costs almost twice as much. . . . I wasn't counting on that.

VALINDIN (*paces, irritated.*)   Irénée, I'm not giving you another cent! We made our agreement and that's final! You'll build that peacock for me, and you'll build it quick! Without the peacock there can't be a show.

BERNIER   Honestly, Monsieur Valindin, I tell you the money isn't enough! I . . . it occurred to me that maybe the peacock could be built out of wood. . . .

VALINDIN (*stops.*)   Wood?

BERNIER   That way it would be easier to paint, and it would be plenty strong.

VALINDIN   And there would be a little something left over for Bernier's pocket. Right?

BERNIER (*smiles sadly.*)   No one can do that to you, Monsieur Valindin.

VALINDIN   Precisely. You and I are going right now to see about these prices. And if you've tried to deceive me, you'll regret it! (*He goes to door upstage center and opens it.*) Go ahead.

BERNIER (*sighs.*)   God be with you, Madame Adrienne.

ADRIENNE And with you, Monsieur Bernier.

BERNIER *exits.*

VALINDIN I'll be back soon, Adrienne. (*He starts to leave.* ADRIENNE *rises.*)

ADRIENNE Louis . . .

VALINDIN What?

ADRIENNE Don't you think you were a bit harsh with him? (*She moves toward him.*)

VALINDIN With whom? Bernier?

ADRIENNE Yes. And with that poor blind boy.

VALINDIN I'm harsh because I like to get things done. You say I'm harsh with you, too. But I'm saving you . . . the same as I'm doing for the rest of them. (*He laughs and pinches her cheek.*) Go back to your knitting . . . my little tramp.

He exits. A pause. ADRIENNE *goes to the alcove and listens. Then she moves, slowly and hesitantly, to the center of the room, where she stops for a moment to look with disgust at her knitting. Finally she sighs and moves rapidly to door right. She starts to open it, then stops as the alcove door opens. Enter* LEFRANC, *followed by* DAVID *and* DONATIEN, *who are carrying their violins.*

LEFRANC I beg your pardon. Isn't Valindin here?

ADRIENNE He just left.

LEFRANC I'd like to leave these two here. Unless you'd rather they went outside.

ADRIENNE They won't bother me.

LEFRANC For the moment it's better like this. Thank you. (*Exits through the alcove, closing the door after him.*)

ADRIENNE (*approaches* DAVID *and* DONATIEN, *intrigued.*) What's the trouble?

DONATIEN He threw us out.

DAVID *moves toward a chair, checks to make sure it's there, and sits. He lowers his head.*

ADRIENNE *(to* DAVID.) I was about to suggest that you sit down. . . .

DAVID   That won't be necessary.

ADRIENNE *(coldly.)* So I see.

DONATIEN   He always learns where the furniture is right away, but it takes me longer. . . .

ADRIENNE   Come. Give me your hand. (DONATIEN *holds out his hand to her and she leads him toward the table. She stops.*) What's wrong with you, boy? You're trembling!

DAVID *raises his head.*

DONATIEN *(upset.)* It's nothing.

ADRIENNE   Here. Sit here. *(She helps him sit next to the table.)* Are you sick?

DONATIEN   No, no! *(He drops his violin on the floor and clutches his hands.)*

ADRIENNE   I'll give you a glass of wine. That will warm you up! *(She pours two glasses and places one in* DONATIEN's *hand.)* Here.

DONATIEN   Thank you, Madame. *(He drinks, nervously.* ADRIENNE *takes the other glass to* DAVID.)

ADRIENNE   Here's yours.

DAVID *(raises his head.)* I didn't say I wanted anything to drink.

ADRIENNE *(stung, she draws back her hand quickly.)* I beg your pardon!

DONATIEN   No, Madame. You're the one who must pardon us. After what happened in there, we don't know what we're saying. . . .

ADRIENNE *(looking at* DAVID, *she goes to the table and leaves the glass.)* Why did they throw you out?

DONATIEN David tried to play harmony on his
violin and Monsieur Lefranc became furious.

ADRIENNE (*sitting at the other side of the table.*)
And what about you?

DONATIEN I . . . tried to follow David.

ADRIENNE But why?

DONATIEN Madame, don't you think we could do
what he wants?

DAVID Why ask her? You know she will just say
the same thing that he said. (*Sarcastically.*) He
did say that you were his wife . . . didn't he?

ADRIENNE (*coldly.*) I don't know what he said.

DAVID Of course. (*He runs his hand over his
violin, which is on his lap. He plucks a string,
which emits a muffled sound.*)

ADRIENNE (*starts to answer him, then thinks better
of it and speaks to* DONATIEN.) How did you
lose your sight, boy?

DONATIEN (*lowers his head, shamefully.*) Can't
you tell?

ADRIENNE (*smoothly.*) Smallpox?

DONATIEN I caught them when I was a baby. I
don't even remember what it's like to see.

ADRIENNE Who taught you to play the violin?

DONATIEN He did. (ADRIENNE *looks at* DAVID.)
When I came to the Asylum, he took charge of
me. He has taught me everything I know. Our
beds are next to each other, and at night he talks
to me about music and about all kinds of
things. . . . He's sort of like my father.

DAVID Can't you be quiet?

ADRIENNE Are you an orphan?

DONATIEN (*after a pause.*) I don't know.

ADRIENNE What do you do in the Asylum?

DONATIEN We spin and weave, we make bread, we beg . . . and we pray all day. That's the way God wills it. (*Each time* DONATIEN *has enumerated a task,* DAVID *has plucked a string of his violin. On the last phrase he stands.* ADRIENNE *does not take her eyes off him. He turns and goes to the door with great self-assurance. After a moment's thought, he places his hand on the latch, without having to grope for it.*) Where are you going, David?

ADRIENNE (*she rises.*) Are you leaving?

DAVID Does it bother you? (*He opens the door and exits, closing the door after him.*)

ADRIENNE He's . . . why, he's . . . unbearable!

DONATIEN I'm the one he's angry with. He says God couldn't have wanted us to be blind.

ADRIENNE Isn't he perhaps just a bit sick in the head?

DONATIEN At the Asylum some people think so.

ADRIENNE And what do you think?

DONATIEN I believe what he says! The others say he's crazy because he knows more than any of us, because he thinks what no one else dares to think.

ADRIENNE (*sits, slowly.*) For example?

DONATIEN Well . . . for example . . . this whole idea that blind people can play music just like people who have eyes. . . .

ADRIENNE What else?

DONATIEN He says we could read and write like they do.

ADRIENNE (*astounded.*) But . . . how on earth could you do that?

DONATIEN I don't know.

The muffled sound of Corelli's Adagio floats into the room.

ADRIENNE *(looks in the direction from which the sound is coming; she appears troubled.)* He's playing——

DONATIEN That means he's sad. . . .

ADRIENNE Are you really so sure he isn't crazy?

DONATIEN *(shaking his head, energetically.)* He knows about a lady. . . . A beautiful lady . . . as beautiful as you are, Madame!

ADRIENNE *(smiles.)* What makes you think I'm beautiful?

DONATIEN *(naively.)* Aren't you?

ADRIENNE Well . . . I'm not ugly. What were you going to say about that lady he knows?

DONATIEN Oh, he doesn't really know her. But he knows that she lives in France and that she's blind. *(He leans toward her, confidentially.)* That lady reads and writes books! And she reads and writes music! And she speaks many languages and she knows about numbers. Her name is Melanie de Salignac.

ADRIENNE *(incredulously.)* And she's blind?

DONATIEN Like us. . . . Can you keep a secret?

ADRIENNE Of course.

DONATIEN I can trust you, because you're good! I know you're good! *(Lowers his voice.)* When he plays that music . . . I know he's thinking about her.

ADRIENNE *(with irony.)* He loves her and he's never even met her?

DONATIEN His dream is to find her some day.

ADRIENNE But . . . can you people . . . love? *(DONATIEN's face darkens.)* Forgive me. . . . How foolish I am. Of course you can love. It's just that I don't know anything about . . . blind people.

DONATIEN   Nobody knows anything about blind people.

ADRIENNE   (*reaches across the table and takes his hand.*)   Will you forgive me?

DONATIEN   (*he begins to tremble; impulsively he takes her hand in both of his.*)   Madame, you're the kindest woman I've ever known! (*He kisses her hand and, without releasing it, begins to sob.*)

ADRIENNE   (*surprised and upset.*)   Calm down, boy! Control yourself!

The alcove door opens. DONATIEN *quickly draws back his hands and tries to hide his face.* LEFRANC *enters.*

LEFRANC   Excuse me, Adrienne. This situation is worse than I had thought.

ADRIENNE   (*rises.*)   Louis still hasn't come back. . . .

LEFRANC   It's just as well. Now the others have decided they won't rehearse without these two. (*Notices the sound of* DAVID'*s violin.*) What's he doing out there?

ADRIENNE   (*coldly.*)   Apparently he likes to play his violin.

LEFRANC   Yes, so I see. Come along, boy. Let's go rehearse.

DONATIEN   Yes, Monsieur. (*Picks up his violin.*)

ADRIENNE   Wait, I'll help you.

DONATIEN   Thank you, Madame. You don't have to. (*He rises and takes a few clumsy steps.* ADRIENNE *takes his hand.*)

ADRIENNE Here. This way. Are you trembling
again?

DONATIEN It's nothing, really. . . .

LEFRANC *goes to door, upstage center.*

ADRIENNE Here, Lefranc, you take him, I'll try to
get the other one to come back. He's in a bad
mood—I don't think you could handle him right
now.

LEFRANC I'll leave him to you. (*Takes* DONATIEN
by the arm.) Come along, boy.

They exit through the alcove. ADRIENNE *closes the
door after them, then goes to door, upstage center.
She opens it quietly and looks out. The sound of
the violin becomes stronger.* ADRIENNE *goes out. In
a moment the violin stops.*

DAVID (*voice.*) Who's that?

ADRIENNE (*voice.*) Monsieur Lefranc asks that you
forgive him and come back to the rehearsal.

DAVID (*voice; sardonically.*) How kind of him!

ADRIENNE (*voice.*) Shall I guide you?

DAVID (*voice.*) Why doesn't he come ask me himself?

ADRIENNE (*voice.*) He didn't want to have to tell
you . . . that the others refuse to work unless
you come back. (*A silence.*)

DAVID (*voice.*) Let's go.

ADRIENNE (*voice.*) Take my arm.

DAVID (*voice.*) That isn't necessary. (ADRIENNE *en-
ters and rests, leaning on the edge of the table.*
DAVID *enters and moves his head back and forth.*)
Where's Donatien?

ADRIENNE The boy? He's already gone back to the
rehearsal. (DAVID *takes a few steps left.* ADRIENNE

watches him, thoughtfully.) That boy seems miserable.

DAVID (*stops.*) We're all blind. (*Continues walking.*)

ADRIENNE (*to stop him.*)   But he doesn't play as well as you. He probably can't console himself with his favorite music . . . as you were doing out there.

DAVID (*has stopped.*) Who said that music was a consolation for me?

ADRIENNE It just seemed that way. . . . I used to sing. . . . I have my special song for those bad moments. . . . (*A silence.* DAVID *turns toward the alcove and starts again to walk. Caught up in a strange anxiety,* ADRIENNE *takes a few steps toward him.*) Can I help you?

DAVID (*stops.*) Yes.

ADRIENNE (*moves closer to him, anxiously.*)   How?

DAVID By shutting your mouth! (*He starts to leave.*)

ADRIENNE (*recoils, humiliated.*) Do you never speak except to insult people? Do you always react like that when someone offers you help and kindness?

DAVID (*turns angrily and goes toward her.*) Let's stop this farce! You're not being kind or generous! You're Valindin's mistress, and the only thing you're worried about is his business!

ADRIENNE (*angered.*) How dare you speak to me like that. . . .

DAVID I'm treating you like he treats us! (*He advances and* ADRIENNE *retreats.*) And what are you getting out of this? A nice low-cut dress? Maybe some jewelry?

ADRIENNE *(she instinctively caresses the brooch which* VALINDIN *earlier placed around her neck.)* You beast!

DAVID You don't fool me. And I advise you not to try to fool that poor boy, either! Don't use your tricks on him. You would only destroy him . . . and if you do, you'll answer to me.

ADRIENNE *(blushing, stammering.)* How dare you imply that I . . .

DAVID What else could I expect from a woman like you?

ADRIENNE Then what kind of woman would you like? Some silly little schoolgirl? A fine lady you've dreamed up for yourself? *(Pause.)*

DAVID *(stiffly.)* What do you mean by that?

ADRIENNE *(laughs.)* Maybe you're not quite as superior as you think you are! What do you know about real, live, flesh-and-blood women?

DAVID *(coldly.)* I know what they taste like and I know they taste good. That's all I ask of them.

ADRIENNE Yes, I know: you pay them and then on your merry way! You're a pig—like all the others!

DAVID You should know about that!

ADRIENNE Yes, I do know about it! I know that you men would rather pay for it and leave, because you don't dare ask any more of a woman! *(Laughs scornfully.)* I hope you'll soon find yourself a woman you don't have to buy! (DAVID *again turns to the alcove.)* A *real* woman! (DAVID *is moving toward the door.* ADRIENNE *takes a few steps toward him and says, her voice suddenly smooth again.)* Wouldn't you like to take my arm? You might run into something, you know.

DAVID *(smiles.)* I know the way better than you do.

I don't even need light to get around.

He goes to the door, opens it without groping, and exits, closing the door after him. ADRIENNE *is upset. She runs to the door, takes the latch in her hand. As she stands there indecisively,* VALINDIN *enters silently through door, upstage center. He smiles and watches her. Finally, he clinks together two keys which he has in his hand.* ADRIENNE *turns around, startled.* VALINDIN *laughs.*

VALINDIN   What were you doing?

ADRIENNE   You frightened me.

VALINDIN   Yes, I must have. You're blushing.

ADRIENNE   Am I? Not really. . . . What are those keys for?

VALINDIN   These, my dear, are the keys to the café. I just purchased an excellent lock and took it to the carpenter . . . but I kept the keys. Here, one is for you.

ADRIENNE   *(taking it.)* For me?

VALINDIN   Keep it here in the house. Just in case I should lose the other one . . . which I won't.

ADRIENNE   Where shall I put it?

VALINDIN   Wherever you like, as long as I know where it is.

ADRIENNE   *(her mind is obviously on something else; she goes to the table.)* Here? *(She opens the jewel box.)*

VALINDIN   Not bad at all. No thief would ever associate it with the café. Not that I'm expecting any thieves. . . . *(*ADRIENNE *puts the key in the box.* VALINDIN *sits with a tired sigh.)* Well, the carpenter brought me some good news. It seems there won't be any midget show this year. With

that competition out of the way, the fair belongs
to us.

ADRIENNE   Were you more worried about the midgets than about the Opéra-Comique?

VALINDIN   Of course. Where are the blind men?

ADRIENNE   They're rehearsing.

VALINDIN   (*rubbing his hands.*)   Like a bunch of
little lambs, eh?

ADRIENNE   Not exactly. . . . There was an incident.

VALINDIN   Don't tell me that lunatic started causing
trouble again!

ADRIENNE   He began to play what he wanted to and
the boy followed him. Lefranc had to throw
them out.

VALINDIN   (*rises.*)   I'll show them who's in charge
around here! Where are they?

ADRIENNE   Calm down. . . . They've gone back to
the rehearsal.

VALINDIN   *snorts and begins to pace sullenly.*
ADRIENNE   *sits and watches him.*

VALINDIN   I can't afford to have some idiot upset
this operation. I have too much at stake. (*He
stops and looks at her.*) Both of us have a lot
at stake, Adrienne. You have to help me.

ADRIENNE   (*amazed.*)   You want *me* to help *you?*

VALINDIN   (*smiles.*)   You know how to handle men.

ADRIENNE   (*brusquely.*)   What do you want?

VALINDIN   Not much. I just want you to win them
over. (*He approaches her and leans over her
chair, his face close to hers.*) Especially the little
one. Do a good job on him. The others are very
fond of him. This should be easy for you . . .

especially since those poor devils don't even know what a woman is.

ADRIENNE (*laughs.*) Can you be serious? Are you really asking me to . . . make love to that boy?

VALINDIN (*laughs.*) Without really doing it, of course. Just play around with him . . . and if things start getting difficult, you dance out of his reach . . . right into my arms. (*He plays with her ear.*)

ADRIENNE (*laughing uncontrollably, she dodges his caress, rises, and moves away.*) And for my reward . . . what? A pretty jewel? Maybe a low-cut dress?

VALINDIN (*laughs.*) Aha! she does look out for herself, doesn't she? Yes, you'll have your jewel. That's the language I like to hear: the language of truth!

ADRIENNE (*her laughter has a slightly mocking tone which* VALINDIN *fails to perceive.*) Poor little blind men!

VALINDIN Exactly. Valindin is going to help them, even if he has to do it by force.

ADRIENNE (*her laughter ceases, little by little. She wipes away a tear.*) Or even if he has to do it by love. (*Smiling.*) What did you decide about the peacock?

VALINDIN (*grudgingly.*) We'll have to use wood. Bernier was right . . . the stubborn old fool.

ADRIENNE Have you told the blind men about their costumes?

VALINDIN Why do you ask that?

ADRIENNE (*laughs.*) You haven't told them anything, have you?

VALINDIN Why should I? They'll see them soon

enough, when we have our final rehearsal in the café. Or rather, they'll touch them. (*He looks suspiciously at* ADRIENNE. *She covers her face with her hands and gives a little laugh.*) All right, we've laughed enough. Now it's time to go to work.

ADRIENNE (*uncovers her face; very seriously.*) For our son.

VALINDIN Exactly. For that son that you don't want to give me.

ADRIENNE Pour two glasses, Louis. Let's have a drink together!

VALINDIN (*happily.*) Bravo! (*Goes to the table and pours the wine.*) Eleven days left until Saint Ovide. Put them to good use, my dear! (*He gives her a glass.*)

ADRIENNE (*in a strange voice.*) Here's to the eleven days!

VALINDIN (*looking at her steadily.*) And to Valindin!

ADRIENNE (*laughing.*) And to our blind musicians!

VALINDIN (*laughing.*) And to my little tramp!

They continue to laugh as they drink.

Curtain.

Act Two

The curtain rises on a dark stage. The lights come up gradually until the downstage area is brightly lit. Two black curtains now hang behind the steps. ELIJAH *and* GILBERT *are seated on the steps, waiting. After a moment the tapping sound of canes is heard.* ELIJAH *and* GILBERT *raise their heads.* NAZAIRE *and* LUKE *enter from left, arm in arm.*

ELIJAH We're over here, brothers.

NAZAIRE All of you?

ELIJAH Gilbert and I. (*Feeling for the steps with their canes,* NAZAIRE *and* LUKE *sit down with their comrades. A pause.*) How do you feel?

NAZAIRE How *you* feel?

ELIJAH I'm afraid.

NAZAIRE I'm not worried. As soon as we smell those women out there . . .

ELIJAH Smelling them is as far as you'll ever get.

NAZAIRE We'll see about that after the fair opens. I haven't bothered with Catherine because I don't like her. She's stupid. And of course, nobody's going to get his teeth into Adrienne. . . . (*Laughs mysteriously.*) Unless it's the little one! She certainly takes good care of him. You never know what these women are going to do. Some of them like boys better than they like men!

ELIJAH She's a good woman.

NAZAIRE They're all good for what I want. (*A pause.*)

ELIJAH How many days have we rehearsed?

NAZAIRE Nine.

LUKE No. Ten.

ELIJAH Ten days. Today's rehearsal in the café makes eleven. That's not much.

LUKE It's hardly anything.

ELIJAH How well do we do it, Luke? You know about these things.

LUKE Not any more, I don't.

GILBERT Why do they have to open the Saint Ovide fair today?

NAZAIRE Because today is the day of Saint Ovide, silly!

GILBERT So what?

NAZAIRE Ah, why don't you . . .

ELIJAH Here come the others.

LUKE I only hear one cane.

ELIJAH But two people.

NAZAIRE Then it must be Adrienne and Donatien. She knows what she's doing!

A tapping is heard. From right, ADRIENNE *enters from the street,* DONATIEN *on her arm.* ADRIENNE *appears worried.*

ADRIENNE Here we are.

The BLIND MEN *turn their faces toward her.*

DONATIEN Are the others here?

ADRIENNE Yes, they're here. Sit down, Donatien. (*She guides him to a spot where he sits.*)

DONATIEN Aren't you going to sit down?

ADRIENNE Yes. (*She moves left and looks around, nervously.*)

GILBERT Sit here beside me, Madame Adrienne.

NAZAIRE   Quiet, silly! Here, beside me, Madame.

DONATIEN   (*rises.*) Say, why are we all sitting?

NAZAIRE   What are you so jumpy about?

DONATIEN   I mean, if we're all here. . . .

ADRIENNE   There's one missing.

GILBERT   Sit beside me, Madame Adrienne. Tell us a story.

ADRIENNE   I'll sit in the middle. (*She does so.*)

DONATIEN   Who's missing?

ADRIENNE   David.

DONATIEN *sits back down.*

LUKE   He didn't eat in the tavern today.

ADRIENNE *listens with great interest.*

ELIJAH   And he wouldn't let them take his violin over to the café with all the others.

NAZAIRE   Really?

ELIJAH   I was there. Monsieur Valindin became angry and told him that as long as we are working for him, none of us is going to get the chance to go play on the streets.

LUKE   He's right.

NAZAIRE   But why didn't David show up for dinner?

GILBERT   (*in his own world.*) Madame Adrienne . . .

But ADRIENNE *pays him no attention; she is absorbed in what the others are saying.*

NAZAIRE   Donatien, do you know?

DONATIEN   I don't know. Sometimes he goes off alone . . . or with friends I don't know . . . or with some woman. . . .

ELIJAH   But he'll come, won't he? He wouldn't pull this on us now!

A burning hope reveals itself in ADRIENNE's *face.*

NAZAIRE If he doesn't show up, I'll break his neck! After all the work we've put in these past few days. . . .

DONATIEN What are you talking about? Didn't he finally agree to play the way Monsieur Lefranc wanted? He'll be here.

ADRIENNE's *face darkens.*

ELIJAH Ah, you always defend him!

A silence. ADRIENNE *looks all around, fearfully.*

GILBERT Madame Adrienne, why did they measure our heads and bodies?

ADRIENNE For your costumes.

GILBERT *(happily.)* Will they be pretty?

ADRIENNE *(troubled.)* Yes.

GILBERT And mine will be the prettiest of all!

ADRIENNE Yes . . . I'm sure it will.

DONATIEN Madame Adrienne, what kind of impression do we make up there on the bandstand?

ADRIENNE *(she is suffering.)* A good impression.

ELIJAH And with the costumes it will be even better.

DONATIEN Do we go up and come down all right? Does anyone stumble?

ADRIENNE No one.

GILBERT I climb up on my bird just like it was my cot at the Asylum. Madame Adrienne, didn't they put that bird in the bandstand because I'm the Little Bird? They don't believe me.

ADRIENNE You may be right. . . .

NAZAIRE What the devil is this bird you keep talking about?

GILBERT I've already told you! A big bird with a huge tail that goes up to the sky!

NAZAIRE Ah, why don't you . . .

ELIJAH Madame Adrienne, tell us the truth. How well do we really do our act?

ADRIENNE (*her eyes are moist.*) You do it very well. . . .

DONATIEN (*anxiously.*) Will the people like us?

ELIJAH Will they think we're good?

ADRIENNE Yes, boys. (*She buries her face in her hands.*)

DONATIEN Oh, I hope so. . . .

ELIJAH It will be good.

NAZAIRE You're damn right, it will!

GILBERT And then Madame Adrienne will tell us the prettiest stories she knows. She's already told me some pretty stories.

NAZAIRE (*listening uneasily.*) David is taking a long time to get here.

ADRIENNE *raises her head and looks at him, then looks all around.*

GILBERT Lots of pretty stories. . . .

ELIJAH Be quiet, Little Bird.

GILBERT I don't want to be quiet! A story, Madame Adrienne! Tell me a story.

ADRIENNE I can't, right now.

GILBERT (*whining.*) Yes, you can! You can!

NAZAIRE (*strikes the floor with his cane.*) Come on, tell him a story! It will do us all good.

ADRIENNE (*places her hand on* ELIJAH'S *shoulder and speaks to all of them.*) Are you nervous?

ELIJAH A little.

ADRIENNE Well . . . if you like, I'll tell you a story.

GILBERT (*gives a squeal of happiness and claps his hands.*) A pretty story! It has to be pretty!

ELIJAH Quiet!

GILBERT (*puts his finger to his lips.*) Shhh! Be quiet!

A silence. ADRIENNE *looks at them sadly.*

ADRIENNE   Once there was a very poor village girl who wanted what she didn't want. . . .

GILBERT   Very poor and very pretty!

DONATIEN   Why don't you be quiet?

ADRIENNE   He's right, I forgot. Once there was a very poor and very pretty village girl who wanted what she didn't want. Now, to want what you don't want is a fine thing if you know how to do it. But the little village girl didn't know how to do it. Do you know what she wanted?

GILBERT   What did she want? (*A tapping is heard.* ADRIENNE *stiffens and looks right with a troubled expression.*) What did she want, Madame Adrienne? What did she want?

ADRIENNE *rises.*

DONATIEN   It's David!

DAVID *enters from right.* ADRIENNE'*s face shows great disappointment. She bows her head.*

NAZAIRE   We're over here, David. You're late.

DAVID   I went for a walk.

GILBERT   Finish the story, Madame Adrienne!

ADRIENNE   We have to get over to the fair.

GILBERT   Finish the story first! David, she's telling a pretty story. Once there was a village girl who had no money and she wanted to . . . to come to Paris! Is that it, Madame Adrienne?

ADRIENNE   We'll finish it later.

DAVID   I know how the rest goes. She came to Paris with the carnival people, and the king thought she was so pretty that he made her a countess and gave her the name Countess Du Barry.

ADRIENNE *looks at him, upset.* NAZAIRE's *noisy laugh breaks the silence.*

NAZAIRE   That David . . . ! (*He rises.*)

ELIJAH   (*rises and elbows* GILBERT.)   Let's get over to the café.

LUKE   Madame Adrienne, why don't you go in front, with Donatien?

The BLIND MEN *rise,* ADRIENNE *approaches* DONATIEN, *takes him by the arm, and starts to lead him out.*

DONATIEN   (*holds back.*)   David, are you coming?

DAVID   I can go by myself.

DONATIEN   Why were you so late getting here, David?

The other BLIND MEN, *who have started to move toward the exit, stop to listen to* DAVID's *reply.*

DAVID   I went to see a friend of mine . . . a student. I wanted to ask him about . . . certain birds.

ADRIENNE   Let's go.

She pulls at DONATIEN *and they exit left. The other* BLIND MEN *follow them.* DAVID *exits last.*

The black curtains behind the steps open. The light comes up gradually and we see the interior of the café. At the front of the café, next to the steps, there is a crude wooden table around which are placed four chairs. At right, there are two delicate little tables with curved, embossed legs. There are two chairs at each of these tables. Other tables, at each side of the café, are only partially visible. A copper chandelier hangs from the ceiling; its candles are not lit.

The bandstand is located upstage center. It is approximately seven feet high and ten feet wide. The platform where the singer is to sit is located next to the bandstand and to its right. This platform is wide at back and narrows down in front. It is slightly higher than the bandstand and is separated from it by a little stairway, placed in such a way that a person who ascends the stairs will do so with his back to the audience. This stairway serves as means of access both to the bandstand and to the singer's platform; from the top of the stairway the actors will step down slightly into the bandstand, or up slightly onto the singer's platform. The musicians in the bandstand are to be placed on two levels. On the lower level will be two violinists. When they are standing, their legs will be hidden by the front of the bandstand; when they sit, they will do so on the second level, which is even with the top of the access stairway. The other two violinists and the cellist will be located on the second level, behind the first two violinists. Occasionally they will sit on a bench which runs behind them. Two music stands with sheet music stick out over the edge of the bandstand; beside each of them is a candlestick. At the moment, the violins rest on the musicians' seats; the cello leans against the singer's platform.

The most eye-catching element of the entire ensemble is the throne on the singer's platform. Its back, approximately five feet high, is the brightly colored, wide-spread tail of a rather crude peacock made of painted wood. A music stand will be attached to the bird's neck and the singer will straddle its body. The bandstand is painted in bright colors, including gaudy purple stripes.

VALINDIN *paces impatiently and looks at his watch. He has removed his cloak and is clad in his under-*

vest. He stops at tables, right, and straightens a chair.

VALINDIN   Catherine! What about that drink?

CATHERINE   (*voice.*) Coming, Monsieur. (*She hurries in from right, carrying a tray with bottle and glass.*)

VALINDIN   (*refers to table left.*)   Put it on that table.

CATHERINE   Yes, Monsieur.

VALINDIN   And do it gently! See if you can do it without breaking anything.

CATHERINE   (*her hands tremble.*)   That makes it worse when you say that, Monsieur! (*She sets down the tray.*)

VALINDIN   All right. You're learning. . . . You'll soon be doing it well. Let's try it one more time. I'll give you an order. Go ahead.

CATHERINE   Now?

VALINDIN   Of course!

CATHERINE   (*addressing an imaginary customer.*) Would the gentleman like to try our aromatic coffee? It's the best in all Paris, Monsieur. We have brought it here directly from the Indies. Or perhaps the gentleman would prefer a glass of Burgundy?

VALINDIN   A bottle.

CATHERINE   The gentleman would like a bottle of Burgundy? (*She looks at him.*)

VALINDIN   Pour the wine.

CATHERINE   (*while she fills the glass.*) Your Burgundy, Monsieur. It's a delicious Burgundy. Our supplier is the same one who provides wine to the Duke of——

VALINDIN   To His Excellency!

CATHERINE To His Excellency, the Duke of Richelieu. . . .

VALINDIN Perfect. With me you'll get somewhere, I promise you. Remember, if they ask you for a different wine, bring them the same one. And our supplier is the one who serves His Excellency. (*He takes the glass and drinks.*)

CATHERINE Yes, Monsieur.

VALINDIN Now listen to me. I want you to go to the palace of the Baron of Tournelle. . . .

CATHERINE I went there this morning. He's in Versailles.

VALINDIN He may have come back! Tell whoever opens the door that Monsieur Valindin respectfully requests an answer to the note he sent this morning. Make it clear that if the Baron condescends to honor me with his presence, I won't open the café until he arrives. Do you understand?

CATHERINE Yes, Monsieur. Shall we rehearse that, too?

VALINDIN Get out of here! (CATHERINE *starts to take the tray.*) Leave that here. (CATHERINE *scurries behind the bandstand to get her cloak.* VALINDIN *finishes drinking his glass of wine and looks at his watch.*) Adrienne still isn't here with those idiots!

CATHERINE (*has started to leave through door left.*) Here they come, Monsieur! (*She exits.* VALINDIN *goes to the door.*)

VALINDIN It's about time! (*He returns to center, followed by* ADRIENNE *and the six* BLIND MUSICIANS.) Why are you so late?

DAVID   Because——

ADRIENNE   (*interrupting him.*)   Because I was late getting there.

DAVID *makes a face.*

VALINDIN   This is no day to be late! All right, there's no time to talk about that. Listen to me, all of you! (*The* BLIND MEN *form a row and all turn to face him.* ADRIENNE *goes right to leave her cloak, then returns to the group.*) You're already familiar with the café. Everything is just as it was when you came to familiarize yourselves with the bandstand, except that now the tables and chairs have been put in their places. On your right they go as far as the door; on the left they go back to the kitchen and the stairs. After the rehearsal you'll have all the time you want to learn where they are. Now, let's get to the important thing. . . . (*He pauses for a moment, watching them.*) I'm very pleased with all of you. Make no mistake, the entire city will soon be talking about your talents. But first we must give the show its final touches: the costumes and movements. Remember that in three hours, at exactly five o'clock, the fair opens and you will make your debut before the most demanding audience in the world. And I don't mind telling you that the success of your show will depend on this afternoon's rehearsal. Your instruments are already in their places. Now you must learn to go to them and pick them up without knocking anything over. And you must do it in your costumes. Adrienne, take their canes. And bring in the costumes. (ADRIENNE *goes among them, collecting*

the canes.) You'll have to take off your coats. The
tunics will cover you well enough.

ADRIENNE *goes behind the bandstand to leave the
canes.*

LUKE   Where is she taking our canes?

ELIJAH   And what are you going to do with our
coats?

VALINDIN   Don't worry. There are nails behind the
bandstand to hang all those things on. Come
now: your coats and hats. (*The* BLIND MEN
*clumsily shed their coats and stand in their
miserable shirts.*) Here, let's have them. Adrienne
will hang them up for you. (*He collects them and
leaves them on table left.* ADRIENNE *returns with
two tunics which she has taken from a chest located at left of the bandstand.*) Your coat, David.
(DAVID *takes off his coat and* VALINDIN *places it
with the others.*) All right, here come the costumes! Believe me, I spent a small fortune on
these things, but I did it because for you I
wanted only the best. Try to take care of them.

ADRIENNE   Here's yours, Luke. And yours, Elijah.
(*She hands them their respective tunics.*)

GILBERT   Let me touch it. (*He runs his hands over
ELIJAH's costume while* DONATIEN *and* NAZAIRE *do
likewise with* LUKE's.)

VALINDIN   They're very simple. Wide sleeves, buttons up the front. Adrienne, help them. . . .

LUKE *and* ELIJAH *put on their costumes.* ADRIENNE
*buttons them up part-way, then goes running off
to get more costumes.*

GILBERT   Where's mine?

VALINDIN (*smiles.*)   Be patient, Little Bird. She's

bringing it. (*To all of them.*) Be careful not to knock over the music stands and candlesticks. . . .

DAVID What music stands?

DONATIEN Candlesticks?

VALINDIN They were put in place this morning. They're at the edge of the bandstand.

DAVID What do we need with them?

VALINDIN They're only there for decoration. . . . They fill out the picture. But of course you wouldn't understand that.

GILBERT Is my costume like this one?

VALINDIN No, Little Bird. You'll wear a cloak and a crown. You're going to look like a king.

GILBERT A king! (*Claps his hands.*) Just like in the stories!

VALINDIN *laughs, then stops abruptly when he sees that* DAVID *is going toward the bandstand.*

VALINDIN David! Where are you going?

DAVID To the bandstand.

VALINDIN You already know what it's like. In just a moment you can all go up there.

ADRIENNE (*returns, loaded down with clothing.*) Your costume, David. (DAVID *comes back to the group, takes his costume, and puts it on.*) Nazaire, here's yours. And Donatien.

They all get dressed; DAVID *is carefully feeling his costume. All the costumes are long, closed at the neck, bright blue with brilliant orange satin folds at the neck and sleeves.*

VALINDIN Bravo, boys! Stunning, simply stunning! Aren't they, Adrienne? (ADRIENNE *goes back to the chest without answering.*) But you'll be even more dignified when you put on your caps. That

will be a beautiful sight: enormous hats that will
make you look like giants! (*He rubs his hands
and contemplates them. Meanwhile,* DAVID *has
again started for the bandstand.*)

GILBERT (*anxiously.*) And mine? What will it be
like?

ADRIENNE (*returns.*) Here it is.

VALINDIN First we must give him his tunic. Here.

GILBERT Yes, yes!

VALINDIN *places on him a light blue tunic which
buttons in back. It is short and does not cover his
calves. Meanwhile,* ADRIENNE *places his cloak on a
chair. On a table she places something which appears to be a rather strange headpiece from which
protrude two long ears.*

VALINDIN My, but you'll be handsome! Button
him up, Adrienne. And you will have a beard, too.
(*He goes to pick it up.*)

GILBERT A beard?

VALINDIN Remember, you're a king! (*He falls
silent as he sees* DAVID.) David, I said you could
go up there when the others are ready to go!
(DAVID *is at the bandstand and is running his
hands over the music stands and candlesticks.*)
Come back here.

DAVID The music is turned around backwards.

VALINDIN (*caught.*) Oh . . . is it? Well, we'll fix
that. (*Laughs.*) Or maybe we'll just leave it like
that! Eh? What do you think, Adrienne? (*Winks
at* ADRIENNE *who lowers her head.*) Yes, that's a
wonderful idea! That way the audience will
know that you're all so good, you don't need
music!

GILBERT Where's my cloak?

VALINDIN Here you are, Little Bird. . . . (*He drapes the large purple cloak over his shoulders and fastens it across his chest.*) Now you're a real king. Just like in the stories!

GILBERT Just like in the stories, Madame Adrienne! (*He feels his cloak.*) It's much longer than your costumes. Here, feel it! (ELIJAH *does so.*) May I have my crown now?

VALINDIN (*laughs.*) Not so fast, boy! First we have to finish dressing the others . . . even if that does violate his majesty's protocol. (*He slaps him on the shoulder and* GILBERT *also laughs.* ADRIENNE *returns from behind the bandstand. She carries five tall conical hats. Each has a slight brim and each is striped with wide bands of orange and silver. Little balls and ribbons hang from the top of the hats. Meanwhile,* DAVID *has begun to go up the stairs to the bandstand.* VALINDIN *sees him. With a brusque movement he pushes* GILBERT *out of the way and goes to the bandstand. At the sound of his voice, all the* BLIND MEN *listen attentively.*) What are you doing up there?

DAVID Can't you see? (*He goes up the steps onto the singer's platform and runs his hands over the peacock.*)

VALINDIN Your place is on the other side!

DAVID I want to be familiar with the whole bandstand. If I stumble, I have to know where to grab. (*He continues to feel the peacock hurriedly.*)

VALINDIN Come down from there! (DAVID *now moves his hands from the peacock's body to its great wooden tail.*) Don't touch it there! You're going to break the tail!

GILBERT What are you doing to my bird?

VALINDIN (*places one foot on the bottom step, preparing to go up after* DAVID.) I told you to come down from there!

DAVID That isn't a bird. It's a peacock.

VALINDIN Precisely. What about it?

DAVID (*after a moment.*) Nothing.

VALINDIN Come get your hat!

DAVID I'm coming. (*Starts down.*)

VALINDIN Give them their hats, Adrienne. (ADRIENNE *distributes the hats; as each man receives his, he curiously explores it with his hands.*) Get used to putting them on. It's very simple: there are strings on each side to tie under your chin. (LUKE *puts his on.* ELIJAH *and* NAZAIRE *experimentally put on and take off their hats several times.*)

DONATIEN It's very tall, isn't it?

VALINDIN Yes, but very steady. It won't fall over.

DAVID *returns to the group under* VALINDIN'S *suspicious gaze.*

ADRIENNE (*going to* DAVID'S *side.*) Here's your hat, David.

DAVID (*taking it and exploring it with his hands.*) Isn't the head more beautiful when it's left uncovered?

VALINDIN What would you know about that? With these caps you'll look like astrologers, wise men, musicians of antiquity. That's it: musicians from the orchestra of King Gilbert. Come, Gilbert. Let's finish getting you ready. First, the beard. (*He goes to pick it up.*)

DAVID Why a beard?

VALINDIN (*stung.*) Because he's the king! You put on your hat! You're the only one who isn't ready! (DAVID *hesitates, then puts on his hat.*) All right, Little Bird, pay attention. You fasten the beard to your ears with these two strings. Like this. (*He puts it on him. The beard is grotesque: blond and shaped like a shovel.* GILBERT *feels it with his hand.*) That's right, touch your beard. You're the very image of a Greek monarch.

DAVID   Greek?

VALINDIN   That's just an expression. (*He turns to* ADRIENNE *and makes an "O" with his fingers over one eye.* ADRIENNE *sighs, goes behind the bandstand, and returns with a little box which she leaves on table left.*)

GILBERT   (*meanwhile.*)   And now, my crown!

VALINDIN   (*picks up the headpiece.*)   His majesty's crown! It's like crowns used to be in the old days: a helmet and two beautiful wings.

GILBERT   Two beautiful wings for the Little Bird!

VALINDIN   Precisely. Lower your head . . . there. (*He places the "crown" on his head. It does indeed consist of a purple headpiece trimmed in gold, from which protrude two donkey's ears.* GILBERT *touches it and laughs happily.* VALINDIN *backs away and looks at him.*) My, there's never been an orchestra like this one! Adrienne, aren't they beautiful? Isn't this a stunning sight? (*He urgently motions to her to agree with him.*)

ADRIENNE   (*avoids his gaze.*)   There's still something missing, isn't there?

VALINDIN   Yes. That little final touch, to ease the solemnity without destroying it altogether. . . .

DAVID *goes to* GILBERT *and feels his headpiece.*

GILBERT   Who's touching me?

DAVID   The wings on this helmet are not wings.

VALINDIN (*he has started for the little box, now wheels around sharply.*) Really? What are they, then?

DAVID They aren't wings. And that peacock symbolizes stupidity.

VALINDIN Does it? I see that you know more about those things than I do.

DAVID (*nervously.*) No. You know more about them than we do.

VALINDIN Then why don't you just shut up!

DAVID You know more than we do, but I do know that's the meaning of the peacock. That's why he's always shown together with the most foolish king who ever lived.

DONATIEN Go on, David.

DAVID King Midas, who was so foolish that he sprouted donkey's ears. That's you, Gilbert: King Midas. You're wearing two donkey's ears on your head.

Murmuring among the BLIND MEN. GILBERT *touches his donkey's ears.*

VALINDIN (*angrily.*) What do you know about it? What could a blind beggar possibly know? Nothing! (*To* ELIJAH, *who is feeling the ears on* GILBERT'*s headpiece.*) They're wings! You can tell that, can't you, Elijah? Wings! Besides, David, you won't be the one who sits on the bird! All right, enough of this nonsense. Listen to me, boys. We still have to give it the final touch. (*He takes from the little box some oversized eyeglass frames, made of black cardboard.*) I want you to pretend that you can see and that you are reading the music. Since your songs are comical, we have to make the whole show as funny as possible. Don't get nervous if the people start laughing at you! On the contrary, I want you to . . . amuse them . . . all you can. We're going to rehearse it now, and I want you to put on these cardboard eyeglasses. (*He begins to distribute them.*) They fasten down over your ears. (*Puts* NAZAIRE's *on.*) Like this. (NAZAIRE *starts to take them off.*) Don't take them off! You have to get used to wearing them. Come on, put them on, all of you. (*To* GILBERT, *who comes forward to receive his glasses.*) You don't have any, Gilbert. Kings don't wear glasses. (LUKE *puts his on,* ELIJAH *and* DONATIEN *toy with theirs, indecisively.*)

DAVID (*nervously feels his glasses, then hurls them to the floor.*)   That's enough! (*A heavy silence.*)

VALINDIN (*icily.*)   Just what do you think you're doing?

ADRIENNE *is frightened; she picks up the glasses.*

DAVID   You're trying to turn us into a pack of clowns!

VALINDIN (*slowly.*)   What if I am? Clowns have an honorable profession. Sometimes they become so famous that the king calls them to come perform for him.

NAZAIRE *takes off his glasses.*

DAVID   We won't be your clowns!

VALINDIN   Then what will you be? Stubborn, proud fools who starve to death?

ADRIENNE   Louis . . .

VALINDIN   You shut up. (*Smoothly.*) You made plenty of people laugh on the street corner, didn't you? What's the difference? Why should you object to making them laugh a little here?

DAVID   We won't have people thinking we're imbeciles!

VALINDIN   Nobody is calling you imbeciles.

DAVID   That's what you're calling us! The peacock, the donkey's ears, the candlesticks, the music stands turned around backwards . . . and our horrible music! The worse it is, the better you'll like it. Right? This show is nothing but a vulgar spectacle for a stupid audience. Come, brothers. Let's go. (*He takes a few steps.*)

DONATIEN   Let's go!

VALINDIN   (*seizes* DAVID *by the chest.*) Stop right there!

ADRIENNE   Louis, no!

DAVID   Take your hands off me!

VALINDIN   (*frees him.*) All right. My hands are off you.

DAVID   Where is my coat?

VALINDIN (*smoothly.*) Yes, where is your coat? And your canes?

The BLIND MEN *move about nervously, instinctively seeking the protection of each other's closeness.*

DAVID   We'll find them!

NAZAIRE   We'll go without them!

DONATIEN   Let's go!

VALINDIN   (*shouts.*) If you go anywhere, it will be to jail!

DONATIEN   Jail?

VALINDIN   You're not going to ruin my show! We have a contract and you're going to carry out your part of it! Whether you like it or not, you're going to be men! You'll carry out your contract, and if the audience laughs at you, you'll put up with it!

DONATIEN   Brothers! David's right, just like he always is!

VALINDIN   And so what? He says you're clowns? All right, you're clowns! What does it matter?

DAVID   A pack of ridiculous blind beggars who think that the awful noise they make can really be called music!

DONATIEN   We're as ridiculous as the donkey and the peacock!

VALINDIN   But you'll eat! Don't you understand? Let them laugh! We all laugh at each other. The world is one big fair. I know what those people want—it's my business to know what they want! Midgets, idiots, blind men, cripples! All right, we'll give it to them and we'll have the final laugh! And we'll eat at their expense! (*With great scorn.*) Now forget about your . . . music. (*Authoritatively.*) All right, get the glasses on and let's rehearse!

The BLIND MEN *hesitate, then the group disintegrates.*

NAZAIRE   (*puts his glasses on.*)   They all ought to be hanged!

ELIJAH *sighs and puts on his glasses.*

VALINDIN   They're all putting on their glasses, David. Adrienne, give him his.

ADRIENNE *puts the glasses in* DAVID's *hands. He toys with them indecisively.*

DAVID   (*puts his hands behind his back.*)   No!

VALINDIN   Who do you think you are, you little son of a bitch? (*Strides up to* DAVID *and shakes him.* DAVID *drops his glasses and his hat falls off.*) And you, imbecile? (DONATIEN *screams frightened by the sudden attack.*) Blind man, cripple—

you don't even deserve to live! Do you know what
they do with blind babies in Madagascar? I saw
quite a bit of that while I was a sailor!

DAVID   No, don't say it!

ADRIENNE   Louis, for God's sake!

VALINDIN   (*shaking* DONATIEN.)   They kill them!
They kill them like mangy dogs!

DONATIEN   (*emits an inhuman scream and breaks
loose.*)   No . . . no . . . !   (*He runs, swept
along by his terror, bumping into chairs, knocking
one over.*)

ADRIENNE   Donatien!   (*She runs to stop him.*)

DAVID   Donatien! Come here, boy!   (*He looks for
him.* GILBERT *whines. The other* BLIND MEN *mill
around, helpless and confused.*)

DONATIEN   Let's do what he wants . . . !   We'll do
what he wants!!! Won't we, David?   (*He falls to
his knees. As* ADRIENNE *tries to pick him up,* DAVID
comes to them.)

DAVID   Donatien!   (*The two of them get him to his
feet.*)

VALINDIN   Leave him alone, Adrienne!

ADRIENNE   What are you . . . a monster?   (*She holds*
DONATIEN *against her chest.*)

VALINDIN   What the devil's wrong with him?

DAVID   (*with a hard voice.*)   I know what's wrong
with him.

ADRIENNE   There, now . . .

DONATIEN   Anything he wants! David, they'll put
us in jail . . . !   They'll kill us! We have to do
what he wants!

DAVID   (*biting his words.*)   We have to get out of
here!

DONATIEN   (*with a scream.*)   No! Let's do what he

wants. . . . (*He again slumps to the floor sobbing. A long silence.*)

DAVID (*with a deep sigh.*) Give me my glasses, Adrienne. (ADRIENNE *gives them to him; her eyes are moist.*) Give the boy his. We're going to rehearse. (DAVID *puts on his glasses.* VALINDIN *sighs also and picks up the glasses which* DONATIEN *has dropped. He holds them out to* ADRIENNE, *who snatches them from him without a word.*)

ADRIENNE Here, Donatien, I'll put them on you. (*She helps him to his feet; he does not resist. She puts the glasses on him.* VALINDIN *takes out a handkerchief and wipes his forehead.*)

NAZAIRE (*mutters bitterly.*) They all ought to be hanged!

CATHERINE *enters from left. When she sees the* BLIND MEN *she stops, stunned, then bursts into laughter.* ADRIENNE, *in vain, motions to her to be quiet.*

VALINDIN (*ill-humoredly.*) Well? What did you find out?

CATHERINE (*unevenly, as she attempts to restrain her laughter.*) The Baron . . . has not returned yet . . . from Versailles. . . .

VALINDIN (*angrily slams his fist into his hand.*) All right! Let's rehearse!

The BLIND MEN *turn and move slowly toward the bandstand.* ADRIENNE *picks up the hat which is on the floor and hands it to* DAVID, *who puts it on somberly as he walks.*

The black curtains slowly close, hiding the bandstand from view, and at the same time the lights come up on the downstage area. In the distance a bell strikes five times. VALINDIN *bursts through the curtains and comes down the steps. He is smiling.*

*He is now wearing a formal cloak—pale green with
silver trim—and an elegant tricorn hat adorned
with officer's stripes, red ribbons, and white feath-
ers. He is not wearing a sword. In his hand he carries a long, elegant baton. Drum roll.*

VALINDIN (*speaks to the audience.*)

If you, dear friends, have seen the world and are
    by naught impressed,

You'll see before you now a show which towers
    above the rest!

A new and worldly spectacle which may not come
    again,

Brought to this great city through the love of
    men for men.

Here the blind musicians sit proudly in their
    places

With eagerness and gratitude reflected in their
    faces.

Their sole desire is that you share with them the
    finer things,

And all of Paris soon will gaily hum the songs
    they sing!

(*Drum roll.* VALINDIN *strikes his baton on the
floor.*) Come right in, beautiful ladies and gracious
gentlemen! Come right in! (*From right enter*
LATOUCHE *and* DUBOIS, *two policemen in civilian
dress.* LATOUCHE *bears a slight resemblance to a
fox,* DUBOIS *to a bulldog.* VALINDIN *bows and motions them to the left.*) Monsieur Latouche! Such
an honor for my humble café!

LATOUCHE (*bows.*) Monsieur Valindin . . . I'd
like you to meet Monsieur Dubois, one of my
men. (*Bows.*) Judging from your publicity, this
show should be quite interesting, indeed. I de-

cided that I simply had to come and see it for
myself!

VALINDIN   If you'll be so kind as to come in,
Adrienne will seat you at the best table in the
house. We were reserving it for His Excellency,
the Baron of Tournelle, who, much as he regrets
it, has found himself unable to come today. . . .
(*Moves to left.*) This way, gentlemen. (*Continuing
to flatter them, he accompanies them to the side
exit.*) I hope you'll forgive me if I don't personally show you to your table. . . . Please ask
for anything you wish. It's on the house. . . . We
consider it our honor to serve you. . . .

LATOUCHE   Thank you, Monsieur Valindin.

LATOUCHE *and* DUBOIS *exit left. As* VALINDIN *returns
to center,* CATHERINE *appears through the curtains
and whispers loudly.*

CATHERINE   Almost full, Monsieur. Only two or
three places left.

VALINDIN *smiles and starts to go up the steps. At
that moment a man enters from right, and* VALINDIN
stops. The man is VALENTIN HAÜY, *twenty-five years
old, handsome. He appears to be an unassuming
bourgeois. He walks with his hands behind his
back and appears distracted.* VALINDIN *motions to*
CATHERINE *to disappear; she does so behind the curtains.*

VALINDIN   Come right in, beautiful ladies and gracious gentlemen! Come right in! See the blind
musicians! See the most philanthropic show in
all Paris!

HAÜY *stops for a moment, listens; then accepting*
VALINDIN's *invitation, he moves across the stage and
exits left.*

VALINDIN *straightens his coat and turns elegantly toward the curtains. They open, revealing the brightly lit chandelier and the customers who sit laughing and chatting at the tables. At the table at left two slightly tipsy* LADIES *and a town* DANDY *are drinking coffee and wine. At the first table right,* ADRIENNE *pours drinks for* LATOUCHE *and* DUBOIS. *At the other table an elderly* BOURGEOIS COUPLE *drink coffee. The bandstand is hidden from view by a green curtain adorned in large silver letters: CHEZ ADRIENNE.* VALINDIN *goes up the steps and places himself before the green curtain. He strikes the floor three times with his baton. The murmuring of the crowd dies away.* ADRIENNE *exits right.*

VALINDIN   Noble audience and honorable citizens of Paris, your attention please! Our great philanthropic show is about to begin! (VALENTIN HAÜY *enters from left. After asking permission of the* DANDY *and the two* LADIES, *he sits in the remaining empty chair.* CATHERINE *hurries to him, takes his order in a low voice, and exits right.*) Ladies and gentlemen, for many years we have wanted to present a show which would be worthy of such a distinguished audience and which would satisfy your impeccable taste. A show which would, at the same time, be happy, humanitarian, and enlightened! This afternoon you are going to see such a show. Ladies and gentlemen, we humbly submit to your superior judgment—our magnificent blind orchestra!

CATHERINE *returns, places a cup in front of* HAÜY, *pours his coffee from a coffee pot, and exits.* VALINDIN *again strikes the floor three times, gestures toward the green curtain, and moves away right.*

The curtain rises. The bandstand is brightly lighted, GILBERT *sits astride the peacock, a wooden scepter raised in his hand.* LUKE *stands with his cello in front of him; beside him are* ELIJAH *and* NAZAIRE. *In the front row, from left to right, are* DONATIEN *and* DAVID. *Except for* GILBERT, *all are standing, their instruments ready. The glasses give their faces an owlish appearance. The two candlesticks have been lit. A murmur of surprise runs through the café. The* BLIND MEN *bow ceremoniously. The violinists sit and grip their instruments. Laughter from the audience.* DONATIEN, NAZAIRE, *and* ELIJAH *pretend to look at the sheet music.*

BOURGEOISE   Look at those eyes!

FIRST LADY   Look at that one on the peacock!

DANDY   He's vanity itself!

GILBERT   (*he is in his glory; he gives the signal.*) One, two, three! (*The instruments play the introduction and he begins to sing. Violins, cello, and singer all perform in unison: a lively, biting melody, delivered loudly, with mechanical precision, without the slightest trace of feeling.* ADRIENNE *and* CATHERINE *cross back and forth, waiting on the customers.* VALINDIN *leans on his baton and watches them, a pleased expression on his face.* GILBERT *beats time with his scepter as he sings.*)

> Corina the little shepherd girl
>   is feeling oh so sad.
> The doctor tells her what she needs
>   is a shepherd lad.
> Her little lambs sing to her,
> "Baa! Baa! Baa!" [*Chorus, pizzicato.*]
> As they dance round and round.

Corina only sighs,
"Ahh! Ahh! Ahh!" [*Chorus, pizzicato.*]
As she turns crimson red.

*The comments and laughter from the audience grow
louder and coarser. Except for* DAVID *and* LUKE, *the
musicians—especially* DONATIEN—*exaggerate their
grotesque gesticulations. After a brief pause, they
plunge into the second stanza.*

SECOND LADY   Their music is turned around backwards!

DANDY (*laughs.*)   But it certainly is well lit!

GILBERT

The pretty little shepherd boy
        can do no more than moan.
Corina smiles though she is sad
        for she wants him for her own.
"Be my little lamb
You! You! You! [*Chorus, pizzicato.*]
And come and play with me."
"I don't know what you mean,
Me! Me! Me! [*Chorus, pizzicato.*]
I only talk with sheep."

BOURGEOIS (*laughing uncontrollably.*)   They look
like little animals!

BOURGEOISE   Maybe they are! Look at the ears!

VALENTIN HAÜY *suddenly slams his fist down violently on the table and leaps to his feet. He is
livid with rage. The* LADIES *scream. The* BOURGEOIS
COUPLE *look at him curiously.* LATOUCHE *watches
him steadily.*

DANDY (*rises.*)   Monsieur!

GILBERT, *still wearing his idiotic smile, begins the
third stanza. The other* BLIND MEN *are confused by
the disturbance and do not follow him.* VALINDIN

hurries over to HAÜY, *whose violent anger prevents him from speaking coherently.* CATHERINE *and* ADRIENNE *stop with their trays.*

VALINDIN   Did you want something, Monsieur?

HAÜY   Yes.

DUBOIS *(to* LATOUCHE; *he starts to rise.)*   Shall I? *(*LATOUCHE *stops him. He himself rises and goes over slowly.)*

VALINDIN   And might I know what it is?

HAÜY   If I told you, you wouldn't like it.

BOURGEOISE   Who is that man?

VOICES   Throw him out!

LATOUCHE *(bows.)*   Police Commissioner Latouche. Your name.

DUBOIS *comes over slowly.*

HAÜY   Valentin Haüy.

DANDY   He's just a drunk!

HAÜY   I'm an interpreter in the Ministry of Foreign Affairs.

VALINDIN *and* LATOUCHE *look at each other.*

VALINDIN *(laughs.)*   Valentin, eh? That's interesting. My name is Valindin. And I'll tell you what you're going to do: You're going to leave this café!

HAÜY   That's exactly what I intend to do. *(Tosses a coin on the table.)*

LATOUCHE   Quick! Get out!

VALINDIN   Here, take your money. It's on the house.

HAÜY   Give it to the blind men. What a circus they would see if they had eyes!

VOICES   Quiet! Throw him out! On with the music!

DAVID   What did he say? *(The* BLIND MEN *whisper among themselves.)*

LATOUCHE   I told you to get out of here!

FIRST LADY That's right! Throw him out!

HAÜY (*turns to the bandstand and raises his voice.*) Did you ask what I said? I said if you had eyes, what a spectacle you would see in front of you! Remember that!

LATOUCHE (*takes his arm and pushes.*) Out! (*The angry cries of the audience grow louder. With a look of disgust,* HAÜY *shakes off* LATOUCHE's *grip and exits left.*)

VALINDIN (*to* LATOUCHE, *in a low voice.*) Thanks. . . . (LATOUCHE, DUBOIS, *and the* DANDY *sit back down.* VALINDIN *goes to the center of the room.*) It's nothing, ladies and gentlemen! (*Laughs.*) Just a lunatic! A misanthrope in this philanthropic age! The great concert of the blind musicians will continue now!

VOICES Yes, yes! On with the music!

VALINDIN (*addressing the musicians.*) Ready up there? (*The* BLIND MEN *poise their instruments.* DAVID *hesitates.*) Ready, I say? (DAVID *raises his violin.*) All right, Little Bird! On with the third stanza! (*Strikes the floor three times with his baton.*) One, two, three!

The music begins. CATHERINE *and* ADRIENNE *go back to waiting on the customers.* VALINDIN *keeps time with nods of his head. The laughter grows louder. The audience joins in on the bleating lines.*

GILBERT

> 'Round the two young sweethearts
>> frolic the little lambs.
> Corina's face still blushes
>> as does her shepherd lad's.
> As Corina draws near him,
> "Baa? Baa? Baa?" [*Chorus, pizzicato.*]

She asks with love's desire.
Soon very close together,
"Baa! Baa! Baa!" [*Chorus, pizzicato.*]
Like little lambs they lie.

A kaleidoscope of hysterical laughter, grotesque faces, owlish expressions in the bandstand, the bouncing cones on the heads of the musicians.
A slow curtain.

Act Three

The reception room at the Asylum of the Quinze-Vingts. SISTER LUCIE *stands next to the blue curtains sprinkled with* fleurs de lis. *At left,* VALINDIN *waits, his hat under his arm. The* PRIORESS *enters, from right, followed by* SISTER ANDREA, *who, after entering, moves back to stand next to the curtains.*

VALINDIN (*bows.*) God be with you, Reverend Mother.

PRIORESS And with you, Monsieur Valindin. Sister Andrea tells me that you have come to deliver the rest of your donation.

VALINDIN Yes, Reverend Mother.

PRIORESS Has the fair ended?

VALINDIN There are five days left. But the day after the fair ends, we leave for the South. I shall have many things to attend to, so I thought it well to settle now with the Asylum.

PRIORESS We thank you.

VALINDIN (*takes out a purse, which he holds out to the* PRIORESS.) One hundred francs. If Your Reverence would care to count them . . .

PRIORESS (*does not move.*) Sister Andrea. (SISTER ANDREA *takes the purse and goes off to one side.*)

VALINDIN (*uneasy.*) And perhaps you could give me a receipt . . . (SISTER ANDREA *stops and looks at him.*) . . . just to keep my accounts straight,

of course. . . . I have such a terrible memory. . . .

PRIORESS   Sister Andrea will bring you the proper
recognition of your donation.

VALINDIN   (*sees that the nun is about to exit; takes
one step forward.*)   Is she not going to count the
money?

PRIORESS   (*smiles coldly.*)   Monsieur Valindin, we
do not doubt that you have already counted your
money to perfection.

VALINDIN   (*bows, humbled.*)   You are very kind.

SISTER ANDREA *exits right.*

PRIORESS   Our poor blind inmates have been praying for you since the first day, Monsieur.

VALINDIN   I know, Reverend Mother.

PRIORESS   And the musicians, are they happy? I
hardly ever see them any more. . . . They return
to the Asylum so late every night. You seem to
have immersed them so completely in worldly
affairs . . .

VALINDIN   Yes, but with admirable results, Reverend Mother! They perform so beautifully that,
if I can say this without excessive vanity, our
show has been the most popular one in the whole
fair! Even more popular than the Opéra-Comique! Would you believe that on four days we
found it necessary to remove the front wall of
the café, so that the crowds who wanted to see
the show would not push it over! To hold them
back we had to call upon a special brigade of
fusiliers which the Chatelet was kind enough to
send us every day for that purpose.

PRIORESS   Heavens!

VALINDIN   Naturally these circumstances forced us

to work especially hard during the day, since I did not want to leave the café open at night.

PRIORESS Then, I take it, you are quite satisfied.

VALINDIN The results have been most pleasing, Reverend Mother. All Paris is talking of us and humming our songs.

PRIORESS My congratulations. But the musicians . . . Are they happy? Have you not had any conflicts, any incidents?

VALINDIN Nothing out of the ordinary, Reverend Mother. Naturally, an occasional shortness of temper during the rehearsals. . . . Nothing serious.

PRIORESS (*after a moment.*) Monsieur Valindin . . . is it true that their violins are locked up during the night in the café?

VALINDIN I see that you are well informed, Reverend Mother.

PRIORESS I should like to ask a favor of you. One of the blind musicians has an especially strong devotion to his music. . . .

VALINDIN (*seriously.*) I know the one you refer to.

PRIORESS The others do not mind so much . . . but he . . . Could you not permit him to keep his violin with him?

VALINDIN Reverend Mother, it saddens me to see that he has complained to you. Believe me, he has no reason to do so. I will tell you confidentially that he is the most mischievous, the most undisciplined of all the men.

PRIORESS I did not intend my remark as a complaint. It is simply a request of his which I am passing on to you.

VALINDIN I already told him that what he wants is out of the question. He says he wants to play for his own amusement, but I ask: Where? He only comes to the Asylum to sleep. The only other place he would have to play would be on the streets, and I cannot permit that. We have a contract, Reverend Mother. You yourself signed it in his name.

SISTER ANDREA *returns with a rolled-up paper.*

PRIORESS (*coldly.*) All right. I shall not insist. (*She looks at* SISTER ANDREA.)

SISTER ANDREA   Your receipt, Monsieur.

VALINDIN (*takes it.*) My most humble thanks. (*Smiling, he unrolls the paper.*) Permit me to read it, Reverend Mother. It moves my heart to think that a simple sheet of paper could embody such piety, so many prayers for me. . . . (*He glances at the paper, sighs, and rolls it up.*) Reverend Mother, I'll not tire you any longer. I realize your time is valuable. With your permission I shall take my leave.

PRIORESS (*does not hold out the rosary to him.*) God be with you.

VALINDIN (*bows deeply.*) May He be with you, Reverend Mother.

SISTER LUCIE   This way, Monsieur. (*The two of them exit left.*)

PRIORESS   Sister Andrea, if that man ever comes back to this house, I shall not be in. Is that clear?

SISTER ANDREA   Yes, Reverend Mother. Is he a nobleman?

PRIORESS (*shrugs her shoulders.*)   He wears a sword. (*Turns and starts to exit right.*)

SISTER ANDREA   The hundred francs were all there, Reverend Mother.

PRIORESS (*stops at the sound of the voice.*) Very well.

She exits and SISTER ANDREA *follows her.*

The curtains open, revealing the room in VALINDIN's *house. The upstage center door opens and* DAVID *enters abruptly. Behind him comes* CATHERINE, *who is trying in vain to stop him.*

CATHERINE But you can't come in here! Monsieur said for all of you to wait in the vestibule!

DAVID The others can wait there if they like.

CATHERINE Please leave!

DAVID You leave. And close the door after you.

CATHERINE If you stay here, I'll have to stay with you. And I still have so much work to do before I go to the café.

DAVID (*smiling, as he moves to sit.*) All of us who work for Monsieur Valindin have a lot of work. For him we're not human beings. We're lemons which he intends to squeeze dry. Catherine, I'm not going to steal anything and I don't drink. Now be a good girl and run along.

CATHERINE Are you crazy? Do you know what he would do to me?

DAVID (*rises suddenly, takes her by the arm and pushes her roughly.*) I want to be alone, do you understand? I want very much to be alone! Now get out!

Frightened, CATHERINE *backs toward the door.* DAVID *pushes her out, then slams the door. With his hand on the knob he listens for a few seconds. Then he sighs and sits, letting his cane slide down between his legs. He passes his hand over his face and closes his eyes. He buries his face in his hands. Very softly,*

*with his mouth closed, he begins to hum Corelli's
Adagio. He is nervous. His humming becomes more
intense. He raises his head and leans back against
the back of the chair, still humming. With his arms
he absentmindedly pantomimes the playing of a
violin. With an abrupt movement he grips his knees
with both hands. He stops humming and listens.
His hands go to his cane.* ADRIENNE's *voice is heard
behind the door, as it opens.*

ADRIENNE (*voice.*) Well, you shouldn't have! He
has no reason to be in here! (DAVID *rises.*) Go
on with your work—I'll take care of him. (ADRI-
ENNE *appears in the doorway carrying a market
basket.*) Here, take this. (*She gives it to*
CATHERINE, *then enters, closing the door. She has
just come in from outside and is wearing a head
scarf and shawl. She turns and looks intently at*
DAVID.)

DAVID All right, don't say anything. I'll leave.

ADRIENNE (*still looking at him as she takes off her
shawl.*) Wait. (*She moves right.*) Did Louis tell
all of you to come here?

DAVID Yes.

ADRIENNE Now?

DAVID In half an hour.

ADRIENNE Then you're early.

DAVID I was looking for some place where I could
be alone. (*She looks at him a moment, then goes
off right to leave her things.*)

ADRIENNE (*voice.*) Why did he tell you to come?

DAVID You mean you don't know?

ADRIENNE (*comes back in.*) No.

DAVID Neither do I. What do you want with me?

ADRIENNE I want to talk. (DAVID *makes a gesture*

of impatience.) You know very well I'm constantly trying to talk with you. It's so difficult at the café, because he's always there. . . . And because you always avoid me. (*A silence*.) Do you really despise me so much?

DAVID   What are you trying to do? Aren't you satisfied with having caught yourself one fool? Isn't Donatien enough for you? What are you going to do with him? Do you plan to keep on wrapping him around your finger? Well, you go right ahead! Play with him and tear him into little pieces at your leisure, and then sit back and laugh afterwards, because I'm completely helpless to stop you. (*His pacing and his speech become increasingly nervous and intense. He stumbles over his words*.) But don't try the same thing on me! I know what you are!

ADRIENNE   No, you don't know what I am!

DAVID   Aren't you getting awfully familiar with me?

ADRIENNE   (*almost in tears*.) But not because I don't respect you!

DAVID   Why, then? (*A silence*. ADRIENNE *sits, unable to reply*.) Suppose you just leave us alone. You and Valindin have gotten what you wanted. We're the laughing-stock of the fair . . . and the others don't even care any longer. They've gotten used to it. We're earning money for you. What more do you want with us?

ADRIENNE   (*faltering*.) I'm not like Valindin.

DAVID   (*after a moment's pause*.) Whore! (*He goes rapidly toward the door*.)

ADRIENNE   Yes, a whore! (DAVID *stops with hand on the doorknob*.) And you're right—he told me to

use my . . . charms on you. That was what I
wanted to tell you.

DAVID   You admit it?

ADRIENNE   Yes.

DAVID   Why?

ADRIENNE   Because I'm not like him!

DAVID *(turns slowly.)*   What are you like?

ADRIENNE   You know I've defended you and tried
to help you! Admit it, David; you know I have!

DAVID   But you still work for him.

ADRIENNE *(rises and goes to his side.)*   And so do
you! I've been around. I know what hunger is!
Remember, you're working for him, too! You
didn't leave when you could have. He's trapped
you, just like he trapped me. You see, our situations are not so different. (DAVID *lowers his head,
finds a chair and sits next to the table.)* I know
that every day you play in the café you become
more and more ashamed . . . just as I do every
day that I stay with him.

DAVID *(with a bitter smile.)*   It's all a matter of getting used to it, isn't it? I think I'll eventually get
used to it . . . and we'll all go on working for
him. . . .

ADRIENNE   No, David. I watch you sometimes while
you're playing. . . . I know you're getting desperate. . . . I know you can't go on much longer.
Even if you don't cry any more . . .

DAVID   What do you mean?

ADRIENNE   I saw you crying that first day, when
those idiots were laughing at you. I wanted to
scream!

DAVID   Be quiet!

ADRIENNE   You shouldn't have cried! Not you!

Leave that for him. . . . He cries too sometimes,
the pig. You should have stood up and insulted
all of them! You should have stirred up the other
musicians! You could have driven Valindin out
of his mind! That's what I expected you to do. I
said to myself: "Now! Now he'll do it . . . !"
I've been waiting for years to see . . . a man.

DAVID   But I wasn't one and I sat there and cried
like a woman. We blind men aren't really men at
all; that's our saddest secret. We're more like
frightened women. We smile without feeling, we
flatter whoever orders us around, we let ourselves
be turned into clowns . . . because even a child
can hurt us. You can't imagine how easy it is to
hurt us! I cried in the café. . . . I knew that
everyone was looking at me. What did it matter?
I was alone then . . . just as I always am.

ADRIENNE   Don't talk like that.

DAVID   Watch your words when you talk to a blind
man. It's almost impossible to help us . . . and
so easy to hurt us.

ADRIENNE   I don't want to hurt you. Or Donatien.
(*She sits at the other side of the table*.) You're
very fond of that boy, aren't you?

DAVID   I love him like the son I'll never have.
Couldn't you at least leave him alone?

ADRIENNE   What's wrong with him?

DAVID   Nothing.

ADRIENNE   But you said——

DAVID   I didn't say anything!

ADRIENNE   You once said, "I know what's wrong
with him."

DAVID   When did I say that?

ADRIENNE   The day the fair opened, when Valindin said that in Madagascar they kill blind children . . . and Donatien screamed so much that you gave in and agreed to play. What's the matter with him?

DAVID   Female curiosity?

ADRIENNE   Call it that if you like.

DAVID   There's no reason for you to know.

ADRIENNE   I want to help you.

DAVID   Fool! You can't help us! Donatien is terrified and no one can change that.

ADRIENNE   Why is he terrified?

DAVID   (*after a brief pause.*)   He's been blind since he was three years old. . . . Smallpox. His father was about as intelligent as the animals he took care of. Since Donatien was of no use in the fields, his father beat him and hardly gave him anything to eat. They lived in Limousin, which has always been one of the most miserable parts of the country. One year, when Donatien was five or six years old, the harvest was especially bad. Donatien was useless and was just one more mouth to feed. So his father took him by the neck one day and tried to kill him while he cursed him for all the trouble he had caused.

ADRIENNE   My God!

DAVID   Donatien managed to break away and struck out blindly, running at full speed across the fields. He was half-strangled but he kept running, slipping and falling, trying to get away from that savage. Two days later he was found, unconscious and covered with blood, at the side of the highway. A passing coach picked him up and took him to the Quinze-Vingts. . . . I bought him a violin. And I have taught him all the music he knows.

A long silence.

ADRIENNE   You haven't told me everything, have you?

DAVID   No.

ADRIENNE   Then go on.

DAVID   Why? You can't help him.

ADRIENNE   How do you know that?

DAVID   (*after a moment.*)   Each of us is like a well, Adrienne. If you insist on looking into it, you may fall.

ADRIENNE   Tell me the rest.

DAVID   (*stammers.*)   For a long time he's been frightened of women. He's a young man now, and he knows that his face is repulsive. He tries to forget about it by laughing and even bragging. . . . He often tells the story of the scrub maid who called to him from the window one day while her master was away, and taught him to make love. At the Asylum they all laugh at him because no one believes him. But I know the story is true because I know the girl. It wasn't hard to check. I know the people in the areas where I play. The girl herself told me about it, the bitch. She laughed the whole time she was telling me.

ADRIENNE   What did she tell you?

DAVID   That Donatien hadn't been able . . . to do it. (*Angrily.*) And she laughed at his smallpox scars, at his clumsiness! She laughed at him and taunted him and threw him out of the house. I heard him crying all night. . . . He sleeps next

to me. Sometimes when he thinks I'm asleep, he
still cries. Since that happened he has refused
to go back to that corner. In fact, that was what
made me suspicious in the first place. (*He falls
silent.* ADRIENNE *sobs.*) You shouldn't cry in front
of a blind man.

ADRIENNE   That hurts you too?

DAVID   That's right. (*Rises and moves away. A
pause.*)

ADRIENNE   (*weeping.*) Why did you tell me all
that?

DAVID   (*laughs.*) You wanted to know, didn't you?
Well, what do you have to say now?

ADRIENNE   (*weeping.*) Is that a challenge?

DAVID   I didn't intend that little story for you!
Get that straight. Sometimes it isn't possible to
keep quiet. . . . Sometimes I have to talk . . .
but I didn't do it for you!

ADRIENNE   Then whom did you intend it for? Melanie de Salignac?

DAVID   (*strikes the floor with his cane.*) So the
little one has been talking too much again! So
you've even squeezed that out of him, you ser-
pent. Yes! I speak to her and I play for her!
And I look for her. I look for that blind woman
. . . who would understand. . . . Oh, my God!
(*Buries his face in his hands.*)

ADRIENNE   (*dries her eyes; with a steady voice.*) A
blind woman who reads books in some mysterious way that you don't even understand.

DAVID   (*raises his head.*) Do you think I give a
damn if you believe in her or not?

ADRIENNE   You're wrong. I don't doubt that she

exists. But I think that she must be very wealthy.

DAVID   What difference does that make?

ADRIENNE   That's the only way she could have ever learned all those things she knows. Blind, yes . . . but not your kind of blindness. She has never been afraid or hungry . . . as we are. (*Pause.*)

DAVID   Damn you!

ADRIENNE   (*rises.*)   Would you really rather go on dreaming about her than find yourself a real woman? (*Brief pause.*) You're not afraid of women. . . . That's obvious. But you don't trust them, do you? You don't dare believe that anyone might have good intentions!

DAVID   Can't you shut up!

ADRIENNE   (*troubled, goes toward him.*)   And that's why you go on dreaming about your Melanie. But what can she do for you? That fine lady, surrounded by all her servants, what can she do compared to a real, living woman?

DAVID   Will you stop?

Silence. DAVID *goes back to his chair. He sits and runs his nervous hands over the cane. She turns and looks at him, moved.*

ADRIENNE   I accept your challenge.

DAVID   There isn't any challenge!

ADRIENNE *goes to the table, looking at him steadily.*

ADRIENNE   I'll teach the boy how——

DAVID   (*trembling.*)   No! You'll destroy him!

ADRIENNE   (*sadly.*)   You're forgetting I have experience. (*She sits.*)

DAVID   What are you after? A triumph for your vanity? Or maybe you enjoy it.

ADRIENNE   Do you think it's not repulsive to me?
It isn't as easy as people think to live my kind of
life. But what difference does one more make?
That's all life is, anyway.

DAVID   (*he is trembling visibly and expresses himself with difficulty.*)   I don't understand! Why?
Why?

He slams his fist down on the table. ADRIENNE *is
now trembling also. Her only reply is to reach
across the table and gently take* DAVID's *hand.*
DAVID *shudders violently, then rises and moves
away.* ADRIENNE *rises also; she is breathing rapidly.
A silence.*

ADRIENNE   A few days ago I asked Louis to let you
keep your violin. He wouldn't even listen to me.
But I'll ask him again. I'll insist. Even if you
play for your blind lady.

DAVID   I don't believe you.

*Silence, which is interrupted by the sudden open-
ing of the door.* VALINDIN *enters and looks at them.*

VALINDIN   What is he doing here?

ADRIENNE   I called him in. . . . We've been talking about the fairs we're going to play.

VALINDIN   Hasn't Lefranc come yet?

ADRIENNE   Is he coming here?

VALINDIN   Who does he think he is? I agreed to
meet him here because he won't even set foot in
the café after our success. And he still makes me
wait for him.

ADRIENNE   What did you want with him?

VALINDIN   You'll see. . . . I don't have time to explain right now. (*Goes to door.*) Come in here,
you! (*He steps aside and the five* BLIND MEN
enter.) Hurry it up, let's go! (*They hurry in,*

awkwardly, and VALINDIN *turns back to the door*.)
Catherine! If Monsieur Lefranc comes, send him
in right away! (*Closes the door and turns to*
BLIND MEN.) All right, boys. Listen to me. I've
called you here because you have already shown
me that you know how to work. You've probably
noticed that our show no longer attracts people
the way it did at first. That's because your ten
songs are old now. Everyone has already heard
them. In a few days we'll be leaving for the
South. In February we'll be back here for the
Saint Germaine celebrations . . . and I thought
that for your own good you should come back
with at least five new songs. But you would have
to learn them here, in the few days that we have
left, so that you could practice them while we're
in the South. That's the only way you can be
sure of an audience in Paris when we come back.
(*Laughs.*) This would mean hard work—you remember how it was at first. But I know I can
ask it of you. What do you say? (*Silence.*) What
about you, Elijah?

ELIJAH I . . . I don't know. See what Luke says.

LUKE We'd have to think it over.

VALINDIN (*laughs.*) That's exactly what we don't
have time to do! Did someone say he was afraid?
Come now, let's decide.

DAVID It's already decided. We won't do it.

VALINDIN (*looks at him coldly.*) The others have
a right to speak, too.

DAVID Our public is large enough already.

VALINDIN (*bristles.*) What do you know about
these things? If you don't give them something
new, they drop you! You and Adrienne were talk-

ing about the fairs—she'll tell you! She knows what they're like! (*Makes frantic signals to* ADRIENNE, *motioning her to help him.*) You tell him, Adrienne! (ADRIENNE *looks at him and says nothing.*)

DAVID   Yes, Madame, you tell us. Or perhaps you don't approve of this plan, either?

VALINDIN *again motions to her.* ADRIENNE *turns and goes to door right.*

VALINDIN   Where are you going? (ADRIENNE *exits.* VALINDIN *starts after her.*) Adrienne!

ADRIENNE (*voice.*)   I don't feel well.

DAVID *laughs.* VALINDIN *looks at him, unnerved. Goes rapidly to door, upstage center, and opens it.*

VALINDIN   Catherine!

CATHERINE (*voice.*)   Yes, Monsieur . . . (*She appears in the doorway.*)

VALINDIN   Hasn't Monsieur Lefranc come yet?

CATHERINE   No, Monsieur. (VALINDIN *dismisses her with a gesture.*)

VALINDIN   And I have to leave! (*Faces the* BLIND MEN.) What do the rest of you say? Don't you have anything to say?

DAVID   There's nothing for them to say. As long as I say no, the answer is no. What you're asking isn't in the contract.

NAZAIRE   Maybe we could at least think about it . . . if Monsieur Valindin agreed to pay us more.

VALINDIN   Unfortunately that's out of the question. There are simply too many expenses . . . and it will be even worse now, with the trip coming up. But you must understand that I'm asking you to make this effort because it's for your own good.

DAVID   No.

VALINDIN *starts to explode but controls himself. He calls, right.*

VALINDIN   Adrienne, I'm going. I'll leave them here with you. . . . Maybe you can convince them that it's for their own good. If Lefranc comes, tell him the details and let him talk to them. And you'll have to take them to the café this afternoon—I won't be back. (*Turns to the* BLIND MEN.) Think about it, boys. And don't take too long.

He exits rapidly. Door slams offstage. NAZAIRE, *sighing, goes to a chair and sits.* GILBERT *and* ELIJAH *sit on the floor.* LUKE, DONATIEN, *and* DAVID *remain standing.*

GILBERT   Madame Adrienne . . .

DAVID   She's not here.

NAZAIRE   Do we have to wait here?

ELIJAH   In case Monsieur Lefranc comes.

DAVID   If we're not going to do what he wants, we don't have to wait for anybody.

NAZAIRE   What if he agreed to pay us more?

DAVID   We're through being his clowns! (NAZAIRE *shrugs his shoulders. Pause.*) Unless . . . (*He falls silent.* ELIJAH *raises his head.*)

ELIJAH   What?

DAVID   Listen to me! This is our last chance! (ADRIENNE *enters silently and stands in the doorway listening, her eyes damp.*) We'll learn those five new songs and we'll go on being the laughing stock of the fairs, if he agrees to let me, and only me, teach you to play harmony. When we come back to Paris in February we'll be a real orchestra, not the trained dogs he's turned us into. There's

still time, brothers! Help me do this. (*Silence.*)
Luke, you once loved music. Say you'll help me!

LUKE   Won't you ever stop dreaming?

ELIJAH   He doesn't even let us keep our violins.

DAVID   He'll let us if we make him agree to my
idea. But we have to ask him together, brothers!
All of us!

NAZAIRE   That's enough! Now I'm the one who
says no. What you want is a crazy dream that I
don't give a damn about! I want money and you
heard him say he won't give us any more. So
just shut up and leave us alone!

DAVID   He has us tied up for a year! Brothers, this
is our last chance to do something worthwhile!
(*Pause.*) No one has anything to say? (*Sweetly.*)
Donatien . . .

DONATIEN   (*coldly.*)   I don't have anything to say.
DAVID'*s face darkens.*

DAVID   You all deserve what you're getting.

ELIJAH   (*starts to rise.*)   I'll close that mouth of
yours . . . !

DAVID *quickly returns him to his seat with an ac-
curate thrust of his cane.* ELIJAH *cries out.*

DAVID   Careful, Elijah! My cane has eyes!

ADRIENNE *comes forward a few steps, uneasily.*

ELIJAH   Lunatic . . . !

LUKE   Don't fight, brothers. We've all said we
won't do it.

ELIJAH   (*rises.*)   Come along, Little Bird.

GILBERT *rises and the two of them go to the door.*

DAVID   (*brings his hands to his head in a burst of
desperation.*)   I must play!

He sobs dryly. ADRIENNE *looks at him with damp
eyes.* DONATIEN *takes a step toward him, then stops.*

ELIJAH *and* GILBERT *stop for a moment at the sound of his voice, then exit.*

LUKE (*sighs.*) I'm coming with you. . . .
Exits upstage center. DAVID *sobs silently. He slowly slumps to the floor and sits next to* NAZAIRE *who places his hand on his shoulder in a timid gesture of friendship.* DAVID *quickly pulls away.*

NAZAIRE Don't bother thinking about it any more, David. We're trapped. But if Valindin hadn't done it, somebody else would have. That's what we're here for. (*Leans over and lowers his voice.*) I'd like to punch their eyes out—all of them! That's what I'd like to do. Not much chance of that. The only way we could handle them would be in the dark, and the world is full of light. Even at night they have their moon to give them light. But nobody can keep me from thinking about it . . . thinking what a pleasure it would be to hang them . . . all of them . . . one at a time. (*Laughs, straightens up, and gives* DAVID *an affectionate slap.*) It's good therapy. I recommend it. Aren't you coming?

DAVID No. (NAZAIRE *exits upstage center.* ADRIENNE *stares intensely at* DAVID *and* DONATIEN, *then crosses silently upstage center. She again looks at them, then exits.*) Who is that? Adrienne?

DONATIEN It must have been her. There's no one here now.

DAVID (*rises.*) I thought you had gone.

DONATIEN I was waiting . . . for you.

DAVID I don't feel like going anywhere right now. You go ahead, boy.

DONATIEN (*slowly.*) I'm not a boy. And I won't leave you alone with her.

DAVID (*comes near.*)   What are you talking about?

DONATIEN   Do you think I don't know what you're doing?

DAVID   That's enough! (*Takes his arm.*) Let's go.

DONATIEN (*frees himself.*)   You don't give me orders!

DAVID   Let's go.

DONATIEN   I'm not going! She prefers *me*!

DAVID   What are you talking about?

DONATIEN   You're in love with her. You want to take her away from me! But you won't do it. . . . I won't let you! (DAVID *slaps him.* DONATIEN *whines. A silence. His lips tremble as he adds.*) I'll never forget that, David.

ADRIENNE *reappears in the doorway and watches them.*

DAVID   Forgive me, boy. . . .

DONATIEN   Don't call me boy!

ADRIENNE (*gently.*)   Why not, Donatien? He loves you very much. More than you think. . . .

DONATIEN (*bitterly.*)   I'm sure he does.

ADRIENNE   David, Catherine has gone out on an errand. Would you step outside? I'd like to talk with Donatien . . . alone.

DONATIEN (*trembling.*)   With me?

ADRIENNE   Yes. (DAVID's *face has altered drastically.*) Will you leave us, David?

DAVID (*with an effort.*)   All right.

He goes toward the upstage exit. As he passes ADRIENNE, *she reaches out and silently squeezes his hand. He stops, surprised. Then he draws back his hand and exits, rapidly.* ADRIENNE *looks at her hand. As the tapping of his cane fades away in the distance,* ADRIENNE *goes to* DONATIEN *and takes his hand.*

ADRIENNE   You're trembling again. There's nothing to be afraid of. You know I'm . . . fond of you.

DONATIEN   I . . . I don't . . .

ADRIENNE   Come, boy. Come with me.

They exit right, closing the door behind them.

Light comes up on the downstage area. DAVID *appears from left. He is stooped and tired. He sits on the steps. He tiredly lets his cane fall at his side, then buries his face in his tensed hands.* LEFRANC *appears from right and starts to cross. He sees* DAVID; *his pace slows and he stops at* DAVID'S *side.*

LEFRANC   Where are the others? Upstairs?

DAVID *(raises his head.)*   Eh?

LEFRANC   I'm Monsieur Lefranc. I asked you if——

DAVID   Yes, I know. Monsieur Valindin has left. He couldn't wait for you any longer.

LEFRANC   What! Blast him! This isn't the first time he's done that. I'm a busy man. If I happen to be a bit late once in a while, it wouldn't hurt him to wait for me. All right, you tell him to call me whenever he likes. I won't be coming back here. *(*DAVID *nods, weakly.* LEFRANC *looks at him, puzzled.)* Is something wrong with you? *(*DAVID *shakes his head;* LEFRANC *shrugs his shoulders.)* Good-bye. *(Starts to exit right.)*

DAVID *(raises his head.)*   Monsieur Lefranc.

LEFRANC *(turns.)*   What is it?

DAVID *(rises.)*   May I have a few words with you, Monsieur Lefranc?

LEFRANC *(comes back to his side, annoyed.)*   Make it quick. I'm in a hurry.

DAVID Monsieur Lefranc, it's true, isn't it, that our show is bad?

LEFRANC It's intolerable. Do you know why? Because you people can't even put a tune together, and yet you're taking work away from the best musicians at the fair. Thanks to our stupid public.

DAVID But you yourself are still helping Monsieur Valindin.

LEFRANC I have to eat too, my friend! Besides, that's none of your concern.

DAVID I want to get out of this mess.

LEFRANC (*looks around and places his hand on* DAVID's *arm.*) Good for you.

DAVID You must help me do it.

LEFRANC (*recoils.*) How?

DAVID Couldn't I get into the Opéra-Comique? Even if I were only the last violinist. . . .

LEFRANC (*scowling.*) You are bound by a contract.

DAVID But if you talk to him, he'll let me go. He hates me. Please help me, Monsieur Lefranc! I could do it, I know I could do it! (LEFRANC *looks at him steadily, his mouth drawn.*) You yourself said that I play well. . . .

LEFRANC (*clears his throat.*) I don't deny you have talent. But that hardly means you would be capable of playing professionally.

DAVID If you would help me, I could study . . . !

LEFRANC By ear? No, David. It's hard for you to see this . . . but one must play far better than you do to get into the Opéra-Comique . . . or anywhere else. (DAVID *seeks the step with his foot and sits.*) I'm sorry.

DAVID Forgive me, Monsieur Lefranc.

LEFRANC (*starts to say something else, then changes his mind.*) God be with you.

He moves right. At the exit he turns and looks again at DAVID, *who has not moved. Then he looks at the floor, troubled, and crosses himself in silence. He exits.*

A pause. Old BERNIER *enters from left and looks at* DAVID *as he crosses. He starts to pass him by, then changes his mind and stops.*

BERNIER I am Old Bernier. Are you waiting for Monsieur Valindin?

DAVID I'm not waiting for anyone.

BERNIER I knocked at his door but no one answered. Do you know whether he plans to come back?

DAVID He said he wasn't coming back.

BERNIER (*sighs.*) That always happens to me. (*Looks at* DAVID.) Aren't you the one they call David?

DAVID Yes.

BERNIER (*hesitates, then sits at his side.*) It's been a bad year, eh?

DAVID Is there ever a good one?

BERNIER Not for me. The gold is pouring into the café and I haven't even been paid yet. And now he wants me to make him a box to take the peacock to the country fairs. Says he'll pay me for everything after all this is over.

DAVID Don't do it!

BERNIER Then he wouldn't pay me anything. I know how he works. (*Lowers his voice.*) I can't afford to have any trouble with him. My family is waiting for me at home . . . starving, all of them. Last year my little one died. They couldn't even find any roots to eat. All they had was bread made from ferns. This year there are more peasants than ever in Paris.

DAVID   Something ought to be done for them.

BERNIER   That's what I say. Here and in the provinces, too. Even if the harvest is good, it doesn't help us. The noblemen and the clergy wouldn't even think of paying taxes, so everything comes out of our hide. We pay the taxes, we work the fields. The women and children have to put on the harnesses and do it themselves because even the animals have died. My boy Blas is sick from doing that. He's working himself to death, but nobody can understand what's wrong with him. (*Sighs.*) And tonight he'll be screaming with terror, the poor thing. . . .

DAVID   Why?

BERNIER   He's afraid of the dark. Tonight there's no moon.

DAVID   (*after a moment.*) So many things need changing!

BERNIER   And somebody will have to change them, hang it all! But he'll have to be careful while he's doing it. Strange things happen to people who talk too much about change. (*A pause.*) You should be careful, David.

DAVID   Why?

BERNIER   (*looks around and draws nearer, lowering his voice.*) I heard them talking about you in the café.

DAVID   You heard who talking about me?

BERNIER   Valindin . . . and the Police Commissioner. Do you know what a sealed letter is?

DAVID   No.

BERNIER It's a paper signed by the king to allow them to imprison someone without a trial. They're sold for a high price. And sometimes they're given in exchange for special favors.

DAVID They sell them?

BERNIER They think no one knows about it, but they sell too many. . . . People know. The old father who's in the way, the jealous husband. . . . (*Snaps his fingers.*) He spends the rest of his life rotting in jail.

DAVID Can that really be true?

BERNIER Anything can be true if you wear a sword. And Monsieur Valindin wears one, even though he doesn't have noble blood. He's a dangerous man, David, and he has friends in the court. I heard him say that if you got in his way, he would have you thrown in jail with a sealed letter. (*A silence.*)

DAVID (*seeks* BERNIER's *hand and squeezes it.*) Thank you, Friend Bernier.

BERNIER Shh! There he comes!

DAVID Who?

BERNIER Monsieur Valindin. (*Rises.*)

DAVID (*also rises, frightened.*)   Are you sure?

VALINDIN *enters hurriedly from right. He sees them and stops.* BERNIER *bows humbly.*

VALINDIN What are you doing here? Don't you know it's almost time to open the café? Get yourselves going!

BERNIER Monsieur Valindin . . .

VALINDIN I don't have time for you now, Irénée. (*Resumes his walk.*)

BERNIER But I don't have anything to eat, Monsieur Valindin!

VALINDIN   You mean you wouldn't have anything to eat if I didn't give you a job!

BERNIER   I could manage with just a small salary advance. . . .

VALINDIN   I already gave you one.

DAVID *steps in front of him.*

DAVID   I . . . I have to talk with you.

VALINDIN   I'm in a hurry. Talk with me at the café. (*Starts to push his way by him.*)

DAVID (*grabs him.*)   It's important——

VALINDIN (*frees himself.*)   Don't you touch me!

DAVID   There's no one in your house. They've all gone.

VALINDIN   So?

DAVID   Just let me tell you. . . .

VALINDIN (*turns and pushes him.*)   Get over to the café. (*He exits.* DAVID *follows him.*)

DAVID (*voice.*)   Monsieur Valindin!

BERNIER *sighs, then turns slowly and exits right. The light comes up in the house. A pause.* VALINDIN *enters upstage center,* DAVID *still hanging on him.*

DAVID   Monsieur Valindin, please come outside with me. . . .

VALINDIN   I told you to go to the café.

DAVID   But you'll have to take me. . . .

VALINDIN (*shakes him off.*)   I'll fix you! You're a raving lunatic! Do you know what happens to lunatics? We lock them up! (*He removes his tricorn hat and puts it on the table.* DAVID *again seizes his arm.*)

DAVID   Listen to me. . . .

VALINDIN (*shoves him.*)   Get out of my house! (*He slips out of his coat and moves rapidly right. As he reaches the bedroom door,* ADRIENNE *comes*

out. She is wearing a nightgown and is very pale.)
What are you doing here? Why aren't you
dressed?

ADRIENNE I felt faint . . . so I decided to lie
down a while.

VALINDIN Get dressed quick. And fix yourself up.
The Baron of Tournelle is finally coming today!
I'm going to put on my good coat and change
my hat. (*He starts to enter.*)

ADRIENNE I'll get them for you. . . .

VALINDIN I know where they are.

ADRIENNE You're all tired out. Sit down and have
a drink while I get your clothes for you.

VALINDIN You worry about yourself. I want you
to get dressed. Quit wasting time.

ADRIENNE But——

VALINDIN Let me by! (*He pushes her out of the
way and goes into the bedroom.*)

ADRIENNE Oh, my God . . . !

DAVID (*softly.*) Did you hide him?

ADRIENNE Not very well.

DAVID (*after a pause.*) We'll leave today.

ADRIENNE You can't! No one can go against his
will. . . . Shh!

She fixes her frightened eyes on the door. VALINDIN
enters, his face contorted with anger. He is dragging
DONATIEN *by the neck.* DONATIEN *is frightened and
trembling; his clothes hang loosely about him.
There is a tense silence, during which* VALINDIN
and ADRIENNE *look at each other sharply.* VALINDIN
hurls DONATIEN *to the floor.* DONATIEN *moans softly.*

VALINDIN (*goes toward her.*) Bitch!

ADRIENNE (*retreating.*) No!

VALINDIN You filthy whore! So you'd do it even

with a stinking, worm-eaten, blind idiot! (DAVID *tries to shield her with his body.*) Don't get in my way, scum! So you were trying to cover up for them, eh? Waiting your turn? Or maybe you've already had it. Have the others had you already, Adrienne?

ADRIENNE   I don't care what you say about me!

VALINDIN   You've turned my house into a brothel! It's been a brothel ever since I brought you here. That's what I deserve for being so stupid as to think you could . . . Disgusting tramp . . . !

He takes her by the arm, pulls her to him, and slaps her. DAVID *is helpless to intervene.* ADRIENNE *screams.* DAVID *tightens his hands on his cane.*

DONATIEN   (*trying to rise.*)   Don't hit her!

VALINDIN *turns and returns him to the floor with a sharp kick.* DONATIEN *screams.*

DAVID   If you hit her one more time, we'll all walk out on you.

VALINDIN   (*turns on him sharply.*)   You'll walk out on me when I say you can and not before! All right, let's not give this incident more importance than it deserves. I think a few little love taps should be enough to straighten her out. That's the only language women understand. And apparently the only one you understand.

ADRIENNE   Louis, we're going away.

VALINDIN   (*hurls himself on her insanely.*)   Bitch! Bitch! (*He beats her mercilessly.*)

ADRIENNE *screams.* DONATIEN *gropes his way toward them.*

DONATIEN   No! Stop!

He tries to strike VALINDIN, *who knocks him across*

the room with his fist. DONATIEN *falls over a chair, howling with pain.* DAVID *raises his cane.*

ADRIENNE (*sees him.*)   David, no!

VALINDIN *turns quickly.*

VALINDIN   You sneaky . . . (*He seizes the cane in mid-air and takes it from* DAVID *with a sharp twisting motion. He throws the cane to the floor; then, seizing* DAVID'S *arm and twisting it behind his back, he forces him to his knees.* DAVID *moans with pain.*)

ADRIENNE   Louis, they're blind!

VALINDIN   That's right, you imbecile. Remember that: You're blind. And you're weak! Don't ever try anything against a man who still has his eyes.

ADRIENNE   You'll break his arm!

VALINDIN   No. (*He frees him.* DAVID *remains on his knees, holding his arm.*) I won't break his arm. Today you play for me. Tomorrow, if you like, you leave. (DAVID *raises his head, surprised.*) You've been causing trouble for me ever since the first day. I could crush you like an insect, but I have no desire to do that. I'm not a vengeful man. The best thing is for you simply to get out. If you want, I'll free you from your contract—I can get by with five in the orchestra. This very night I'll give you your release. Agreed? (*Pause.*) All right, think it over. But I warn you: for your own good, it's best that you leave. (*He moves right.* DAVID *is weeping silently.*)

ADRIENNE   Louis . . . I'm leaving, too.

VALINDIN (*looks at her steadily.*)   Nobody walks out on Valindin unless he says so. If I have to, I'll tie a chain around your neck and each day

I'll give you the lashes you deserve . . . until
you drag yourself at my feet . . . like a dog!
Get dressed!

He exits right. ADRIENNE *runs to help* DAVID *up,
then throws herself, sobbing, into his arms. He
embraces her desperately.*

DAVID Don't cry, Adrienne. You haven't done
anything wrong. You mustn't cry.

DONATIEN *gets up and gropes his way toward them.*

DONATIEN What are you doing? (*He realizes that
they are embracing and tries to separate them.*)
No! Was he right, after all? Was he right?

ADRIENNE *pulls away, looks painfully at the two
of them, and begins to walk away.* VALINDIN *appears
in the doorway.*

VALINDIN Didn't you hear me? (*He takes* ADRIENNE
by the arm and drags her with him.) I told you
to get dressed! You two wait here. You're going
to the café with me.

He takes ADRIENNE *into the bedroom. A pause.*
DAVID *quietly goes to the door and listens. Then
he goes to the table, finds the jewel box, and opens
it.* DONATIEN *hears him and turns.*

DONATIEN What are you doing?

DAVID Nothing. (*He silently removes something
from the box and puts it inside his clothing.*)

DONATIEN What did you pick up?

DAVID (*closes the jewel box.*)   Nothing.

DONATIEN Yes, you did. You took something. . . .

DAVID (*moves away from the table.*)   You've hated
me for quite a while, haven't you?

DONATIEN (*weakly.*) No.

DAVID You won't have to put up with me much
longer. I'm leaving tomorrow.

DONATIEN Alone? (DAVID *does not answer.* DO-
NATIEN *moves toward him.*) You're going alone,
aren't you? (*Pleading.*) David, you are going
alone, aren't you? Alone!

*The lights fade slowly as the black curtains close
on the upstage area. The first part of Corelli's
Allegro begins to play, very softly. Suddenly, a
bell strikes two o'clock.* DUBOIS *enters downstage
left, carrying a glowing lantern. He stops and raises
the lantern, while his free hand goes to his belt.*

DUBOIS Halt! Who's there? Oh, it's you, Monsieur
Valindin. I wasn't expecting you tonight.

VALINDIN *enters from right. He, too, carries a lantern. He is obviously intoxicated.*

VALINDIN Tonight's just like any other night.

DUBOIS Not exactly. Tonight there's no moon.
. . . It's black as pitch out here.

VALINDIN So?

DUBOIS The plaza isn't lit. You might have some
trouble, walking around here at this hour.

VALINDIN I can take care of myself.

DUBOIS Why don't you come with me to the guardhouse for a while?

VALINDIN I'd rather go to my café.

DUBOIS Good crowd today, eh?

VALINDIN (*solemnly.*) One of our best days.

DUBOIS Where will you go now?

VALINDIN To the South! Going down there and
take all the money they've got!

DUBOIS Taking the blind men?

VALINDIN Naturally. (*He reels.*)

DUBOIS (*holding him up.*) Looks like you hit it
pretty hard today.

VALINDIN Yep. I suppose I did.

DUBOIS   Why don't you go on home? I'll keep an eye on this area. That's what I'm here for.

VALINDIN   (*rejecting the suggestion.*)   I want to go sit in my café. Mine!

DUBOIS   You'd be better off in your own bed. That's yours, too. I'd sure like to be in mine right now.

VALINDIN   Bah! Bed! For all I care they can burn my bed. . . . They can burn my whole house! This is where I belong. . . . This is where I celebrate my successes . . . and suffer my failures. My dear friend, it's so wonderful to be alone!

DUBOIS   (*laughs.*)   Then I'll leave you, Monsieur Valindin.

VALINDIN   (*places a coin in his hand.*)   Go to the guardhouse and drink to my health.

DUBOIS   Thank you, Monsieur. If I can be of any service to you, you know where to find me.

He bows slightly. VALINDIN *gestures to him vaguely, and exits left, unsteadily. As he exits he fumbles in his pocket for a key.* DUBOIS *raises his lantern to watch him leave.* DUBOIS *then exits right, and the black curtains open.*

At the back of the stage the noise of a key in a lock is heard, then a lantern casts its yellow glow across the interior of the café. The bandstand and its giant peacock are outlined in the dim light. A door slams, then again the sound of a lock. VALINDIN *appears from left. He stops at center, raises his lantern and looks around. Then he moves right and exits. He is heard opening and closing another door. The lantern's glow projects his enormous shadow on the walls. He reappears with a bottle.*

*He goes to the bandstand and walks around it,
caressing it all the while. He returns to center,
sighs, sets the lantern and bottle on the table left
and begins to take off his coat. Halfway through
that operation he stops, absorbed in his thoughts.*

VALINDIN The devil take all the women in the
world! Bitches. . . . (*He finishes removing his
coat and drops it on a chair. He pulls up another
chair and sits heavily. He takes the bottle, removes the stopper, and drinks deeply. He runs
his hand over his eyes.*) Don't feel sorry for them,
Valindin. You've been drinking and you're not
a young man any more. Devil take them. . . .

*He drinks again, sets the bottle on the table, and
buries his face in his hands. A pause. Something
moves vaguely in the dim light. Behind the music
stands the figure of a man emerges. His hands rest
lightly on the wooden edge of the bandstand.* DAVID's
voice is clear and smooth in the heavy silence.

DAVID Monsieur Valindin. (*A pause.* VALINDIN
raises his head, unable to believe his ears.) It's
David, Monsieur Valindin.

VALINDIN *gets up quickly and looks toward the
bandstand. He takes the lantern and goes toward
it.* DAVID's *face can be seen clearly now. He wears
the trace of a smile.*

VALINDIN What are you doing here? How did
you get in?

DAVID With the key.

VALINDIN What key?

DAVID Your extra. I'll give it back to you.

VALINDIN Aha! So Adrienne gave it to you!

DAVID (*laughs smoothly.*) She doesn't know anything about it . . . not yet. I was in the hallway the day you gave it to her. . . . I heard where she put it.

VALINDIN (*he is struggling against the effects of the wine.*) Have you come here to rob me?

DAVID If I had come to rob, I wouldn't have called you.

VALINDIN What do you want? Your violin?

DAVID I wouldn't have called you for that, either.

VALINDIN Well, whatever it is, you shouldn't have come here. You can't just walk into my café like that! I'll make you regret it! (*He moves left.*)

DAVID Where are you going?

VALINDIN I'm going to call the watchman.

DAVID He's not out there. You sent him to the guardhouse, remember? Wouldn't you like to know why I've come?

VALINDIN I don't have anything to discuss with you! Come down from there and get out of here. We'll just forget about it this time.

DAVID Monsieur Valindin, I came to tell you that I accept your offer.

VALINDIN What offer?

DAVID You said I could leave the show.

VALINDIN And for that you stole a key and came here in the middle of the night?

DAVID There's more. I wanted to tell you a secret . . . something that concerns you . . . and Adrienne. (*Silence.*)

VALINDIN Come down from there.

DAVID (*making his way to the stairway.*) I'm glad you're going to listen to me. (*With his stick he finds the top step and starts to come down.*) It would be a shame if we parted ways forever without ever having had a chance to talk. (VALINDIN *watches him descend the steps. He is still amazed.* DAVID *reaches the floor and moves to the table.*) Isn't this where you were sitting? (*He feels the bottle.*) We'll be more comfortable here. (*He calmly sits on one of the chairs.* VALINDIN *comes up slowly and leaves his lantern on the table.* DAVID, *as if startled by the sound, reaches out and feels the lantern.*) What's that? Oh . . . your lantern. (*He pulls back his hands.*)

VALINDIN (*places his hands on the table.*) All right. . . . What is it you want to tell me? (*A silence.*)

DAVID You've taught me a great lesson and I wanted to thank you. When the Reverend Mother told us about you, I said to myself, "At last! I'm going to help that man . . . and I'll worship him as long as I live." Afterwards I found out that I was only supposed to make people laugh. But, after all, I suppose we're all clowns, aren't we? (*Laughs.*) Thank you for turning me into a clown. It has been an unforgettable experience.

VALINDIN (*smiles.*) You lunatic. You make me laugh. (*Sits, picking up the bottle.*)

DAVID I'm glad! (*Laughs.*) That's very important, you know. (*He grotesquely pantomimes the playing of a violin.*)

"Her little lambs sing to her.
'Baa! Baa! Baa!'"

VALINDIN That's it, lunatic! Good, good! (*As he speaks he slaps the table with his open hand. He laughs and* DAVID *laughs with him. Then he drinks.*)

DAVID   That's the only way to fight off fear. Well, there is another way, but it's no good for most people. Most people have to fight it off by jumping around like little circus animals. Or by dreaming.

VALINDIN   Say, what about that secret you were going to tell me?

DAVID   You'll get it in a minute. I was telling you that I used to hide from my fear by dreaming. I dreamed about music. . . . I dreamed I loved a woman I'd never even met. . . . I dreamed I would never harm anyone and no one would ever harm me. . . . I was quite a dreamer, wasn't I? To dream things like that in a world where people can starve us to death . . . or turn us into ridiculous clowns . . . or hurt us . . . or have us imprisoned for the rest of our lives with a sealed letter. (VALINDIN *looks at him, his face quite serious.*) Dreams like the groping of a blind man.

VALINDIN   Why do you say that?

DAVID   No reason. . . . It's always irritated me when people laughed at a blind man who was thrashing around with his cane. Because I may be a dreamer, Monsieur Valindin, but I'm not a fool. Do you remember that time in your house when I hit you on the foot with my cane?

VALINDIN   (*looking at him steadily.*)   Yes.

DAVID   I've become very good at that. I can put my stick right where I want it.

VALINDIN   Now, just a minute, you scoundrel!

DAVID   (*holds up his hand.*)   Wait! There must be some reason why I told you that, don't you think?

VALINDIN   (*raps the table with his knuckles.*)   I

want you to tell me that secret and get out of here!

DAVID (*sighs.*) What a shame this place is so big . . . and so dark. When there's no moon you can't see a thing.

VALINDIN What difference does that make to you?

DAVID To me it makes no difference at all . . . but it does to you.

VALINDIN To me?

DAVID This afternoon you told me never to try anything against a man who has eyes. That was good advice. Now I'm going to repay it with some of my own.

VALINDIN (*laughs.*) You're going to give me advice? (*Picks up the bottle and starts to drink. He stops as* DAVID *speaks.*)

DAVID You should never hit blind people . . . or women.

VALINDIN (*after a moment's silence he bursts into laughter.*) Are you threatening me? (*He laughs and drinks.* DAVID's *agile hands dart quickly to the lantern, open it, and put out the candle. There is absolute darkness on stage.*) What are you doing? (VALINDIN's *hands are heard on the table as he gropes for the lantern.*) Where is my lantern?

DAVID (*his voice now comes from a different part of the stage.*) Yes, where is your lantern?

VALINDIN *rises noisily and clumsily.*

VALINDIN Give it to me, you idiot!

DAVID Now I'll tell you that secret. You're never going to see Adrienne again.

VALINDIN What are you talking about, you fool? She'll be mine as long as I live!

DAVID But Valindin . . . You are not going to
live very long. (*Silence.*)

VALINDIN (*weakly.*) What did you say?

DAVID You have exploited your last blind beggar.

VALINDIN You bastard! When I catch you . . .
(*He stumbles around noisily, knocking over
chairs.*)

DAVID (*from a different place.*) The more you
move, the more you'll stumble.

VALINDIN (*stops moving.*) Do you want to . . .
kill me?

DAVID Don't move. Don't say anything. Every
time you do, my stick knows exactly where the
back of your neck is. (*A silence.*) I hear you.
Stay away from that door. (*A silence.*) What
does it feel like to be afraid, Valindin? (*A
silence.*) The blind have prayed long enough
for your soul. Now it's your turn to pray . . . if
you know how.

VALINDIN Son of a dog! (*He hurls himself furiously
toward the voice and falls over something.*)

DAVID (*laughs.*) It's no use, Valindin. I'll never
be where you think. But I'll always know right
where you are. Because you're fat . . . you
breathe loudly . . . and you stink. I'm through
talking, Valindin. (*A silence.*)

VALINDIN (*a trembling in his voice.*) David . . . !
(*After a silence, with his voice broken by weeping.*) David . . . you don't understand. . . . I
wanted to help you. . . . I'm not like you think
I am. . . . You're ingrates, all of you. . . . (*Silence. Suddenly* VALINDIN *runs, sobbing desperately, toward the door.*) No . . . ! No . . . !
Help! Adrienne . . . help me!

A sharp blow drops him in his tracks. Two more blows follow. A complete silence; then the black curtains close.

Lights come up full on the downstage area. It is morning. ADRIENNE *and* CATHERINE, *at left, are listening to* LATOUCHE *and* DUBOIS, *at right.*

LATOUCHE Believe me, Madame, I am sorry to have to bring you such bad news.

ADRIENNE How did it happen?

DUBOIS It seems that last night he was drinking rather heavily. So much that he even forgot to lock the door when he went into the café. Apparently he climbed up onto the bandstand— perhaps to look over his possessions—and then lost his balance and fell head-first onto the steps.

LATOUCHE That's where we found him. The broken lantern was lying at his side.

DUBOIS He had removed his coat, I suppose in order to be more comfortable. In the pockets we found the two keys to the café, and quite a bit of money.

ADRIENNE Two keys? (*She instinctively glances upstage.*)

LATOUCHE Weren't there two? Or were there more?

ADRIENNE No, no, there were two. It's just that he always left one of them here . . . in the jewel box. He must have taken it without telling me. We had a little disagreement . . . personal matters, you know. . . . He must have taken the key because of that.

LATOUCHE Yes, that must have been the reason. Can you tell me where Monsieur Valindin kept his money?

ADRIENNE   He deposited it with Legrand.

LATOUCHE   Does anything in the café belong to you?

ADRIENNE   No.

LATOUCHE   (*to* CATHERINE.)   Or you?

CATHERINE   No, Monsieur.

LATOUCHE   Then, everything there belonged to Monsieur Valindin?

ADRIENNE   Yes. That is, everything except the musical instruments. They belong to the blind men.

LATOUCHE   Do they still live at the Asylum?

ADRIENNE   Yes, Monsieur. In the Quinze-Vingts.

LATOUCHE   I must ask you all these questions, Madame, because we have gotten in touch with the brother of the deceased. Did you know he had a brother?

ADRIENNE   Yes, I knew.

LATOUCHE   All that Monsieur Valindin left behind now belongs to his brother. That includes this house—which means that you can no longer stay here. I hope you understand.

ADRIENNE   I understand.

LATOUCHE   You must stay here, of course, until the brother arrives. Then you can arrange for the removal of your own personal property and all of you can ask him for any back pay which you might have coming. I shall leave one of my men at the door, in case you need anything. Once again, my condolences.

ADRIENNE   Thank you, Monsieur.

LATOUCHE   God be with you, ladies.

Bows from LATOUCHE *and* DUBOIS, *curtsies from* ADRIENNE *and* CATHERINE. *The* POLICEMEN *put on their hats and exit.*

A pause.

CATHERINE   So now it's back to the streets.

ADRIENNE   What difference does it make?

A silence. Knocking at the door.

CATHERINE   They're back!

ADRIENNE   Go let them in.

The black curtains open, revealing the room.
CATHERINE *goes up the stairs and exits.* ADRIENNE
*goes up the stairs and to the jewel box. She opens
it and looks inside, apprehensively. She closes it.*
CATHERINE *appears in the doorway.*

CATHERINE   It's David, the blind man.

ADRIENNE   *(without looking at her.)*   Catherine, we
have nothing for lunch. Go out and buy whatever you like, then take it to the kitchen and
prepare it.

CATHERINE   Very well. What should I do with the
blind man?

ADRIENNE   Bring him in here. (CATHERINE *exits.
Moments later* DAVID *appears in the doorway. A
door slams offstage.)* Come in, David. No one
else is here. (DAVID *enters.* ADRIENNE *goes to the
door, looks out, and closes it.)* Have you been at
the Asylum?

DAVID   Yes.

ADRIENNE   *(watching his face.)*   David, the Police
Commissioner was just here. Something terrible
has happened. Have . . . have you heard anything?

DAVID   *(after a moment.)*   Adrienne, I'm leaving
Paris.

ADRIENNE   Answer just one question for me. Did
you take that key from the jewel box?

DAVID   Yes.

ADRIENNE   Oh, David! (*She throws herself, sobbing, into his arms.*)

DAVID   That's what I came to tell you. If you want to turn me in, do it. I'll do whatever you say. But you have to be the one who does it. I'll never turn myself over to their justice.

ADRIENNE   We'll leave here. . . . No one will know anything. . . . I'll stay with you as long as I live . . . or as long as you want me.

DAVID   (*gently frees himself from her grasp.*)   Don't decide anything yet.

ADRIENNE   (*weeping openly.*)   I've loved you since the first time I saw you!

DAVID   The last word he spoke was your name. (ADRIENNE *weeps, then sits next to the table.*) He loved you, Adrienne. And he beat you . . . he beat all of us . . . because he loved you. Now you have to turn me in.

ADRIENNE   No!

DAVID   (*explodes.*)   Adrienne, I've killed a man! I wanted to be a musician and I've ended up a murderer.

ADRIENNE   He was the murderer! He was killing all of us . . . little by little.

DAVID   Because he loved you!

ADRIENNE   (*raises her head.*)   Perhaps. Maybe God will forgive him. But he wouldn't convince me if he called me with his dying breath. (*Bitterly.*) I learned long ago not to trust his tears and his sweet words. I don't even care any more whether they were sincere. (*Goes to him.*) He probably never even knew, himself. (*Puts her head on his chest.*) David, together we can forget all this.

DAVID   I'll never forget.

ADRIENNE   Then let me help you bear the memory.

DAVID   You'll come with me?

ADRIENNE   Yes.

DAVID   But I have nothing to offer you! All you'll get from me is hunger and misery!

ADRIENNE   I need you.

DAVID   I'm a blind beggar!

ADRIENNE   And I'm a wretch.

DAVID   (*embraces her passionately.*)   Adrienne, Donatien is going to suffer.

ADRIENNE   Both of us have done all that we can for him. Now we have to think of ourselves. David, this life is all we have!

DAVID   And it's nothing. . . .

They remain embraced for a moment. Suddenly ADRIENNE's *eyes grow wide with fright.*

ADRIENNE   Oh, my God!

DAVID   What is it?

ADRIENNE   (*she breaks away from him.*)   I think I've made a terrible mistake!

DAVID   What are you talking about?

ADRIENNE   They told me they had found two keys in his coat pocket, and I . . . Oh, David.

DAVID   For God's sake, Adrienne, what is it?

ADRIENNE   I told them that was odd, because he always left one of them here for me, in the jewel box. (*Paces, distraught.*) How could I have been so stupid?

DAVID   I put them in his pocket. I knew there were two keys and I knew it would look suspicious if one of them disappeared. And I certainly couldn't take the chance of bringing the other one back here, since it might already have been missed.

ADRIENNE   (*nervously.*) My story goes all right with that. But . . .

DAVID   What did you tell them?

ADRIENNE   I told them what I actually believed. I said that we had a fight, that he must have taken the other key because he was angry with me. . . . They seemed to believe me. . . .

DAVID   They have no reason to suspect anything. And least of all to suspect me. How could a blind man kill someone with eyes?

ADRIENNE   Yes! How did you . . . ?

DAVID   I put out his light. He couldn't see me but I could hear him. It was all thought out ahead of time. Even blind men can think.

He sits, slowly, beside the table. ADRIENNE *looks at him tenderly.*

In the street, downstage right, CATHERINE *appears, carrying a shopping bag. She is followed by* LA-TOUCHE *and* DUBOIS, *who are leading* DONATIEN *by the arm. As they reach the exit, left,* DONATIEN *holds back.*

DONATIEN   No, please!

LATOUCHE   (*smiles.*) Don't you want to go up there?

DONATIEN   No, no!

DAVID   All carefully thought out. . . . (ADRIENNE *moves closer to him.*)

LATOUCHE   Turn him loose, Dubois. (*To* CATH-ERINE.) And you, remember: As soon as we enter the house, you go straight to the kitchen without a word to anyone.

CATHERINE   Yes, Monsieur.

LATOUCHE   Let's go.

They exit. DONATIEN *sits on the stairs and buries his face in his hands.*

DAVID (*sighs.*) Thinking has been a pastime of mine ever since I was a child. . . . I used to eavesdrop on my master's children, just to hear them talk about the books they were studying. And then at night I'd lie awake for hours thinking about what I had heard. . . . (ADRIENNE *strokes his shoulder.*) My mother would call to me, "David, are you asleep?" And I never answered her. . . . One day I asked her, "Who was my father?" and then she didn't answer me. . . . You see, I can't even tell you about my life. I only remember how happy I was when the music teacher taught me a little about the violin. . . . I was so happy that when I lost my sight, it didn't really bother me because they gave me a violin to console me.

ADRIENNE   How did you lose your sight?

DAVID   Playing with fireworks during a festival in the castle where we lived. My mother was the washerwoman there. . . . Then we left the castle. . . . I don't know why. She and I wandered for years, singing in the towns we came to. . . . And then my mother died one night while we were sleeping in a haystack.

ADRIENNE   David, I can sing.

DAVID   I'm tired. Empty. Such a nightmare. . . . I don't understand anything. I only know that I can't see, that I'll never see . . . and that I'm going to die.

ADRIENNE   Our children will see. . . .

DAVID (*excitedly takes her hand which is on his*

shoulder.)   Adrienne, what I wanted to do is not impossible! It can be done. I know it can! Some day blind men will read! Some day they will play beautiful music!

ADRIENNE (*weeping*.)   Others, perhaps.

DAVID (*sadly*.)   Yes . . . others.

Suddenly LATOUCHE *and* DUBOIS *burst into the room through the door, upstage center.* ADRIENNE *screams.* DAVID *leaps to his feet and stands, tightly clutching his cane.*

LATOUCHE   Stay where you are! Are you the one they call David?

DAVID   I am.

LATOUCHE   What time did you return to the Asylum last night?

DAVID   I don't remember. . . .

LATOUCHE   Then let me tell you: at three o'clock. Your bed was empty till then. Where were you?

DAVID   Wandering around the streets. . . .

LATOUCHE (*laughs*.)   And did you by any chance wander through the Place de Louis Quinze?

DAVID   Why would I go there?

LATOUCHE   To kill Monsieur Valindin.

ADRIENNE   But that was an accident!

LATOUCHE   You be quiet! (*He goes to the table, opens the jewel box, and crisply snaps it shut*.) Yesterday afternoon you took the extra key to the café from this jewel box and then left it with the other key after you had killed him.

ADRIENNE   Louis took it with him!

LATOUCHE   No, Madame. This man took it. I know that for a fact.

DUBOIS (*takes* ADRIENNE *by the arm and shakes*

her.) Are you trying to cover for him? Were you his accomplice?

LATOUCHE   Let her go! If she had been his accomplice, she wouldn't have told us about the key. (DUBOIS *releases her, grudgingly. To* DAVID.) The best thing you can do is confess.

DAVID   How could I have killed him? I can't even see.

ADRIENNE   That's right, Monsieur Latouche! He can't see! And Louis was strong! Why, he would have knocked him over with one blow. . . . (*Laughs confidently.*) Obviously, he couldn't possibly have done it. . . .

LATOUCHE   He did it.

DAVID (*laughs.*) How?

LATOUCHE (*with a sinister smile.*) That's what you are going to tell me.

DAVID's *face grows solemn.*

ADRIENNE (*looking at* LATOUCHE.) No . . .

LATOUCHE   Let's go!

DUBOIS *goes to* DAVID *and snatches his cane from him with a quick movement. Then he takes him by the arm and pushes him toward the door.*

ADRIENNE   Don't take him away! He didn't do it!

DUBOIS   Out of the way!

ADRIENNE   No! I won't let you take him! (*She throws her arms around* DAVID's *neck.*)

LATOUCHE   Well, well! What have we here?

ADRIENNE   Let him go . . . !

DUBOIS   Maybe that was the motive for the killing. . . .

LATOUCHE (*he roughly pulls* ADRIENNE *aside, in spite of her resistance.*) You don't leave Paris without permission. Understand? (*She continues to struggle; he throws her back again.*) Let's go, Dubois. (*They exit with* DAVID.)

ADRIENNE   No . . . ! (*She runs after them. Her voice is heard from offstage.*) No . . . ! Have mercy on him! He's blind! Have pity on him. Don't torture him! He's the best man in the world! In God's name, I beg you . . . ! Have mercy . . . ! He didn't do it . . . ! (*At the sound of her cries,* DONATIEN *rises and tries to appear innocent. He is trembling.* LATOUCHE, DUBOIS, *and* DAVID *come into the street at left.* ADRIENNE *follows them; she passes by* DONATIEN *without noticing him.*) Have mercy . . . ! (*With an anguished cry.*) David . . . !

DAVID *wheels around suddenly and runs to* ADRIENNE. *They embrace and kiss desperately.* LATOUCHE *and* DUBOIS *pull them apart.*

DUBOIS   That's enough!

LATOUCHE   Let go of him.

LATOUCHE *takes* ADRIENNE's *arm. In spite of her sobbing refusals, the two men separate the lovers. Their hands are still locked;* LATOUCHE *breaks them apart with a final pull.* DUBOIS *drags* DAVID *away.*

ADRIENNE   (*weeping.*) David . . . !

LATOUCHE *takes* DAVID's *other arm.*

DAVID   Tell the little one I forgive him.

DONATIEN *shudders.* LATOUCHE, DUBOIS, *and* DAVID *exit right.* ADRIENNE *falls to her knees, weeping inconsolably. A pause.* DONATIEN, *behind her, takes a few hesitant steps, then stops, undecided. He comes to her side.*

DONATIEN   He doesn't have anything to forgive me for. I didn't . . . do what he thinks. (ADRIENNE *stops weeping. She raises her head and listens to him without turning around.*) I was wandering around here. . . . They caught me and asked me questions. . . . I had to tell them he was late returning to the Asylum. . . . But I didn't mean to hurt him. . . .

ADRIENNE (*rises; she turns to* DONATIEN, *her eyes flaming.*) You told them he took something from the jewel box yesterday!

DONATIEN (*trembling.*) I don't remember. . . . Maybe I did. . . . They asked me so many questions. . . .

ADRIENNE Liar! (*Furious, she starts to exit left. He hears her move, runs after her, and holds on to her dress.*)

DONATIEN You have to believe me!

ADRIENNE *pulls away angrily.*

ADRIENNE Judas!

DONATIEN Please believe me! You have to believe me. I can't live if you don't . . . ! I need you . . . ! Don't leave me! (ADRIENNE *spits in his face, turns and exits quickly.* DONATIEN *trembles violently. The light fades while he follows her, without hope, his arms outstretched.*) Adrienne . . . Adrienne . . .

The black curtains close. Downstage right a white spotlight comes up slowly on VALENTIN HAÜY, *who is holding some papers. He is no longer the young man who once went to hear the blind orchestra play at Valindin's café. He is now fifty-five years old. His hair is almost white and he is dressed in the style of 1800. A melancholy smile floats across his face. He speaks simply and calmly.*

VALENTIN HAÜY (*reading.*) "Almost thirty years

have passed since an outrage against humanity, carried out publicly against the blind inmates of the Quinze-Vingts and repeated each day for almost two months, provoked the laughter of certain completely insensitive individuals. In September of 1771, a café at the Saint Ovide fair offered to the public a spectacle composed of unfortunate creatures whose only livelihood consisted of begging for their daily bread in the city's streets, with the help of a musical instrument. . . ." (*Looks up.*) Sometimes I think that no one would still recognize me as that excited young man who stood up and shouted in the café that day. . . . I have been worn down and changed by the years and by people. But that was where it all began. When I saw those poor wretches subjected to such humiliation, I realized that my own life had a meaning. At the time I was unheard of: Valentin Haüy, linguist and music lover. A nobody. But the most obscure individual in the world can do wonders if he so desires. That's what happened in the Place de la Concorde. . . . Quite a few monstrosities were punished there, you know. A king lost his head—poor devil, he wasn't really so bad as he was weak—and then his judges lost theirs: Danton, Robespierre. . . . A lot of blood was spilt during those years. But they were no worse than the years which had preceded them and brought them about, the years when all through France people were hungry and the fairs went gaily on. . . . (*Reads.*) "Yes, I told myself with noble enthusiasm: I'll make this ridiculous farce come true. I'll teach the blind to read. . . . I'll place in their hands books which they themselves have printed. I'll teach them to trace out the letters and then read their own writing. And I'll teach them to play beautiful music." (*Looks up and takes a few steps left.*) It isn't easy, but we are getting there. If they are given time, they will achieve their goal, even though I may not be alive to see it. They want to do it, and some day they will. (*Lowers his voice.*) Still, one thing troubles me. You see, I never did go back to the fair. I didn't want to know any more about those poor blind devils who were playing there. . . . I began my work with others. But I heard, not so long afterwards, that one of them had been hanged. I wonder if it's true. . . . Sometimes I try to find out from another blind beggar . . . an old man who has been playing on the street corners for years. I think he could tell me. Who knows—he may even have played with that horrible little orchestra. . . . But he never answers my questions. His face is terribly deformed with smallpox scars. . . . And he seems a bit crazy. I'd like to help him . . . but of course he's too old for my school. . . . (*A violin begins to play Corelli's Adagio.* HAÜY *turns his head and listens.*) There he is. That's the only thing he ever plays: Corelli's Adagio. And he's always alone. (*Sighs.*) It's true that I'm opening up new lives for the blind children in my school. But if it's true that they hanged one of those blind musicians, who will answer for that death? Who can give it a meaning? (*He listens to the music.*) I'm an old man now. Sometimes, when I'm alone as I am now, I like to wonder if perhaps . . . if perhaps

music is not the only answer to some questions.
. . . (*He raises his head and listens to the music.*)

A slow curtain.

Condemned Squad

A DRAMA
IN TWELVE SCENES

By Alfonso Sastre

Escuadra hacia la muerte
Translated by Leonard C. Pronko

Characters

The action takes place during the Third World War.

Part One

Scene 1

Interior of a gamekeeper's lodge, seen through a vertical cross section. A background of dense forest. In the foreground a clearing.

This is the only room of the building. A fire in the fireplace. In disorder about the fire, the sleeping bags of six soldiers. In one corner, arranged on a stand, four rifles and a machine gun. Ammunition boxes. A barrel of water. A field phone. An electric battery. A huge pile of wood for the fire, and a first-aid box with a red cross on it.

A door at the back and a large window in the oblique wall at the edge of the stage.

It is twilight. Around the fire, JACK, RUDY, *and* PETER, *sitting on their rolled sleeping bags, are playing dice.* GADDA, *lying on his sleeping bag, is dozing. Sitting apart, Corporal* GOBAN *is carefully cleaning his rifle.*

RUDY (*throwing the dice.*) A pair of aces.

PETER (*the same.*) One. Your turn, Jack.

JACK (*who seems lost in his thoughts.*) Hm?

PETER Your throw.

JACK *says nothing. He drops the dice into the dice box and throws them without watching.*

RUDY Lose. Try again! (JACK *throws again.*) A pair of queens. Throw again. (JACK *puts three*

141

dice into the dice box and throws.) Four. Good.
(JACK *holds on to the dice box.*) You going to
give me the box?

JACK Oh, here. . . . I'm sorry. (*Gives it to him
and* RUDY *throws the dice.*)

PETER What's the matter with you? Don't you
feel well?

JACK I just . . . have a slight fever. I feel sort of
warm. (*He touches his forehead.*)

PETER Lie down a while, and see if you feel better.

JACK No. I'd rather not. . . . If I lie down it's
worse. . . . I'd rather stay up. I'll get over it.
Whose turn is it?

RUDY Mine. (*He throws. Annoyed, he throws the
five dice again.*) Three kings.

PETER (*playing.*) Two. . . . (*He throws again.*)
And four. (*To* RUDY.) Your turn.

RUDY I know. (*He yawns, throws, laughs.*) A flush.
That's good enough for me.

PETER (*playing.*) Lousy. (*To* JACK.) Your turn.
(*But* JACK *is not listening. He has his head between his knees, clasped firmly between his fists.
He is perspiring.*) Hey Jack, what's the matter
with you?

JACK (*groaning.*) My head is killing me. (*He
raises his head; we can see tears in his eyes.*) It
must have been yesterday while I was on guard
duty . . . I got chilled. . . . It's easy for me
. . . always has been. (*He groans.*) God, it hurts!

PETER Wait a minute. (*He gets up and goes to
the first-aid box at rear, opens it and takes out
a tube from which he takes a pill. He takes a*

cup from his pocket and fills it with water, putting the pill in it.)

GOBAN (*without turning.*) What you doing?

PETER It's a pill . . . for Foss. He's not feeling well.

GOBAN (*without raising his head.*) What's the matter?

PETER He has a headache. He's sick.

GOBAN (*moving his head.*) We can't waste our medicine.

PETER But Corporal . . . He's——

GOBAN (*smiling icily.*) I mean as a general rule. If he has such a headache, go ahead and give him the medicine, and be done with it. I'm humane too, even though you may not always think so. What I'm trying to tell you is this situation may last a long time, and we have no right to ask help from headquarters. They gave us food and medicine for two months. For those two months we're dead as far as the outside world is concerned. They've written down the date when we begin to count again . . . February first. . . . In the meantime anyone who knows we're here is thinking about other things. (*He looks up.*) Well, what are you waiting for? (PETER *clicks his heels and returns to the others.* GOBAN *continues his work.*)

PETER (*giving the glass to* JACK.) Here, take this.

JACK (*drinking it.*) Thanks. (*He sits against the wall.*)

PETER (*to* RUDY.) Cigarette?

RUDY Sure. (*He lights it.* GOBAN *has begun to hum to himself.*) That guy's singing again.

PETER   Yes. It's obvious he likes that song.

RUDY   Yes. It drives me crazy to listen to it.

PETER   Why?

RUDY   I don't know. I just don't like it, that's all.

PETER *adds a log to the fire.*

PETER   Feels good here, doesn't it? Near the fire. (*He smokes. He pokes the fire.*) It reminds me of the town I came from. This time of day the whole family used to gather around the fire.

RUDY   I'm from a small town, too. But I've lived almost all my life in the capital.

PETER   I left home when I was eighteen, and I've never gone back. That was eleven years ago.

RUDY   What did you do?

PETER   I worked in a factory. You?

RUDY   Business. (*Pause. They smoke. He lowers his voice.*) Say, doesn't that guy ever get cold?

PETER   (*finger to mouth.*)   Be quiet. He'll hear you, and he's a rough customer.

RUDY   Yeh, I know. What the hell do I care? Why doesn't he sit around the fire with the rest of us? I don't like his kind. The bastard thinks he can walk all over us. (*The* CORPORAL *continues humming.*) I'll bet he really thinks he's somebody, and all he has is a stinking corporal's chevron. He's one of those noncoms who think they're generals.

PETER   You going to shut up? (*Pause.*)

RUDY   (*with a brusque gesture, he throws down his cigarette.*)   Three days we've been here, and it already seems like eternity.

PETER   If after knowing each other only five days we've already begun to . . . it's not a very good sign.

RUDY   Begun to what?

PETER   To get on each other's nerves.

RUDY   Bah!

PETER   This doing nothing . . . just waiting . . . isn't very pleasant. . . .

RUDY   No, not pleasant at all. Especially when you know what's in store for us . . . unless someone does something about it.

PETER   What do you mean?

RUDY   Nothing.

PETER   Good. I think it's better not to get upset thinking about what is or isn't in store for us. Because we don't really know what's going to happen. . . .

RUDY   I was thinking maybe the offensive won't take place after all.

PETER   Possibly. Personally, I hope it does.

RUDY   You mean . . . ? You'd rather . . . ?

PETER   Yes. What I can't stand is this doing nothing. For three months now the front has been silent, and I don't like it.

RUDY   So now you're going to be a great patriot!

PETER   No. I'm not a patriot. It's just . . . Oh well, it would take too long to explain. It's not worth it.

RUDY   Why did they put you in this squad anyway? We all know we're here for some reason. This is . . . I guess they call it a punishment detail. A dangerous outpost . . . and not much chance of telling anyone about it. Well, why are you here? Not because you're a virtuous man, huh? A little angel?

PETER   No, of course not. . . . I . . . I mistreated some prisoners, at least that's what they say.

RUDY   What did you do to them? Peel off their skin? Or carefully extract their eyes?

PETER   Nothing like that. What do you care? Leave me alone.

RUDY   You hate them, don't you? The enemy . . . the mysterious enemy. (*With irony, as though repeating a propaganda slogan.*) Oriental souls . . . refined and cruel. You hate them, don't you?

PETER   Yes . . . I think I do.

RUDY   You must have your . . . private reasons.

PETER   (*with emphasis.*) Yes, very private. Extremely . . . private. (*He gets up and paces nervously with hands in pockets. He goes to the window and looks out.*) Must be very cold out, huh Corporal? What weather!

GOBAN *shrugs his shoulders. He puts the bolt in his rifle and rises. He leaves the gun in the corner, stretches, while* RUDY *observes him silently.* GOBAN *approaches the sleeping* GADDA *and kicks him.*

GOBAN   Hey, you! You've slept enough! (GADDA *stirs weakly.*) Do you hear? Get up now! (*Kicks him again.* GADDA *sits up, takes his glasses from his pocket and puts them on.*)

GADDA   What's the matter?

GOBAN   You've had enough sleep. Do you think you're on vacation here?

GADDA   (*he has gotten to his feet and assumed an attitude similar to "attention."*)   No . . . I just had nothing to do.

GOBAN   Is being ready for any eventuality doing nothing? Pick up that machine gun. (GADDA *gets it and returns to the* CORPORAL.) It's dirty. Clean it.

GADDA Yes, sir. (*He sits and tries to clean it, indifferently.*)

GOBAN And what's the matter with this fellow? Is he still sick? (RUDY *shrugs his shoulders.*) You! That's enough of this foolishness. (JACK *does not open his eyes.* GOBAN *strikes his face with the back of his hand.*)

JACK (*half-opening his eyes with great effort.*) It still . . . hurts terribly. As though I had something inside. On one side. A throbbing pain.

GOBAN Don't worry. You'll forget it on guard duty. It's your turn now.

JACK (*looks at his watch.*) My turn? (*He tries to get up.*)

GOBAN Yes, your turn. Does it surprise your excellency? (*He changes tone.*) We've got to follow the schedule—you know that already. I hope this won't happen again. . . . You might get into trouble. I'm not a schoolmarm, and you're not a schoolboy. You're wearing a soldier's uniform, kid. If you haven't realized that yet, we're not going to get along together.

JACK *has gotten to his feet. At the price of great effort, he puts on his cloak and belt. He takes his rifle and when he tries to hang it over his shoulder, he reels. The gun falls to the floor.*

GOBAN (*with a roar.*) What are you doing, imbecile? A soldier never lets his gun fall! (*In his teeth.*) Never!

PETER Corporal, Foss is really sick. I'll do his guard duty.

GOBAN You be quiet. . . .

PETER But if——

GOBAN I said, shut up! And keep out of business

that's none of your concern. Now get on out
there, you. I won't have my men carrying on like
schoolgirls. It's time for relief, and that's sacred.
JACK *goes out unsteadily. There is a gust of wind
when he opens the door. A silence.* PETER *is staring
fixedly at the* CORPORAL. *The latter sits by the fire
and lights a cigarette. He looks at* GADDA's *work.*

GOBAN   That lock isn't clean. (GADDA *picks it up
and looks at it.*) You can clean it better than
that, can't you? (GADDA *doesn't answer. He simply shrugs his shoulders and cleans it again.*)
Ricker, bring me the barrel.

PETER *picks up a little barrel and takes it to* GOBAN.
RUDY *approaches and* GADDA *puts down the machine
gun in order to take a folding cup out of his pocket.
All are waiting for something. With a dipper,*
GOBAN *serves a small portion of liquid to each one.*
RUDY *savors it slowly.* PETER *drinks it in two swal-
lows,* GADDA *in one.*

RUDY (*when he has savored the last drop voluptu-
ously.*)   Corporal, I don't think just one more
drop of cognac would hurt us. Just a little . . .
with this cold weather . . .

GOBAN (*drinking his own.*)   The little we drink is
because of the cold. We must be careful with alcohol. I've seen magnificent soldiers lose respect
for their uniforms, just because of alcohol.

PETER   Have you . . . been a soldier all your life?

GOBAN (*finishing his cognac.*)   Yes.

PETER (*trying to converse with him.*)   How long
have you been in uniform, Corporal? Which is
just another way of asking how old you are.

GOBAN   I'm thirty-nine. . . . When I was seven-

teen I joined the Legion, but I was already a
soldier when I was just a kid. . . . I liked it.

PETER *(laughing.)*   You're a man who's never worn
a tie, Corporal.

A pause. PETER *stops laughing. A silence.*

GOBAN   These are my real clothes. And your "real
clothes" now too, forever. The clothes you're going to die in. *(He laughs at the others' expressions. They look at each other uneasily.* GOBAN's
expression grows hard, and he adds.) These are
men's clothes: a soldier's uniform. Men have always dressed this way. . . . Rough shirts. . . .
Clothing that protects one neither from the cold
nor the heat. . . . Leather straps. . . . Rifle
over the shoulder. . . . Any other kind of clothing is for women . . . the shame of the human
race. *(He looks intently at* GADDA, *who pretends
that his glasses have fogged up and takes them
off to clean them.)* But it's not enough to wear
this uniform. . . . You've got to be worthy of
it. . . . That's what I'm going to get out of you
men . . . make you real soldiers, so you can die
like men. A soldier is just a man who knows how
to die, and you're going to learn just that with
me. That's all you've got left: to die like men.
And that's exactly what we teach in the army.

PETER   Corporal, I heard that in the army they
taught men how to fight . . . and how to win,
in spite of everything.

GOBAN   To fight and win, first you've got to forget
about living. You haven't forgotten it, have you?
You're still hanging on to a stinking shred of
hope. You're not soldiers. You're the castoffs, the

garbage, I know that . . . men who want nothing but life and don't know how to submit to discipline. Undisciplined cowards! All right! You're going to swallow Corporal Goban's discipline, the discipline of an old legionnaire. I need a squad of soldiers who are ready to die. And I'll get them. I'll make you into those soldiers. The Command knows what it's doing, putting you under my orders. I'll be with you to the end. I'm going to die with you. But you're going to meet death clean, in perfect dress formation. And the last thing on earth you're going to hear is my voice, commanding you. You're going to bear with me to the end, no matter how little you like it.

RUDY (*in a hoarse voice.*)   Corporal.

GOBAN   What?

RUDY (*with a mocking smile.*)   I know what kind of guy you are. You're one of those people who think war is beautiful, I'll bet.

GOBAN (*looking fixedly at* RUDY.)   If you don't like it, just try to leave. You'll see what happens. (GADDA *murmurs something to himself.*) Did you say something?

GADDA   No, I just . . . hurt my finger putting this lock back on.

GOBAN   I understand you're a professor. You must have theories about this, and about almost everything, I suppose. Explain your fine theories to us. It's about time we had some amusement. Come on. Speak up!

GADDA (*nervously.*)   Listen, Corporal, I don't care to talk about anything, you hear? I'm here, and I obey you. What more do you want?

GOBAN *(cutting him.)* Eh, eh, careful. Cut the airs. I won't tolerate that tone . . . Professor.

GADDA Excuse me. . . . I'm . . . just nervous.

GOBAN You certainly are. The Professor is a very nervous man, and besides that, a real cad. I think it's about time that we got to know each other.

The door opens and JACOBS *appears, wearing the collar of his cloak turned up, gloves on his hands, and carrying his rifle. He approaches* GOBAN.

JACOBS Reporting sir.

GOBAN Sit down.

JACOBS Corporal, I wanted to tell you that Foss doesn't look fit to take over guard duty. I'm afraid he's not well.

GOBAN Forget it. I've already looked at him and he's all right. There's your cognac.

JACOBS *takes off his cloak and belt, sits down, and avidly drinks his cognac to the last drop.*

GOBAN You've arrived just in time to hear a fine story. We're talking about the Professor.

GADDA That's enough of that. Leave me alone.

GOBAN *(looking fixedly at* GADDA.*)* From the start I knew we weren't going to get along together. We don't belong to the same race. I hated you even before I knew you, from the moment a week ago when they called me up and I held your file in my hands. It's strange to think that a week ago none of you knew each other. But I knew all of you already. And you couldn't even dream of my existence, could you? And yet, now there's nothing more real for you than me. *(He laughs.)*

JACOBS You mean . . . they gave you our files?

GOBAN Yes, your inspiring biographies. (*There are looks of uneasiness.*) Private Herbert Gadda. From the Fifteenth Infantry Regiment. Operations to the south of the Black Sea. Isn't that right?

GADDA (*nodding.*) Yes, I'm from there. It was a hell of shell fire, something . . . frightful. (*He covers his ears.*)

GOBAN Don't worry. This is another hell. Private Rudolf Lavin, Second Antitank Company. . . . In the South. Do you remember?

RUDY (*somberly.*) I haven't forgotten.

GOBAN Andrew Jacobs. A rookie. Straight from the training camp at Lemberg to a punishment squad. That's you, isn't it?

JACOBS That's right.

GOBAN Private Peter Ricker. The river Kar. . . . The winter offensive, many prisoners—huh?

PETER Yes.

GOBAN But you're a real soldier, Ricker. . . . I congratulate you. If we get out of here, I'd like to see you again some day.

PETER (*seriously.*) Thank you.

GOBAN In case you're interested, I'm not here to punish you. I'm being punished myself. I'm no saint. If I were I wouldn't be here. (*A cold smile.*)

PETER (*daringly.*) They told me you . . . had once been something more important in the army. I mean . . . you were broken. You used to be a sergeant, didn't you?

GOBAN Who told you that? What do you know about me? Come on, say it.

PETER Not much.

GOBAN   I hope it's nothing I'll be ashamed of. Go
ahead, speak up!

PETER   They told me you have three black crosses
by your name.

GOBAN   Three black crosses? What do you mean?

PETER   It's obvious. You've taken care of three.
Is it true, Corporal? (GOBAN *looks him in the
eye.*) When you were a sergeant. You killed two
of your own men during the war, and one in
training. Is that right?

GOBAN   (*after a silence.*)   Yes. I killed two cowards.
One because he was trying to run away. That
was in the last war. And the same thing happened again this time. . . . He refused to get
out of the trench. (GADDA *lowers his head.*)

PETER   And the third?

GOBAN   (*somberly.*)   The third . . . was an accident.

PETER   An accident?

GOBAN   Yes! (*He gets up. Gloomily, he paces.*)

PETER   What kind of accident?

GOBAN   (*pacing.*)   During instruction, while I was
explaining hand-to-hand combat . . . and bayonet tactics. . . . It was his fault. . . . He was
stupid, got nervous. . . . He didn't keep his
guard up. . . .

PETER   You killed him? Right there . . . he died?

GOBAN   I didn't realize what I was doing. The kid
was trembling and turned pale. It made me furious. I threw him to the ground with one blow,
and then I don't know what came over me. It
was like an attack. I finished him off myself . . .
right there. I stabbed him with the bayonet. He
drove me out of my mind. He was clumsy—a

pale kid, with freckles . . . (*His tone changes.*) . . . and now I think of it, I seem to remember that he had . . . (*His mouth twists.*) . . . a sad look in his eyes. . . .

Darkness has been falling.
Blackout.

Scene 2

The light gradually comes up again. It is morning. JACK is lying down, GADDA seated near him. PETER is sweeping the floor, and JACOBS is shaving before a small mirror near the window.

GADDA Don't worry, son. It's nothing serious. You've just caught cold. . . . Your temperature's gone down. . . . That's a good sign.

PETER (*sweeping.*) Leave him alone now. Let him try to get some sleep.

GADDA (*rising.*) Did you hear how delirious he was last night?

PETER Yeh, poor kid. . . . He must have had at least 104 degrees. . . . The things he was saying. . . . (*Sweeps.*) God, he gave me a scare when I went to relieve him—lying there in the snow . . . out cold.

JACOBS (*finishing his shaving.*) That man's a savage. Why did he make him stand guard if he was sick? And you, why did you let him go?

PETER And why did you come back when you saw

he could scarcely stand up? You should have
brought him back.

JACOBS And leave the guard post alone? That
man would have killed me. He's mad. He doesn't
know anything but military orders. You go talk
to him about pity and brotherly love!

GADDA (*he speaks weakly.*) Andy is right. His only
morality is written in the military ordinances.
If that were all . . . but he's aggressive, cutting.
He tried to make fun of me last night, telling
stories that interest no one. What can he say
about us? Didn't you understand that, last night?
He seemed to be threatening to tell what he
knew about each of us. I don't think anyone is
interested in anyone else's life.

JACK *says something which is not understandable.*

PETER (*approaching him.*) What?

JACK (*making an effort.*) I don't mind telling you
why they put me out here. I refused to be part
of a firing squad. That's all. I couldn't kill in
cold blood. They called it insubordination or
something. I don't care. I'd do the same thing
again. . . .

PETER All right, now be quiet. You mustn't talk
now. It's bad for you. You need to rest.

JACK I . . . wanted to tell you——

PETER We heard. Be quiet now.

GADDA *is now standing a bit off from the others.
He lights a cigarette and smokes, standing there
motionless.*

JACOBS (*has put away his shaving things, and is
sitting on his bedroll.*) When you think about
it, what's happened to us, for one reason or another, it's pretty awful, isn't it?

GADDA   It certainly is.

JACOBS   We're in a rat trap with no way out. No salvation is possible.

GADDA   (*with a contorted look.*)   That's the truth. We're a squad of men condemned to death.

JACOBS   No . . . it's even worse than that. . . . We're men condemned to *wait* for death. Condemned men are killed. But we are still alive . . . waiting.

PETER   There are many squads like this one all along the front. Don't think we're in a special situation. What's happening to us has no importance at all. It's nothing to be proud of. It's what they call a security squad . . . a corporal and five men like any other.

JACOBS *is not listening.*

JACOBS   (*with a shiver.*)   We're five kilometers ahead of our front lines alone in this forest. I don't think it's anything to take lightly. It strikes me . . . as a terrible punishment. Our only mission is to blow up a mine field and die, so the good boys on the front line will know what's happened and prepare the defensive. But what does the defensive matter to us? We'll be dead already.

PETER   That's enough, Jacobs. You're a cheerful guy, aren't you?

JACOBS   But it's true, Peter. . . . It's true. . . . What do you want me to do about it? Sing? You can't close your eyes. I . . . I'm afraid. Remember . . . I've never been under fire yet. . . . This will be the first time . . . and the last. I can't even imagine what being in combat is like. God, it's frightening.

PETER A combat is nothing. You've already been through the worst part.

JACOBS What's . . . the worst part?

PETER Training camp. Instruction. Six, seven hours marching under a blistering sun, when the sergeant doesn't give a damn about what happens to you. One, two! One, two! And all you want is to fall in your tracks like a hunted-down animal. But nobody cares. Left, right; open ranks; one, two! Quick step; one, two! one, two! That's the worst of it. Long, senseless marches. Roads leading nowhere.

JACOBS (*slowly*.) For me, the worst part is this endless waiting.

PETER Four days isn't endless, and already you can't bear it. Just imagine if this goes on for days and days. . . . It seems to me we have to control ourselves, bear up . . . for the time being. . . . We'll see. . . .

JACOBS (*nervous*.) Didn't they say the offensive would come off any day now? I had already gotten used to the idea of dying, and it didn't even matter: they liquidate us, and that's it. But out here it doesn't even seem like there's a war going on. . . . Silence. . . . We know that in front of us, behind the trees there are thousands of soldiers armed to the teeth and ready to fall on us. Who knows if they've already discovered us, and are just making us a temporary present of our lives? They've got us now, and they're laughing at us. That's what's happening—caught in a rat trap. We want to hear something . . . and there's only silence. . . . It could go on for months. . . . Who can take that?

GADDA (*in a grave tone.*) People say they're ferocious and cruel. . . . But we don't know how cruel. . . . It's part of the unknown . . . and the unknown is what frightens us most. We know they think in a way different from us . . . and that bothers us, because we can't measure them, reduce them to objects, dominate them in our own minds. . . . We know they believe fanatically in their own strength and their own truth. . . . We know they believe we are corrupt, sick, incapable of the smallest act of faith or hope. They've come to exterminate us, burn out our very roots. . . . They're capable of anything. But, just what *are* they capable of? What? If we knew we might be afraid . . . but I'm not afraid. It's like a kind of torture. . . . To die fighting isn't the worst thing that could happen. . . . What terrifies me now is surviving . . . falling prisoner . . . because I can't imagine how they would kill me.

JACOBS You're right. I know what you mean. If we were fighting French soldiers . . . or Germans . . . it'd all be different. We know them. We've seen their movies, read their books. We know a little of their language. It's different.

GADDA These people are frightening . . . this country. . . . We're so far away. . . .

PETER Far away from what?

GADDA I don't know. . . . Far . . .

A silence. PETER, *who has looked at his watch, begins to put on his cloak and belt. He takes his rifle.*

PETER See you later.

JACOBS   Yeh. (PETER *goes out. A silence.*) What can the Corporal be doing?

GADDA   Taking a long walk in the woods. . . . Watching . . . or inspecting the mine fields. He can't sit still a minute. (JACOBS *takes out a cigarette. Offers one to* GADDA *and they smoke.*)

JACOBS   (*after a silence.*)   When the Corporal was talking about us last night, I noticed you turned pale. (GADDA *doesn't move.*) I didn't like it much either. It's just that . . . well, what we've done is no one else's business, is it?

GADDA   No. No one's.

JACOBS   I prefer to keep out of other people's business and let them keep out of mine.

GADDA   So do it.

JACOBS   You can tell everything to a friend, even your deepest secrets, but he has to be a real friend.

GADDA   Of course.

JACOBS   But it's hard to make friends when you're fighting. We all become too selfish, don't we? We only think of ourselves, of saving our own skin, no matter what happens to the others. I mean most people. I'm not talking about the heroes.

GADDA   (*smiles.*) That's what we need . . . to do away with the heroes, and we wouldn't have any more wars. (JACOBS *laughs.*)

JACOBS   The others say you're unfriendly, that you think you're better than the rest of us, but I don't agree. Is it true you were a university professor?

GADDA   Yes.

JACOBS   Professor of what?

GADDA Of metaphysics. (JACOBS *laughs*.) Why are you laughing?

JACOBS At that. It's funny. A professor of metaphysics. And now you're as grubby as I am. And I never made it past my second year at the university! Now we're both together . . . in the common ditch.

GADDA Yes, it is funny.

JACOBS I didn't like to study—I mean, I guess I got drunk too often. I had the d.t.'s. Couldn't stay in the class or answer seriously the professor's stupid questions. Even my parents got sick of me, so I left home. I was twenty-six and still hadn't gotten beyond second year. (*He laughs*.)

GADDA You left home? Where did you go?

JACOBS I began my own home. I mean I got a girl friend and set up housekeeping. I wasn't capable of earning enough to eat, but I kept getting drunk with my friends. Tavern fights, street fights, the police station . . . bruises, blood . . . the usual thing. I left my woman . . . and lived alone. . . . At last I could drink without giving accounts to anyone . . . without causing anyone to suffer. . . . (*His eyes seem to have become moist*.) A vulgar story, you can see. The only thing that comforts me is to think that the work I didn't do wouldn't have been any use anyhow. . . . It's funny to see you here, in this horrible house, you with your brilliant university career; always bent over your books, I'll bet . . . and into polemics! An exemplary life which ends up just like the life of a tramp or an incorrigible drunkard incapable of earning an honest living.

It looks to me like it wasn't worth the bother, buddy, don't you think?

GADDA   Perhaps . . . perhaps it wasn't worth the bother. I studied because I had to take care of my mother and pay for my brother's schooling. I wanted the future to be bright and clear. I wanted to "earn an honest living," as you say. They had sacrificed themselves for me, and it was up to me not to disappoint my father . . . or my mother's confidence and love. . . .

JACOBS   What did your father do?

GADDA   He worked in a bank. He dreamed of a brilliant, dignified future for me. He never lived to see it. He died before I got my first check from the university.

JACOBS   But couldn't you see that you were working for nothing? Didn't you realize this would happen? This war—the third world war of the twentieth century and perhaps the last—was in the air. So many books, and still you didn't realize the most important thing.

GADDA   No. I didn't realize it. I was in the library. There, time didn't exist. The warnings of the newspapers seemed like pure journalism. Down deep, I was convinced the world was solidly organized, that nothing was going to happen, and that what I had to do was to fight for a living.

JACOBS   I didn't have that feeling of solidity. I felt we were living in a world that could disappear at any moment. I realized we were in a boat that was sinking fast. It wasn't worthwhile working, and that suited me just fine.

GADDA   You understood everything, didn't you, Jacobs?

JACOBS   At least that's what I say now. It seems that when I think back on it, I'm completely justified. At a time like this, you feel you need to justify your actions.

The door opens. RUDY *enters, swearing. He takes off his cloak.*

JACOBS   What's the matter?

RUDY   I'm fed up!

JACOBS   Some kind of directive from the Corporal?

RUDY   He's doubled my watch duty tonight.

JACOBS   Why?

RUDY   He says he saw me sitting down in the guard box.

JACOBS   Weren't you?

RUDY   Yes, but what the hell does that matter? (*He sits.*) Besides, he's disgusting. . . . He spies on us. . . . He watches our smallest movements. You can't live that way. I'm fed up. Just now, as he walked away, I felt like shooting him in the back.

JACOBS   I don't think it's worth that.

RUDY   Yes, shoot him down . . . and have done with him. . . . We'd be able to relax. We could enjoy the little time we have left. . . . No one would ever know. . . . And even if they did, what would it matter to us?

JACOBS   What are you talking about? Have you gone mad?

RUDY   No. I'm not mad. I'm serious. It wouldn't matter to me. I've done worse things. . . . I want to live in peace, do what I feel like doing. This (*He laughs gloomily.*) is my last request.

When he sees the expressions on the others' faces, he laughs again. Just then GOBAN *comes in. The soldiers react uneasily, avoiding the looks of* GOBAN.

GOBAN What's the matter with you? What were you talking about?

JACOBS (*after a pause.*) Rudy was telling us a joke, but I didn't find it very funny. Did you, Gadda?

GADDA (*looking at* RUDY.) No, not funny at all.

Blackout.

Scene 3

In the darkness GADDA *lights a match and with it, a candle. He is obviously upset. He sits on his bed-roll. In the candlelight we see the sleeping forms of* GOBAN, JACK, RUDY, *and* JACOBS. GADDA *takes out a small notebook, puts it on his knees, and writes with a pencil.*

GADDA "I, Herbert Gadda, Private in the Infantry, request that whoever finds my body make known to my mother, whose name and address appear at the end of this note, the known circumstances regarding my death, softening them in such a way that, without obscuring the truth, the news may be as easy for her as possible; and moreover that she be told where my remains are at rest. We have now occupied this place for two weeks. The situation is becoming rapidly unbearable. The offensive has still not taken place and our nerves are about to snap. Only the Corporal remains unmoved. We get up at six every morning, for what reason I cannot say. We follow a rigid schedule for meals and watch duty. He requires us to clean the equipment and the house. We must shave each day and shine our weapons and our boots. All of this is stupid in any case, and even more so in ours. During these days I've come to see how things really are. We seem to be still, closed up in a house, but in reality we are marching, day after day we are moving. We are a condemned squad, marching under strictest discipline, and obeying the voice of a madman, Corporal Goban."

JACOBS *stirs. He lights a match and looks at his watch.* GADDA *stops writing.* JACOBS *yawns, gets up with difficulty, swearing under his breath. He sees* GADDA.

JACOBS What you doing there?

GADDA I can't sleep. I'm writing a letter.

JACOBS A letter? What for? There's no post office here. (*He has put on his cloak, and now picks up his rifle.*) The delightful hour of relief . . .

He goes out, staggering. GADDA *passes his hand over his forehead, and begins writing again.*

GADDA "May whoever finds this notebook know that I am a coward. This is a story that I don't dare tell the others. When they drafted me, I tried to hide, and since then they've got me down as a deserter. I've even managed to embellish this record with various shameful acts. During training I never dared throw the hand grenades. Then, in action, I lost my nerve and cried when I had to leave the trenches. But the one thing I can't forget is that one day, during a retreat, when a wounded friend fell beside me, I heard him saying to me, 'Go on, go on, don't stop for

me!' As though I had ever thought of stopping!
. . . No! I hadn't even thought of stopping by
his side to ask him, 'Do you have something for
your mother? What shall I tell your wife?' I fled,
fled like a hysterical madman . . . and I scarcely
turned my head to see my friend . . . lying with
his face in the dirt, wounded to death!"

Someone moves. GADDA *looks up. It is* GOBAN.

GOBAN (*in his sleep, extremely agitated.*)   It was an
accident! An accident! I didn't want to do it! It
was . . . an accident! (*He groans and turns
over.*)

GADDA (*writes again.*)   "Our devil of a corporal has
something to forget, too. As a matter of fact,
we're all here with guilt in our hearts and remorse on our consciences. Perhaps this is the
punishment we deserve, and in the moment of
death, we may be at last a squad of purified,
worthy men."

JACK (*from his bed.*)   Gadda! Gadda!

GADDA (*looks up.*)   What is it?

JACK (*moaning.*)   I feel awful.

GADDA   Can I get you something?

JACK   No. . . .

GADDA   Try to sleep.

JACK   I can't. . . . (*He turns over and remains
motionless.* GADDA *returns to his notebook.*)

GADDA   "As I look back, I'm surprised at my des-
picable selfishness that made me think only of
my survival when the war broke out. If, as I
believe, this war is an ignoble conflict, I too have
been trying to flee, clinging grotesquely to life,
as though I were the only one worthy of living,
while others are giving their blood, giving gen-

erously and with resignation, happy to die, asking no explanation, with generosity and unself-
ishness. This is my sin. This is my punishment.
Now all I hope is that we can fight, that I can
die in the struggle, and my soul be saved. (*He
stops writing a moment.*) As I sign this declara-
tion, I think of my mother. I know she is awake
and weeping. . . . For this nothing in the world
can ever console me. . . . No one can ever dry
from my eyes . . . the tears of my mother."

The door opens and PETER *appears. He is coming
off guard.*

PETER   That damn Jacobs! I thought he'd never
get there. I was freezing. (*He sits down and rubs
his hands.*) What you doing?

GADDA (*with an unsure voice.*)   I was . . . writing
a letter. . . .

Blackout.

Scene 4

*In the blackout we hear the blasts of a whistle. It
is daybreak, and as the lights come up we see* GOBAN
*standing in the middle of the room, putting away
his whistle.* PETER, JACOBS, *and* RUDY *are getting up.*
JACK *is stirring.* GADDA *is not there.*

GOBAN (*shaking* JACK.)   Get up! Enough sick leave!

RUDY (*putting on his boots.*)   The Corporal's right.
Yesterday he had no fever.

PETER (*yawning.*) Come on, kid. That's the best way to get back your strength.

RUDY (*pouring water into a washbowl.*) How many hours of guard duty do you owe us, Jack? You could have got sick some other time. It's been rough on us. God, I'm tired. (JACK *has gotten up silently.* GOBAN *hums to himself while washing.*) Goddamn it! That's the worst part of it! To get up at this hour . . . in this freezing cold dump . . . and with that musical background. . . . (GOBAN *does not hear him.* JACK *has, with much labor, put on his boots, and stands up. He staggers.*)

PETER How you doing?

JACK I guess . . . I'm all right. . . . (*He walks about staggering slightly. He goes up to* GOBAN *and stands at attention.*) Reporting for service, sir.

GOBAN (*looks at him from head to foot.*) That's more like it. Go wash, and take up your regular duties. We go back to the same schedule we had before you were sick.

PETER *is throwing wood on the fire and* RUDY *is preparing coffee.*

PETER Ugh! What a day. Looks like we'll have snow for Christmas.

JACOBS (*who has gotten up silently, in a bad humor, and is now ducking his face in washwater.*) It's so damn cold in the morning. I can't stand this. Later on I warm up, but at this hour . . . God! (*With a shiver.*) At this hour . . . I feel sick. (PETER *laughs.*) It's nothing to laugh about. (PETER *laughs again.*)

PETER *(lighting a match and putting it to the fire.)* You're right, it's colder today. Hey, Rudy, bring the coffee. The crackers . . .

RUDY *and* PETER *have sat down near the fire.* JACK *approaches them.*

JACK   I feel fine now. A little weak, but fine.

PETER   Sit here. (JACOBS *throws the towel on the ground and stamps on it.*) What's wrong with him?

RUDY   He's probably gone mad.

JACOBS *has gone over to* GOBAN.

JACOBS   Corporal!

GOBAN   What is it?

JACOBS   Corporal, I've got to tell you something: this is unbearable! I don't see why we have to get up at such an hour. There's absolutely no reason to make us do this. . . . (*The others look on, uneasily.*) I've intended to say this several times. I don't agree with this stupid schedule. You may want to see us suffer, but I'm not ready to give in to your whims. Do you understand? I'm fed up with——

GOBAN *(coldly.)*   All right. Now, shut up.

JACOBS   No. I'm not going to shut up. I've started and I'm going to finish. I'm cold at this hour of the morning. Cold and sleepy. Why? Because a guy with one miserable stripe has the idea we have to get up at six in the morning. I'm sure the others agree with me. Don't you, boys? There's no reason for you to—— (GOBAN *grabs the collar of his jacket.*)

GOBAN *(in his teeth.)*   Shut up, you fool. Shut up!

JACOBS   Let go of me! I'm fed up with your god-damned——

GOBAN *punches him in the stomach.* JACOBS *groans and doubles over. As he doubles over,* GOBAN *strikes him in the face, and he falls to the ground.* GOBAN *kicks him in the chest.* JACOBS *remains motionless.* GOBAN *leans over and pulls him up, and strikes him again, letting him drop to the floor.* PETER *(who has gotten up, somberly.)* Corporal. That's enough.

GOBAN *looks at* PETER, *who stares him down. The others have also risen.*

GOBAN *(to* RUDY.) Give me some coffee.

RUDY *slowly pours coffee into a mug and gives it to* GOBAN *who drinks it, then takes his rifle and goes out. A pause.*

RUDY Now you see . . . what a vicious maniac he is.

PETER *(who is taking care of* JACOBS.) Jack, bring me some water. (JACK *brings water.* PETER *throws it on* JACOBS' *face. He appears to be coming to. He moans.)* He really let him have it. It'll be a miracle if he didn't break a rib.

JACOBS *(complaining of his right side.)* He was killing me. . . . And none of you did anything to stop him.

PETER Try to get up.

JACOBS *gets up, with* PETER's *help. He walks, bent over, toward his bedroll, his hand clutching his side. He sits down.*

JACOBS That bastard . . . is going to pay for this. . . . This time . . . I won't have to be drunk to . . . to kill a man. The other time I was drunk.

PETER The other time? When?

JACOBS I'm here because I killed a sergeant.

Didn't you know that? If I kill that guy it won't be the first time I've had blood on my hands.

RUDY Where was it?

JACOBS What?

RUDY That you . . . killed the sergeant?

JACOBS In training. I got drunk, and went back to the barracks after lights out. The stupid sergeant got mad, and I slipped a knife between his ribs before I even knew what I was doing. It wasn't my fault. I didn't know what I was doing. But this time I'll know. I don't pick fights with anyone, but I can take care of myself. It might bother me, but I'll kill him. He kicked me like he thought I was an animal. (*He puts his hand to his mouth, then takes it away apprehensively. He looks at it, turning pale.*)

JACK What's the matter?

JACOBS (*his voice choked.*) It . . . it may not be anything. Don't worry. It's probably unimportant. The best——

JACK Sure, kid, don't worry. Blood is frightening, but sometimes it's better to bleed a little. If the hemorrhage stays inside it's worse. (JACOBS *has lain down on his back.*)

JACOBS (*weakly.*) Let me alone. Don't talk about it. I'd rather . . . not talk about it. . . . (*Trying to seem unworried.*) It's nothing. And besides, what does it matter? If we're going to die, I'd just as soon die spitting blood. (*He tries to laugh.*) I don't know why, but I can't help thinking of before. I never liked to get into fights. I was one of those guys who always leave when the atmosphere gets too tense. I've always liked things quiet. But look what happens to me?

(*He laughs.*) I always get into rough scrapes. . . . I've been stabbed . . . and I've killed a sergeant . . . and here I am. . . . It's strange, isn't it? It's (*He coughs.*) very (*Coughs.*) strange.

He continues a fit of coughing.

Blackout.

Scene 5

A projector illuminates the figure of GADDA *on guard. He wears a cloak with the collar up, and holds a gun between his gloved hands. His lips scarcely move and his voice drones monotonously.*

GADDA I can see nothing . . . but shadows. From one moment to another the forest might come alive . . . soldiers . . . gunshots, cries—dead, six disfigured dead men, pierced with bayonet wounds. . . . It's horrible. . . . No, there's nothing there. . . . The tree's shadow is moving. . . . These glasses are good for nothing . . . and I can't get new ones. . . . It's over. . . . Footsteps? It must be Rudy coming to relieve me. It's about time. (*He shouts.*) Who goes there? (*No answer; only the echo in the forest.*) Who goes there? (*Echo.* GADDA *raises his rifle and looks about nervously.*) It's no one . . . no one. . . . I thought . . . it must be the wind. . . . Where's Rudy? What could have happened to him? Could something be the matter? Perhaps they took them by surprise in the house. I haven't heard a thing, and yet . . . At this moment I may be the only one left, surrounded. . . . I'm afraid. . . . I should think about something else. Think about something else. It's Christmas. It's come at last. . . . December. . . . Mother is probably alone. Tomorrow is Christmas Eve. If I start thinking about that I'll cry. . . . It doesn't matter. I need to cry. . . . It'll do me good. . . . I've taken a lot. . . . Cry. . . . I'm crying. . . . It's so cold. . . . Mother used to put a scarf around my neck and tell me to keep my mouth closed when I went out into the cold. . . . "Now don't catch cold." If she knew I'm dying of cold here . . . This guard post . . . The wind strikes to the very bone. . . . Why doesn't Rudy come? Why doesn't he come? I've been here more than two hours. One, two. One, two! A death squad. One, two! We were already that even before the war broke out. A generation stupidly condemned to the slaughterhouse. We were studying, getting excited about life, and already, without realizing it, we were part of a gigantic squad marching toward death. Generations condemned. . . . It's cold. This can't go on much longer. . . . We're dead already. . . . No one remembers us. . . . One, two! We'll go down in perfect formation, one by one. I don't want to be taken prisoner. No! Not a prisoner! To die! I'd rather (*With a hoarse sob.*) die! Mother! Mother! I'm here . . . far away. Don't you hear me? Mother! I'm afraid. I'm alone! I'm in a forest, far far away! There are six of us, Mother. We're . . . alone . . . alone . . . alone . . . ! (*His voice, choked, dies*

out and is re-echoed in the forest. GADDA *has not moved since he said, "It's no one."*)
Blackout.

Scene 6

In the darkness we hear a Christmas carol, hummed by several men. The lights come up. There are oil lamps about, and in the center of the stage a Christmas tree. Around it JACOBS, PETER, RUDY, *and* GADDA *are standing, motionless, humming the song. When they finish,* GADDA *goes to his bedroll, sits on it, and buries his head in his hands.*

RUDY   What's wrong with him?

PETER   I don't know. Tonight . . . it really makes you think. (*He moves off also.*) It makes you think more than usual. It always happens to me. I feel sad on Christmas Eve. I start remembering all sorts . . . (*He ends the sentence unintelligibly.*)

JACOBS   Thinking of your family, huh?

PETER   Thinking . . . (*A sad grimace.*) . . . I was thinking of my wife.

JACOBS   Where is your wife?

PETER   At home, in Berlin. I was working there. They paid well. . . . When the war began, Berlin was a hell. They entered our section . . . and there were atrocities. . . . I was in Belgium investigating some machines our factory was go-

ing to buy. . . . When I could finally get back
to Berlin I found out what had happened. . . .
I found my wife . . . had been . . . violently
. . . (*Hides his face in his hands.*) I went to
war only to kill. Nothing mattered any more,
not one idea or another. Kill everyone . . . who
was wearing that uniform. Any one of them
might be . . . that savage.

RUDY   What did you do with those prisoners?

PETER   I don't know—they screamed. . . . It was
like a sudden attack of madness. Those uniforms!
I had more than a hundred prisoners in that old
building. . . . It calmed me down. . . . Now I
feel better. . . . Much better. . . . (*A silence.*)

JACOBS   Men, tonight I'm going to get drunk. It's
Christmas Eve!

PETER (*looking up.*)   What you going to do?

JACOBS   Have a drink!

PETER   You're right. We can ask the Corporal's
permission and have a Christmas Eve celebration.
That's the best——

RUDY   Ask his permission! What for! He wouldn't
give it to us.

PETER   But if we tell him——

RUDY   Nuts! "Alcohol is the enemy of discipline,"
and all that crap. Jacobs, if you want a drink, go
ahead and take it. I'll join you. Anyone who's
afraid can spend his time in pure contemplation!
Come on.

PETER   Just a minute. I intend to have a drink,
too, but first we have to decide what we're going
to tell the Corporal.

JACOBS   We'll tell the Corporal (*He has poured
cognac into his cup and drinks.*) that we were

thirsty. Here. (RUDY *takes the cup and drinks slowly.*) Good, huh?

RUDY   Great!

PETER   Okay. . . . If I drink with you it's just so you won't be alone when the Corporal comes back. (*Laughter.*) Give me some.

JACOBS   Here. (*He fills the three cups.*) Hey, Gadda, aren't you going to drink with us?

GADDA   (*shrugging his shoulders.*) All right. . . . (*He rises and goes to them. They pour him cognac.*)

JACOBS   Come on. . . . Bottoms up. . . . (*They drink, except* PETER.) Come on, Peter. Don't we deserve this little party?

PETER   Sure . . . (*He drinks.* JACOBS *pours them more cognac and now they drink silently.* RUDY *soon breaks into laughter. He laughs for a long time until his laughter catches on with the others. Soon they find themselves all laughing for the first time. It seems that they see each other in a different light now, as though everything else had been a bad dream. They calm down.*) What were you laughing at?

RUDY   Nothing. . . . Suddenly I realized that . . . we're not so bad off out here! So . . . pour us some more! (*They drink.*)

JACOBS   (*indicating* RUDY.) He's a good guy, isn't he? (*The others assent.*) A real buddy . . . the kind you can count on. . . .

PETER   (*who has quickly become taciturn.*) I don't think he's a good buddy.

During the following dialogue the drinking continues.

JACOBS   Why?

RUDY   He's right. How could I be a good buddy?

PETER   (*to* RUDY.)   You shouldn't have told me that the other day. I liked you . . . before.

RUDY   Boys! Peter's talking about my lurid past. If you want to know about it, I——

JACOBS   (*interrupting.*)   I don't give a damn about your lurid past. Forget it!

RUDY   I'm not a good buddy. . . . I don't care. . . . I left my unit without bread and I was as calm as—I let the wheat leak out. . . . (*He laughs.*)

PETER   He sold his buddies' rations, and he——

RUDY   No, no . . . wait a minute. . . . The head of the business was a staff sergeant. . . . I was just the intermediary, the helper—the sergeant hadn't had much practice, and I had to explain to him. . . . It was embarrassing. . . . The organization had its defects. When I saw things were getting bad, I denounced him. They shot him, and sent me out here. Okay now, . . . give me something to drink. . . .

PETER   Here. Get drunk. You're the kind who gambles with the poor people's hunger, you bastard! (*He is drunk now.*)

RUDY   (*drinking.*)   Don't . . . don't treat me that way. . . .

PETER   You lousy, filthy——

JACOBS   Leave the guy alone, man. Leave him alone.

PETER   What did you do before the war? Business, you call it. What do you call business? You're one of the people who are responsible for our being here, you . . . and your business. You'd do anything. . . . Soldiers without food, but what the hell did you care? Let them die! Isn't that right? Let them die! We're all of us, even the Corporal, real men, but you . . . you're a dirty bastard. (*He tries to hit him.* GADDA *and* JACOBS *hold him down.*)

JACOBS   That's enough. . . . We're celebrating Christmas Eve. . . . You're messing up everything, Peter. . . . You're ruining it all.

PETER   All right. . . . I'm sorry. . . . I didn't want to ruin everything. . . . I just got angry. . . . I don't know why. . . . (*He tries to walk and staggers.*) I'm . . . drunk! I've hardly had a drop . . . and I'm already drunk! Rudy, will you forgive me? I was a pig. I take it all back. What shall I do . . . so you'll forgive me?

RUDY   Nothing. . . . You were right. . . . (*They embrace.*)

JACOBS   Great. That's more like it. Gadda, what's the matter with you?

GADDA   Nothing. (*He laughs.*) I'm fine.

JACOBS   Your eyes are wet.

GADDA   It's nothing. (*He laughs.*)

JACOBS   All we need now—hey, listen everybody. . . . All we need now is some girls. (*A sudden silence. They are all motionless.* JACOBS *tries to continue.*) Four . . . four girls, huh? (*No one answers.*) But there aren't any. (*A silence.*) We're alone.

PETER   Shut up, will you? Just be quiet. . . . (*A silence.*)

JACOBS   (*he sits.*) It's . . . a beautiful night, isn't it? (*No one answers.* RUDY *rises.*)

RUDY   Okay. We're going to drink . . . the last toast . . .

But he stands nailed to the spot; the door has opened and GOBAN *is standing there, his rifle stuck into his shoulder strap. With a glance he takes in the scene and strides to the center, darkly. There is a slight motion of drawing back.*

GOBAN　What's going on here?

PETER　(*taking a staggering step forward; he speaks with conviction.*)　Nothing.

GOBAN　Lavin, come here. (*He is taking the rifle out of the shoulder strap.*)

RUDY　(*approaching; he is pale.*)　Yes, sir.

GOBAN　You're drunk, the lot of you.

RUDY　Don't think . . . don't think . . .

GOBAN　You can't even speak. Women! You're not even worthy of the uniform you wear. You deserve a whipping. . . . You'd like that too, wouldn't you?

PETER　Corporal, we thought we'd celebrate——

JACOBS　That's right. . . . Merry Christmas, Corporal. Don't get mad today. It's a day of forgiveness and . . . happiness. . . . Peace on earth . . . and glory to God in the highest. . . . All that. . . . Let's celebrate Christmas Eve. "Forgive us our debts as we forgive our debtors . . ." and so on.

RUDY　(*smiling, impudently.*)　It's a night that the church orders us to celebrate, Corporal.

JACOBS　I'll forgive you the kick you gave me the other day, if we can celebrate today. Okay? Do you agree? (*He goes toward the cognac barrel.*)

GOBAN　Stand where you are, Private. Don't go a step nearer to that barrel. (*His voice sounds menacing;* JACOBS *stops.*)

JACOBS　I'll beg if you want. . . . I'll beg you——

GOBAN   That's enough. Get out of here.

RUDY   There's nothing to beg for, Jacobs. That's all over with. You want a drink?

JACOBS   *I* do.

PETER   Yes, sure.

GADDA   (*seconding the others.*) Yes.

RUDY *approaches the barrel.*

GOBAN   Lavin, get away from there. You're asking for trouble. (*He approaches* RUDY. GOBAN *is holding his rifle by the trigger guard and the neck.* RUDY *pours himself some cognac.* GOBAN *strikes him on the collarbone and throws him to the ground. To the others, threateningly.*) You asked for it. Now get up, you. That was nothing.

RUDY *gets up with difficulty. He pulls out his knife. When he attempts to throw himself on* GOBAN *he loses consciousness, and simply rolls on the floor.* PETER *then draws his knife, and immediately* JACOBS *does the same.* GADDA, *seeing the others, takes out his.* GOBAN *is cornered against the wall. No one moves.*

PETER   You shouldn't have done that, Corporal. You had no reason. We just wanted to celebrate Christmas Eve.

JACOBS   That was a mistake. (*He takes a step forward. The others do the same.*) After this we could never live with you.

GOBAN   (*gravely.*)   Get out of here. There's wood to be cut. On the move! (*To* GADDA.) You, it's your turn on guard duty. (GADDA *doesn't move.*)

JACOBS   Guard duty will have to wait.

GOBAN   Gadda, don't you hear me? Get to the guard post.

JACOBS   Don't go, Herb. Stay for the show. Corporal Goban doesn't seem to realize we're drunk. We're dead drunk.

He laughs madly. GOBAN, *without giving the slightest indication of nervousness, raises his gun and advances, his back to the audience, toward the door. The others do not move. When he arrives near* JACOBS, JACOBS *throws himself on him and cuts him in the face.* GOBAN *raises his hand to his face, and his rifle falls to the floor. Blinded by the cut,* GOBAN *attempts, with his right hand, to take out the knife he carries at his belt. He has it out. But* RUDY, *who has risen, strikes him a terrible blow on the head with his knife.* GOBAN *reels but does not fall.* PETER, GADDA, *and* JACOBS *strike him. Slowly he falls to the floor, first on his knees, then face downward. They stand a moment looking at him.*

JACOBS (*as though stunned.*)   He's dead.

PETER (*leans over him, looks up with a scornful stare.*)   Dead.

Anguished, GADDA *looks at the knife which he still holds in his hands, while the curtain falls.*

*It is morning. The house is dark. Outside—in the clearing—*PETER *and* GADDA, *each leaning on a pickax, are watching while* JACOBS *and* JACK *shovel earth into the hole in which* GOBAN's *corpse is lying.* JACOBS *throws on the last shovelful and goes toward the house.* PETER *and* GADDA *follow him wearily.*

JACK I don't mean to imply anything, but it seems to me . . . (PETER *stops and listens.*) that a man shouldn't just be buried like a dog.

PETER What do you want us to do?

JACK I think . . . a prayer . . .

PETER You're right.

JACOBS What for? If we've sent him to hell, there's no help for it now.

GADDA A prayer? Yes . . . even if it's useless. You say one, Jack. I couldn't go away easy just leaving him like that without a word. After all, a man is a man.

JACK (*taking off his cap.*) God, we ask you to receive the soul of Corporal Goban and give him the peace he never found in life. He wasn't a bad man, God, and neither are we, even though we haven't been able to love each other. May his soul and ours be saved through thy mercy, and

181

the love of our Lord Jesus Christ. Have pity on us. Amen.

ALL (*who have slowly taken off their caps.*) Amen.

JACOBS All right. That's it. Let's go. (*They leave slowly.*)

GADDA (*to* JACK.) I'm glad you did that. It makes me feel a little better. . . .

He goes toward the house. At this moment PETER *and* JACOBS *are entering the hut. The weak morning sun is lighting up the interior, where* RUDY *reclines, half sitting up.*

RUDY All done?

PETER Yes.

RUDY Ufh . . . at last. . . . I thought last night would never end. I couldn't sleep with that man lying out there in the clearing, uncovered. . . . It was as if he hadn't finished dying.

JACOBS No one was going to go dig a grave last night. What a wind. . . . And the rain. . . . A night to make you think. . . . The body lying out there, rain falling on it. . . . I'm glad it cleared up this morning.

GADDA *enters the house and sits down apart from the others.*

RUDY A clear, quiet day at last. . . . The dog's dead, the rabies ended. That's just what you have to do with a mad dog, kill it. He was a dirty pig. Yesterday he would have killed me, finished me off. (*He spits.*) A dirty pig!

PETER Shut up. Let's forget it.

RUDY What's the matter with you fellows?

JACOBS *yawns.*

PETER Nothing!

JACOBS   I couldn't sleep either. I'm really tired.
(*He lies down. A pause.*)

GADDA   Now what are we going to do?

PETER   There's nothing to do. Just wait, as though
nothing had happened.

JACOBS   As though nothing had happened! And
we've cut off our last retreat. (JACK *appears. He
stands in the doorway as though afraid to enter
into the conversation with the others.*) After
what's happened I suddenly realize that the time
might have gone by, and the offensive never arrived . . . and in February they might have
called us back from this post . . . and pardoned
us. . . . We've served term . . . back to our
units, to share the usual risks with our buddies.
. . . I thought of all this, suddenly, when it was
too late. We've cut off our own retreat. If there's
no offensive there'd still be a Court Martial.

RUDY   Court Martial! Why? If we're lucky enough
for this calm to last till February, then no one
has to know what's happened here. We'll just
tell them the Corporal died of a heart attack.

JACOBS   (*shaking his head.*) I don't know much
about such things. But I should think that whenever the head of a punishment squad dies there
must be someone who suspects that it wasn't
a natural death. . . . They'll investigate the
cause of death. . . . They'll interrogate all of
us very cleverly, and look for the body. . . .
They'll dig it up and . . . (*A grim look.*) The
broken skull . . .

RUDY   Then he fell. . . . Or disappeared.

JACOBS   (*ironically.*) Just vanished into thin air!

RUDY   He was on guard, and the enemy must have caught him. He's probably a prisoner somewhere, or, who knows . . . dead. . . .

PETER   (*who has listened silently to this dialogue, rises.*)   Don't wear yourself out, Rudy. If we live till February, there'll be a Court Martial. I can promise you that now.

RUDY   Why?

PETER   Bah. . . . It's still too soon to worry about that. Just an idea I've got. . . . Besides, what's sure is that we won't live till February. We still have forty days here, and if there's going to be an offensive, I hope to God it begins before those forty days are up.

RUDY   You've gone mad.

PETER   We'll see. For the time being, if all of you agree, let's keep to the same schedule.

RUDY   (*facing him.*)   Peter, a man has died here, and that man was the Corporal, and if you think that everything is going to go on as if nothing had happened, you're wrong! I'm going to do just as I please and I'm taking orders from no one. We're through with orders and schedules. As far as I'm concerned, guard duty is over, and from now on nights are for sleeping.

PETER   You're wrong, Rudy. This squad is still at its post. And if you don't agree, just try to leave.

RUDY   You hear that, boys? We've got a new corporal. Self-appointed. (*He laughs, then is suddenly serious.*)   Listen, Peter. If you want to get the same treatment the other one got, just keep on this way.

PETER   Is that a threat?

RUDY   A warning.

PETER   Well now you know how I feel. If it comes to a showdown, we'll have a showdown. I'm the oldest one here and I'm taking over command of this squad. Any objections?

JACOBS   As far as I'm concerned, you can take command of the whole division.

GADDA   It's all the same to me.

JACK   No, Peter. I have no objections.

PETER   (to RUDY.)   You hear that?

RUDY   If that's the way it's going to be, I just may decide to take a walk.

PETER   What kind of walk?

RUDY   A long walk through the forest.

PETER   Where do you want to go?

RUDY   I don't know yet.

PETER   Then . . . ?

RUDY   If I feel uncomfortable here . . .

PETER   You're not considering . . . ?

RUDY   What?

PETER   Giving yourself up!

RUDY   I didn't say that! I said, a trip.

PETER   Listen, Rudy. Don't you ever think about leaving this post, do you hear me? Don't even think about it. Unfortunately, when you already have blood on your hands, one more dead man doesn't add to the stains.

RUDY   Now you're the one who's threatening.

PETER   No. I'm just protecting myself.

RUDY   All right. You know what I think? We're stupid fools. If we don't agree, that's no reason to get angry, is it? We've got to try to understand each other and reach an agreement, like good friends. Right, Peter?

PETER Yes. (*Transition.*) I don't know if you understand me. What I want to avoid is our degenerating into a wretched bunch of murderers. When you have nothing left to do, nothing useful to do for others, it's easy to deteriorate. We've got a stupendous chance: we've got a mission to accomplish. And we'll accomplish it. I don't want us to end up a band of fugitives. I'm not a criminal . . . and even less a murderer. . . . Neither are you. . . . We've just been unfortunate in life, that's all. . . .

JACK (*speaking for the first time.*) It's horrible this has happened, isn't it? We've got to take it into consideration, but . . . it's horrible. It would have been better to suffer the whims of the Corporal rather than having to think about this . . . death.

JACOBS You don't have to think about anything, Foss. You don't even have to butt into our conversation. Just leave us alone. You've got nothing to do with what happened here.

JACK No. Don't say that. I'm one of you, Jacobs. I'm in this with the rest of you.

JACOBS It's useless. However much you'd like to, you *can't* be one of us. You weren't here when it happened. You didn't draw your knife. You didn't feel that shudder that goes through you when you kill a man.

JACK No. . . . But I would have drunk with you. I would have grabbed my knife and I would have struck him just as you did, if I had been here!

JACOBS I don't know. You can't tell.

JACK   I'd have stuck by you.

JACOBS   Sure, I know.

JACK   I swear——

JACOBS   Don't worry. There's nothing to worry about. . . .

JACK   It's not my fault I had guard duty at that time.

JACOBS   Of course not. No one's blaming you.

JACK   You won't believe me.

JACOBS   You're wrong. I do believe you.

He gets up and leaves JACK *alone.* PETER *has begun to hum something.*

RUDY   (*covering his ears.*) Peter, would you be quiet?

PETER   What's got you? Can't anyone even sing?

RUDY   No. . . . Sing whatever you like. . . . But that tune . . . that's the song Goban used to sing. And I can't stand listening to it!

Blackout.

Scene 8

All except PETER. *They are lying on the floor, dirty, unshaven.* RUDY *budges. He looks at the others. He has a feverish look. Suddenly he shouts almost hysterically.*

RUDY   No! This is unbearable! It can't go on! We can't go on like this! Day after day, lying on the ground wallowing like pigs in this filth. . . .

Why don't we do something? An expedition or something . . . a reconnaissance patrol—something!

JACOBS And where do you think we're going to go?

RUDY Anywhere. It doesn't matter. Anywhere. This is insane: just sitting here . . . not moving.

JACOBS I can't even sleep any more. I keep thinking that I can't do anything *but* sleep. I'm dead tired. Yet I can't go to sleep. It's terrible.

RUDY You're pale, and your eyes have dark circles around them.

JACOBS I've got a fever.

RUDY (*getting up and going to the window.*) What's the date? Do you know?

JACK January tenth.

RUDY It seems to me much longer than that. (*A pause.*) Last night I thought I heard shooting in the distance, and I was glad. I started listening to see if it was true . . . wanting it to be. Because that would mean that there's someone else in the world besides us.

JACK I thought I heard shooting too.

JACOBS I didn't hear anything.

RUDY It was my imagination, I'm sure. The wind in the trees. . . . At night it's as though the whole forest was alive. . . . You hear noises. . . . At first it gave me gooseflesh, but now it doesn't—you get used to everything. . . . (*The dull bell of the field phone rings.*) Gadda, would you get the phone please? You just have to reach out your hand, whereas for most of us, it would require a great effort. (*It seems that* GADDA *does not hear. The bell continues to ring.*) The phone,

Gadda. Just as a favor to the rest of us. It's sure
to be our dear friend Peter, who's dreamed up
something for tonight. A wild party . . . wine,
women! You know Peter, boys! (GADDA, *who has
heard these last words, picks up the phone un-
willingly.*)

GADDA Yes, Peter! What? Yes. . . . (*Suddenly,
shuddering, his hand tightens on the phone.*)
Yes, I understand. . . . Good. (*Pause.*) I'll repeat your words. (*Pause.*) An enemy party is
visible in the distance. (*Pause.*) Probably a
company (*Pause.*) reconnoitering. (*Pause.*) It
may be the vanguard of the attack. (*Pause.*) Listen carefully to instructions. (*Pause.*) You'll remain at the post. (*Pause.*) At the right moment,
you'll give the signal to blow up the mine field.
(*Pause.*) Rudy at the battery. (*Pause.*) When
the mine field blows we all come out . . . each
one to his position. (*Pause; with a slight smile.*)
We have to make them pay for every inch. Good.
. . . (RUDY *has taken his position near the battery.* JACK *and* JACOBS *have nervously picked up
their weapons and form a group around the
telephone.*) Right. . . . We just wait for your
signal. . . . (*Passes his hand over his forehead,
with a slight unsteadiness.* JACK *tries to steady
him.*) It's nothing, thanks. . . . It's all right. (*He
stays there listening. A long suspenseful pause.*)

JACOBS He's stopped talking? (GADDA *nods.*)
What're we supposed to do? Wait?

RUDY Sure. (*To* GADDA.) As soon as Peter gives you
the sign, just say "now." I'll pull the switch and
we'll make for the trenches. Okay? (*Pathetic nod
of assent.*) Can't you hear anything?

GADDA (*listening.*) No.

JACOBS Say something. Ask Peter what's the matter.

GADDA Peter, what's the matter? Are they advancing? Can you see them better? (*Listens.*) No answer.

JACOBS Try again.

GADDA Peter! Is something happening? Why don't you answer? Are you there? (*Silence.*) Nothing. . . .

JACOBS (*looking at the others apprehensively.*) I wonder why?

RUDY That's strange. . . . Maybe he's left the instrument for a minute.

JACOBS Maybe they took him by surprise? (*A grave silence.*)

RUDY I don't think so. . . .

JACOBS If they've taken him, they may be coming here now and we won't even know it until they're on top of us.

RUDY Shut up. Wait.

JACOBS We can't just stand here with our arms folded! We've got to do something!

RUDY (*in a muffled voice.*) Be still.

JACOBS It'd be better to get out to the trenches now! They're going to massacre us! We can't just wait here!

RUDY Be quiet, calm yourself. You're just nervous; you've got to get a hold of yourself. Nothing's the matter, see? Now just wait.

JACOBS (*wringing his hands, he whines.*) I can't wait!

He sits hunched over, trying to control his nerves. He cannot. There is a long pause. Everyone is

watching GADDA*'s face, which is now imperturbable.*
Suddenly.

GADDA Yes, what is it, Peter? (*He listens.* JACOBS
   looks anxiously at GADDA.) A company, yes. . . .
   It just passed by. . . . No one was following
   them. . . . A false alarm. . . . So long. . . .
   Blackout.

Scene 9

*The five men. They are finishing a meal, with the
exception of* GADDA, *who is lying down, silent.*

RUDY (*eating the last mouthful.*) You have a cigarette?

PETER (*giving him one.*) The last package. (*He
   puts it away.*)

JACOBS The crackers are stale and there's hardly
   any water left. A few more days and we'll have
   to supplement the rations somehow.

PETER If we're careful, we've got enough for a
   week. Till February. After that, it's not up to
   us. Don't worry about it.

RUDY (*smoking.*) Well, it looks like things are
   going to turn out better than we thought. (*He
   laughs.*) The offensive has vanished into thin air.
   (*Laughs again.*) We'll have to start thinking
   about other things. Is it possible that our misery
   is coming to an end? Don't you understand? It's
   over, friends. We've served our time. We've been
   lucky after all, and I guess we can't complain.

I'm sure they'll take us out of this place and pardon us. We've had our punishment. It's not our fault we weren't killed out here. We were sent here to die in the offensive. If there was no offensive, what can we do about it? I don't think they'll send us to another punishment squad.

PETER It's strange, Lavin, how you can consider yourself clean and ready to live peacefully, just as though nothing had happened. There's an account to be settled. An account we can't forget.

RUDY The Corporal, huh?

PETER Yes, the Corporal. I don't know if we've been here long enough to lose all remorse for what we did. But I do know that now we are still guilty of killing a man.

RUDY Are you sorry for killing that bastard Goban?

PETER No. And it's even possible that if it all happened again, I'd kill Goban again with you, but that doesn't change things. I'm one of those people who believe you can kill a man. But when you do, you have to stand up to your crime like a man. That's what I mean.

RUDY Peter, I don't say we've got to forget what happened to Goban and go on living happily. If anyone has pangs of conscience, that's fine, let him have them, and keep them all his life if he wants. Each one according to his own conscience. But now we've got to decide what we're going to do when this is over. We've got to figure out a story about the Corporal's disappearance. That's what I'm talking about. "We just don't know what happened to him"—huh? How does that sound?

JACOBS Yes, that's best. He went out Christmas morning and we haven't seen him since.

RUDY We've got to remember: Christmas morning. Don't forget it. After breakfast, about eight o'clock.

JACOBS About eight o'clock, yes. He said he was going out to look around. He was going to reconnoiter, and if he wasn't back by supper time not to worry. . . . I don't know whether they'll believe the Corporal would leave us alone for so long a time.

RUDY Sure, why not? He was worried. He had heard strange noises the night before.

JACOBS He could have sent any one of us.

RUDY He didn't trust us. He preferred——

PETER (*getting up.*) You can go on making up stories, but it won't do you any good.

RUDY Why?

PETER Because I intend to describe the Corporal's murder just as it happened.

A long pause; they all look at each other.

JACOBS No, Peter. You're out of your mind.

PETER That's just what I intend to do.

RUDY You're kidding, aren't you Peter? You can't be talking seriously. . . . (*He tries to smile.*) Are you? You don't really mean to do what you said. Don't even think . . . of such a thing. . . .

PETER Docs it surprise you?

RUDY Peter! (*He approaches him.*) This is serious business.

PETER I'm talking seriously too. I'm not afraid of the consequences of my acts. I can face up to them. I insist on facing up to them. That's the way I am.

RUDY   No, Peter! You won't do this! You can't! How did you ever think of such a thing? You're playing with fire, Peter.

PETER   Playing! I don't know how to play.

RUDY   (*sits down; somberly.*)   You can't do it. You can't . . .

PETER   (*without looking at him.*)   What can't I do?

RUDY   Just because you're tired of living, you can't drag the rest of us with you.

PETER   I'm not dragging anyone. I'm just doing what I have to do. The rest of you can do as you like.

RUDY   It's suicide. It's like walking in front of a firing squad.

PETER   No. It isn't up to me to turn myself over for execution. It's simply up to them to decide whether I should die or not. My role is simply to tell them what part I had in the crime . . . that took place here on Christmas Eve. Is that clear?

RUDY   You're disposing of our lives, too, Peter. What are we supposed to do?

PETER   I don't intend to discuss it, Rudy. I think there are more important things than life. I would be very ashamed to go on living now. I could never be happy.

RUDY   Peter, we were drunk. Remember . . . alcohol . . .

PETER   No, that's unimportant. We were drunk— alcohol. . . . Yes, it's true. I won't lie. I'll tell everything just as it happened.

RUDY   It's a useless sacrifice.

PETER   To hide what happened here, just in order

to earn a few more miserable years of life . . .
that's what seems a useless sacrifice to me.

RUDY   I understand you now, Peter. It's not what
you're saying at all. It's not that you're a better
man than the rest of us. It's not that you give a
damn about what happened, or that you feel you
deserve punishment. You want to die! You simply
want to die. You don't want to go home, because
you couldn't go on living with your wife after
what happened. Even if you don't want to admit
it, that's the truth of the matter. That's all there
is to it!

PETER   (*with a bellow of rage.*)   What are you talking about? What are you talking about? If you
don't shut up I'll . . .

RUDY   You see? It hurts because it's true. But we
want to go on living. You can't understand how
anyone could want to go on living, can you? But
we . . . we want to!

A pause; PETER *sits down, dejected.*

JACOBS   Peter, what are you thinking about?

PETER   Nothing. You know how I feel now. In-
terpret it any way you like. I'm going to give myself up to the Court Martial. Whoever doesn't
want to follow me can leave. I don't want to
drag you into something you don't think . . .
is best. . . . (*He closes his eyes. Slowly.*) I've
thought a lot about this. This is the road I've
decided to take. I can't see any other way . . .
for me. . . . So that some day my life won't be
something I'll feel ashamed of, and have to throw
away in order to save myself. . . . I don't know
about the rest of you. . . . I . . . I've finished
with living. . . .

JACOBS I understand you. You're taking things into your own hands, but I understand you. I want to live, but I understand you. You're making things hard on us, because we'd have to kill you to keep you quiet, and that would mean even more blood. . . . We're not so bad as that, can't you see?

RUDY Shut up, Jacobs. Or speak for yourself. Don't include me in your pity and understanding. I'm ready to save myself, and at any price. (*He grabs a rifle and cocks it.*) Peter, I'm ready to take care of anyone who wants to take things into his own hands. You wanted it this way.

PETER (*sitting calmly.*) But just let me tell you one thing: think about it a little before you do something stupid. I don't advise you to wipe me out. It wouldn't work. You'd have to give too many explanations afterward . . . and it's almost certain they'd never believe you. After the things that have happened, I think it'd be best to reflect before making a decision. Are you sure the others agree with you? Won't they leave you alone when you do it—the moment you press the trigger?

RUDY Jacobs, what do you think?

JACOBS No, Rudy. I don't think you should do it. Wait. We'll think about it.

RUDY And the rest of you?

GADDA (*shrugs his shoulders.*) I'd like to go home again, but it looks to me like that's going to be very difficult. I'm ready to accept whatever happens . . . whatever is going to be . . . in spite of all our efforts. Don't count on me for anything. I'd like never to have to speak again.

RUDY *(an impatient gesture.)*   Bah! Foolishness!
Why should we give ourselves up as lost? Without Peter, we've got a long life ahead of us. What
shall we do with him? *(No one answers. Exasperated.)* You, Foss, what do you think? Naturally, it'll be all the same to you too. You've
got nothing to fear from the Court Martial, huh?
That's what you think! Everything depends on
what we say. If we want, the whole thing can
be your fault. Understand? You killed him . . .
at your guard post. Deny it, if you like! No,
Jack, we're not going to say that. But I just
want you to understand that you have to help
us. (JACK *turns his head away.*)

PETER   You're all alone now.

RUDY, *discouraged, throws down the gun, sits down
and hides his face in his hands.*

Blackout.

Scene 10

All but PETER *are there.* GADDA *is lying down.* RUDY
in an attitude similar to that at the end of Scene 9.
He raises his head and speaks.

RUDY   Where's Peter?

JACOBS   He just went out.

RUDY   Good. I wanted to say something to all of
you. In spite of everything, in spite of your fears
and your scruples, Peter has to die. It's our only
way out. It's useless to try to convince him. We've

got to finish with him, if we still hope to get something out of life. On the other hand, it's not so horrible, if what upsets you is . . . the actual doing of it. I'll do it alone. And I don't mind doing it, because I know he wants to die, and he's waiting impatiently for the minute he can walk in front of the firing squad. I suppose . . . you've all thought about it and . . . no doubt—

JACOBS I'm against it, Rudy. We've spilled enough blood. Let's forget it.

RUDY (*shuddering.*) Today's the thirtieth. In a few hours the patrol may come. It's getting dangerous even to stay here. I thought it would be easy to explain Peter's disappearance. He simply . . . went away with the Corporal. "Both of them prisoners of the enemy, without any doubt."

JACOBS Shut up, Lavin! It's useless.

RUDY (*darkly.*) All right. Then there's nothing to do but leave this place, right now. And where can we go? Through the forest? . . . Into the mountains? This whole country is a deathtrap for us. But . . . there may be one possibility of saving ourselves.

JACOBS What's that?

RUDY We could organize ourselves . . . in no man's land. Become guerrillas, stealing provisions from the villages and living in the mountains. We're listed as missing, and that's that! I know of groups who've lived that way for years. And it might be a pretty good life.

JACOBS No, Rudy. I don't agree with you there, either. I want to live, but I don't feel like fighting. . . . I haven't got the strength any

longer. . . . I've decided to go over to the other
side. It's not a pleasant solution, but at least I'll
be alive. You can live in the prison camps.

RUDY Is that all you can think of?

JACOBS Yes.

RUDY Well you're a damn fool! Listen, Jacobs.
You're all driving me crazy. What do you want?
You're all against me. You're giving up . . . to
fate, aren't you? But our only fate is the one we
make for ourselves. What's the matter with you?
You don't want to live, do you? None of you!
You say you do, but you're lying. Listen to me.
In the mountains to the north we can live. Soon
it'll be spring, and there'll be plenty of fruit in
the abandoned orchards, and animals to hunt
in the hills.

JACOBS No. I know I'm not made for that kind
of life . . . hiding out . . . until some patrol,
from one side or the other, hunts me down. I
want to rest. In the camp at least I can lie down.
Understand? Ever since the Corporal kicked me
here (*On his chest.*) I haven't been well.

RUDY But don't you know how they work you in
the camps? Like animals. They'll work you to
death in a stone quarry or in a mine.

JACOBS At night I can sleep.

RUDY No. . . . You'll end up like so many others,
throwing yourself against the electric fences that
surround the camps, electrocuting yourself—if
you can. Because you probably won't even be
able to do that. Come with me.

JACOBS Against the fences! . . . You make me
laugh. . . . To throw yourself against the fences,
you have to want to die, and I——

RUDY You *do* want to die, and if you don't now, you *will*.

JACOBS No. . . . To live . . . no matter how. . . .

RUDY How do you think the guards at the camp will treat you? With whips!

JACOBS We'll see. . . .

RUDY Some of the prisoners can't even move; they don't even feel the whipping. . . . They're like sick plants . . . lying there. . . . They do everything to them and they don't even move—living in their own filth. . . .

JACOBS They can rest, at least.

RUDY Besides, who tells you you're going to get as far as the prison camp? They'll probably shoot you down when you approach their lines.

JACOBS I'll carry a white flag. I don't think they'll shoot.

RUDY Jacobs don't you see how much we could do together? For a man alone, it's difficult . . . but an armed group—we could do so much. . . . There are hiding places in the mountains. . . . It'll be worth it. . . . We may even get to like it. Listen!

JACOBS I've already made up my mind, Rudy.

RUDY And what about the rest of you? (PETER *enters.*) Foss, what about you?

JACK I'm staying here, with Peter. If I were sure I could be of any use to you, I'd go along. But I'd just be a hindrance. We would have to commit crimes in the towns, stealing . . . even killing perhaps if the peasants stood up against us. I'm no good for that kind of thing. Forgive me.

RUDY I wasn't counting on you anyway, Foss. You don't have to justify yourself.

JACK You're right to despise me, Rudy. You have every right to.

RUDY Forget it! And you, Gadda? (GADDA *does not answer*.) You staying?

GADDA Yes.

RUDY You know what that means, don't you? The firing squad!

GADDA Yes, I know . . . although they may not shoot *me*.

RUDY Not you? Why?

GADDA That's my business.

RUDY Is Peter going to witness in your favor?

GADDA No. It's not that. Peter likes to tell the truth. Don't you, Peter? (PETER *does not answer*.)

RUDY Then?

GADDA Leave me alone. You and Jacobs are both foolish. You speak with horror of being shot by a firing squad, and yet you're going to let them hunt you down like animals . . . or lynch you in some village. . . . He (JACOBS.) wants to live, so he's going to let them shut him up inside the barbed-wire fences of a prison camp. It's funny. They're *all* . . . roads to death. Don't you see? It's useless to fight back. The last word has already been spoken, and it's useless to struggle. Actually everything was useless . . . from the very beginning. And from the very beginning the last word was already spoken. You still want to fight against the destiny of this squad . . . which isn't simply death, as we thought at first . . . but a shameful death. . . . Are you so stupid you haven't realized that yet?

PETER (*standing apart*.) But you know, I was hoping for something. That things would turn out differently. That everything would end here in this house, facing the enemy, cut down at sword's point . . . after having warned the front line. Now that we aren't going to end up that way, all I hope is that at least there will never be an offensive in this sector, so our suffering will have helped spare some of the bloodshed that seemed inevitable all along the front.

RUDY (*getting up; he yawns.*) I'm going to see if I can sleep. When it gets dark, I'm leaving this place. In the first town I come to there'll be someone who wants to go to the mountains with me. I need to find a companion, and I'll find one. (*He lies down to sleep.*)

JACOBS I'll go with you. If it's all right with you, we can go together as far as the edge of the forest. There, we can shake hands and . . . good luck! I'm going to lie down a while . . . even though I don't think I can sleep. (*He lies down.*) JACK *is looking out the window.* GADDA *is seated, his eyes on the floor.* PETER *is walking back and forth, pensively. Suddenly he stops and speaks to* GADDA.

PETER So you've come to this? Thinking.

GADDA (*shrugs his shoulders.*) I don't know what you mean.

PETER Ever since "that" happened, you've been thinking, hesitating. You think I haven't noticed? While the rest of us were trying to act in our own way, you were watching us . . . curiously . . . almost as though you were a doctor looking at us through a microscope. . . .

GADDA (*laughs dryly.*) Except that I'm one of the bacteria in the drop of water, too . . . this drop of water that's falling into nothingness. A bacteria who knows what's happening to it, can you imagine anything more frightful? (*A silence.*) Yes, you're right. All this time, ever since we killed Goban, I've been investigating . . . trying to answer certain questions I couldn't help asking myself. . . .

PETER   And so?

GADDA   Now I know. . . . I've found the answers. . . . My work has concluded successfully. I've (*With a slight smile.*) succeeded . . . from a scientific point of view. . . . I've reached conclusions.

PETER   What conclusions?

GADDA   Goban's death wasn't an accident.

PETER   I don't understand what you mean.

GADDA   It was part of a vast plan of punishment.

PETER   That's what you've decided?

GADDA   Yes. While he was alive we were almost living happily. All we had to do was to obey and suffer. We could believe we were purifying ourselves and could some day redeem ourselves. Each one of us remembered his sin, a sin with a date and specific details.

PETER   And since then?

GADDA   Goban was here to punish us, and he let himself be killed.

PETER   Let himself? Why?

GADDA   So our torture would continue and intensify! That's why he was here! He was here so we could kill him! And we fell into the trap. And as if that weren't enough, we've even been denied our last opportunity, the offensive. An ignominious death was decreed for us from the very beginning, I don't know where. That's all.

You say you had a hope that we might die in the fight. . . . Poor Peter. . . . And you're still hoping, aren't you? . . . hoping I don't know what. . . . How did you say it? That "our suffering will have helped . . ." It's like praying. . . .

PETER Yes, it's like praying. Maybe that's all there is left to do. . . . When everything seems lost, we still have a few moments left to pray.

GADDA (*laughing roughly.*) We're marked, Peter. We're marked. Pray? What for? To whom? Pray . . .

PETER How can you say that! Then you believe that someone . . . ?

GADDA Yes. Someone is punishing us for something . . . for something. . . . There must be . . . yes, after all, we *have* to believe that . . . a cancer . . . with us from the beginning . . . A mysterious and horrible sin . . . which we can't even understand . . . Perhaps a long time ago . . .

PETER You may be right . . . but stop thinking about it. . . . It must be wrong—no, don't worry about it. . . . We've got to try to be calm . . . so we can face what's coming.

GADDA Yes, but I can't help it. . . . I *have* to think, don't you understand? (*Smiles weakly.*) It's . . . my vocation. . . . Ever since I was a child . . . while all the other children were playing happily . . . I was sitting alone, calmly . . . thinking. . . .

Blackout.

Scene 11

*In the darkness, the noise of the wind. We can
scarcely distinguish two shadows among the trees
in the foreground. We hear the frightened whispers
of* RUDY *and* JACOBS.

JACOBS   Wait. . . . I'm tired. . . . We've been
walking a long time.

RUDY   What's the matter with you?

JACOBS   We've gone so far. . . . Where are we?

RUDY   This is where the forest ends, don't you
see? And over there are the mountains.

JACOBS   And where . . . are the enemy lines?

RUDY   Just opposite us . . . over there. . . .

JACOBS   Let me sit down. . . . I'm tired. . . .
(One of the shadows sinks to the ground.)

RUDY   Come on, don't sit down now. . . . We've
got to hurry. . . .

JACOBS   You go on, go on . . . if you want. . . .

RUDY   No, not alone. . . . Come with me. . . .
You're out of your mind to try to get to the
enemy lines . . . insane. . . . *(A gust of wind.)*

JACOBS   What did you say?

RUDY   You're out of your mind. . . . *(A long gust
of wind.)*

JACOBS   You know what I wish? That we'd never
left the house. . . .

RUDY   What do you want? To go back now?

JACOBS   No. Not now.

RUDY   Are you coming or not?

JACOBS No. . . . I'll stay here. . . . When I feel better, I'll go over to the other side. . . . When (*Choking.*) I feel better. . . .

RUDY Jacobs, come with me! I'm afraid of what I'm doing, too! But together . . . !

JACOBS They won't do anything to me, you'll see! They won't hurt me!

RUDY If that's the way you want it, then. Goodbye and . . . good luck!

JACOBS Good luck, Rudy!

The shadows separate. Another gust of wind.
Blackout.

Scene 12

The lights come up; it is twilight. JACK *is alone.*
Soon PETER *enters.*

PETER Jack!

JACK What's wrong?

PETER (*taking down a rifle.*) What was Gadda doing this afternoon?

JACK Nothing. Just sitting over there. Then he got up and went out. He said he was going to take a walk in the woods. Why?

PETER Did you notice anything strange about him?

JACK No. Just . . . that since Rudy and Jacobs left last night he hasn't said a word.

PETER He won't ever again. I just found him in the woods. He's hanged himself!

JACK What! He . . . ? Dead?

PETER Yes. Just fifty yards from here. From a tree.

I ran across him as I was coming back here.
. . . He was swinging back and forth. . . . A
sad ending for poor old Gadda. I had to climb
the tree to get him down. . . . He's out
there. . . .

JACK Hanged himself!

PETER He didn't have the courage to go on. I'm
sure he'd been thinking about it for some time.
And now that the patrol is due to arrive, it
seemed absurd to him to continue. . . . Or he
was afraid. . . . And since it was all the same in
the end . . . he decided to end it himself.

JACK But it's not the same. To end that way is
worse. To condemn yourself to death.

PETER He felt condemned already. He thought
he was damned. He thought too much. And this
is where it brought him . . . to this kind of
ending.

JACK (*with a frightened voice.*) It really does
seem that this was a condemned squad, Peter.
Where do you suppose Rudy and Jacobs are
now? Could they have gotten far?

PETER (*shrugs his shoulders.*) Forget them. It's as
though the earth had swallowed them. Good
riddance. (*A silence.*)

JACK We're alone, Peter. Alone in this house.
What will happen to us now?

PETER I'll disappear, too, Jack. Only you will go
on living.

JACK No, Peter. I don't want to live if all the rest
of you leave me. There was no reason why I
should be excluded. Peter, please tell them:
"Jack was with us that night. Jack killed him
too."

PETER No. You stay here, in this world. Perhaps that's your punishment. To stay, to go on living, keeping in your heart the memory of this event.

JACK But I won't be able. . . .

PETER Yes you will. The war will end, and you'll go back to living. You'll find new friends. You'll fall in love. . . . You'll get married. . . . You have to accept it all. Others will never know why, at times, you're suddenly sad for a moment . . . as though you were remembering. . . . Then you'll be thinking of the Corporal, of Gadda and Rudy, and Jacobs and me. . . . Jack, don't feel sorry for us. Feel sorry for yourself . . . for the long sentence you still have to serve: your life. . . .

JACK Peter, why did all this happen? What did we do before? When did we do something that made us deserve this? Or did we deserve it, Peter?

PETER Bah! Don't ask. Why? There's no answer. (*He looks at the sky.*) The only one who might have spoken is silenced now forever. Tomorrow the patrol will certainly come. Why don't you go to sleep? I'll stand guard tonight.

JACK No. You sleep, Peter. I'll stand guard.

PETER Then . . . we'll stand it together, we'll talk. . . . You must have lots to say. . . . This is surely the last night we'll spend here. I'm sure this is over.

JACK (*who has looked intently at* PETER.) You know? I hardly ever talk—there are many things I don't like to say—but today, since we're alone here, I have to tell you that I admire you. And

I'm very fond of you. I love you as though you
were my older brother.

PETER Come on, kid. . . . You're crying. . . .
Don't cry—it's not worth it. (*He takes out a
package of cigarettes, with only two left.*) Look.
Two cigarettes. The last. Do you want to smoke?
(*He wrinkles up the empty package.*)

JACK No. I never smoke.

PETER Then let this be the first time. (*They light
up and smoke.*) Like it?

JACK *nods yes, wiping his eyes, as though from the
smoke.* PETER *looks at him tenderly.*

PETER Your first cigarette. . . . You'll never forget it. . . . And when all this is over and seems
like a dream, as though it had never happened
. . . when you want to remember . . . If some
day, a long time from now, you want to remember me again . . . you'll have to light up a
cigarette . . . and when you taste the tobacco,
this house will exist again, and Gadda's body
will be lying outside there, and I . . . I'll be
looking at you . . . like this. . . .

It is growing dark.

The curtain falls slowly.

The Blindfold

By José López Rubio

La venda en los ojos
Translated by Marion Holt

Characters

CARMEN
EMILIA
AUNT CAROLINA
UNCLE GERARD
THE BUYER
BEATRIZ
VILLALBA
HENRIETTA
QUINTANA
MATILDE

The play takes place in an apartment on Almagro Street in Madrid in the present. The first act, one morning in early spring; the second act, the following morning; the third act, the afternoon of the same day.

Act One

The living room of a comfortable apartment in a building not of the most recent construction. The furnishings are a mixture of styles with a few modern details. A door at the rear opens onto a hallway which leads at the left to a vestibule and entrance of the apartment and at the right to other rooms. Another door at right and one at left. There's a living room suite with a coffee table; at the right an open secrétaire *with a telephone. At one side, a chair; on the wall, a mirror; a good painting or two. It's eleven thirty in the morning. When the curtain goes up* CARMEN *and* EMILIA *in maid's uniform are doing a bit of cleaning.* CARMEN *is still young enough to be a chorus girl.* EMILIA *is somewhat older and, as is natural, has had more experience with life.*

CARMEN   (*scandalized by what* EMILIA *has just told her.*)   How awful! Why, I can't believe it.

EMILIA   You can't believe it—well, you haven't heard anything yet! As it happens, her husband has a girl friend and since Madam knows it, she's fixed herself up with a gigolo for outside activities. Of course, the husband has his problems, too—what with all the uproar at home and him not working. But his girl friend is rolling in money, so she lends a hand.

CARMEN   She does what?

EMILIA   Silly, I mean she makes a contribution.

CARMEN   (*amazed.*) The gentleman takes money from her? (EMILIA *looks at* CARMEN *surprised by the question and answers after a moment of thought with a gesture of superiority.*)

EMILIA   You did tell me the train doesn't run through your town?

CARMEN   But a woman giving money like that to a man!

EMILIA   Well, you do the same thing. For example, your boy friend—where does he get his cigarettes?

CARMEN   It's not the same thing. We're talking about society.

EMILIA   The only difference is that they pay more for their cigarettes. The truth is, there are men at all prices. Take the man who asks for a car, just like that.

CARMEN   Will they give it to him—just like that?

EMILIA   No, first they ask what model he wants.

CARMEN   What can women see in some men?

EMILIA   Well, it's not too difficult. You stop at cigarettes because your means are limited.

CARMEN   Yes, but on my Sundays off who do you think pays the check?

EMILIA   That proves my point—I mean, that proves his point.

CARMEN   (*convinced.*) It's true.

EMILIA   Men—through the years—have come to realize their value because women have acted like a bunch of idiots and they have caught on. And when there's a demand, the price goes up. It's like in my town where there were some dirty-looking rocks that were good for nothing except

building walls until somebody found out that
they could be used for war. You wouldn't believe
how much they paid for them.

CARMEN But men can't be used that way.

EMILIA No, in wartime they're free. But after the
war, the price goes up like everything else.

CARMEN Well, tell me the rest of the story.

EMILIA You'll get it. . . .

CARMEN They must keep it all hush-hush.

EMILIA For what? The whole world knows it. The
only thing that's missing is a performance on the
telly.

CARMEN On the telly?

EMILIA You do watch the telly?

CARMEN Of course I do. I like movies.

EMILIA Well, let it pass. The husband takes his
handout from the other woman, who's the one
who really supports the home.

CARMEN She must have a lot.

EMILIA Of money? Well, if she doesn't her husband does.

CARMEN (*stupefied.*) Is she married too?

EMILIA Of course. It's the proper thing, isn't it?

CARMEN If the real wife knows where all the money
comes from . . .

EMILIA Nobody knows where money comes from.
We're lucky if we know where it goes.

CARMEN Then she looks the other way.

EMILIA You're learning, dear. The husband doesn't
work at all but come pay day, he's first in line.
Oh, that house is no ordinary home. The cook
has bought herself a cottage in the mountains for
one thing.

CARMEN (*marveling.*) You don't say.

EMILIA   Indeed I do! And Madam spends her part, too. Take a look at my stockings. (*She lifts her skirt to enhance the effect and shows her leg.*) And all the rest is just as nice. Later I'll show you my trunk. It looks as if I just got back from Tangiers. And you should see their sons.

CARMEN   What do they do?

EMILIA   The older one says he sells motorcycles.

CARMEN   Well, that's nothing special.

EMILIA   Don't be so sure—they're quite the thing now. And the younger one wants to be a professor.

CARMEN   He must be very clever.

EMILIA   Well, he's still young—he doesn't know much about life. But he'll wake up. To look at them you'd think they were royalty—the kind that marries Americans. The daughter is the one who wins at poker—but that doesn't even buy her drinks. But the children get along famously.

CARMEN   That's nice.

EMILIA   They're even on good terms with Daddy's girl friend.

CARMEN   There's no reason to be nasty to the poor thing—she is the one who opens her purse every month!

EMILIA   Call it gratitude, or courtesy, or what you will—that's the way things are. But it's not the life for me, you know.

CARMEN   I should think not!

EMILIA   That's why I gave up my job and left that house. I couldn't take it any more.

CARMEN   And what's it like here?

EMILIA   This is another setup—you'll be seeing for yourself. Here it's perfect—everything you'd expect from a respectable house.

CARMEN   There's no hanky-panky?

EMILIA   (*doubting.*)   Well, not exactly hanky-panky . . . you'll see. Beginning with the niece . . .

She breaks off; she's heard footsteps. A quick gesture to CARMEN *and the two continue their cleaning.* AUNT CAROLINA *appears at the left. She's a woman of sixty; quick-witted. She is wearing a simple dress.*

AUNT CAROLINA   (*to* EMILIA.)   What are you two doing?

EMILIA   We're finishing the cleaning—if Madam has no other orders.

AUNT CAROLINA   (*to* EMILIA.)   Does the new girl know what her duties are?

CARMEN   Yes, madam.

AUNT CAROLINA   (*to* EMILIA.)   Have you told her that we're all utterly mad?

EMILIA   I was just going to when Madam came in.

AUNT CAROLINA   Well, that's the first thing—so that she'll know how to play the game. (CARMEN *looks at her amazed.*) Don't look at me that way—we haven't eaten any of our maids yet, have we, Emilia?

EMILIA   No, madam, not as far as I know.

AUNT CAROLINA   (*to* EMILIA.)   Get my costume ready —you know which one for today.

EMILIA   Yes, madam, right away. (*She starts toward the door at the rear.*)

AUNT CAROLINA   (*to* CARMEN.)   And you, dear, get Master Eugene's room ready. My niece has gone to the airport to meet him. (*From the door, so*

that she can't be seen by AUNT CAROLINA, EMILIA
indicates to CARMEN *with a gesture that she should
pay no attention*.)

CARMEN   Very well, madam.

AUNT CAROLINA   And when he arrives, bring up his
bag. (EMILIA *from the door at the rear repeats
her negative gesture to* CARMEN. CARMEN *looks at
her over the shoulder of* AUNT CAROLINA *who notices it*.) Emilia?

EMILIA   Madam?

AUNT CAROLINA (*to* EMILIA *without turning around*.)
Why are you making signs that Master Eugene
isn't coming?

EMILIA   I, madam?

AUNT CAROLINA   Yes, you! I don't want this girl to
think I'm a fool besides. . . . (*To* CARMEN.)
Don't you think that would be too much? (*To*
EMILIA *without turning around*.) Is it that you
have some reason for supposing that Master Eugene isn't coming today?

EMILIA   No reason at all, madam.

AUNT CAROLINA   Well, then?

EMILIA   But since I've been working here . . .

AUNT CAROLINA (*turning around to face* EMILIA.)
Since you've been working here, haven't you
gotten used to the most unexpected things happening?

EMILIA   Exactly, madam—but since that is the most
expected thing in the world . . .

AUNT CAROLINA   Come now, go do what I told you.

EMILIA   Yes, madam. (*Exits through the rear right*.)

AUNT CAROLINA (*to* CARMEN.)   And you—don't let
your morale sag.

CARMEN (*upset*.)   No, madam.

AUNT CAROLINA   An organized house is one that's
prepared for any eventuality. . . . If eight strange
people turn up and stay for dinner, or someone
needs quite suddenly a pair of skates, or the
elevator decides to run properly—do you understand?

CARMEN   *(who doesn't understand at all.)* Yes,
madam.

AUNT CAROLINA   Here we always have a package of
confetti on hand and a street map of Copenhagen
and a traffic light. . . .

CARMEN   *(amazed.)* What for?

AUNT CAROLINA   Girl, one never knows what may
happen. My husband has taken care to buy any
useful things that he finds in catalogs. American
aid came too late for us—we have everything.

CARMEN   *(just to say something.)* When one has
the means . . .

AUNT CAROLINA   And we do. My husband says that
we must always be prepared. Just yesterday he
signed a nonaggression pact with the neighbors
across the hall. They're ceding us bases in the
laundry room. *(The signer of the pact appears
in the doorway at right. He is* UNCLE GERARD, *a
gentleman of about seventy. He is relaxed and
tidy. He wears a dressing gown of good quality
and slippers. Under the dressing gown a starched
collar and tie. He has in his hand a strange little
apparatus which he manipulates with curiosity.
On seeing him enter, to* CARMEN.*)* Be ready in
case my niece returns.

CARMEN   Very well, madam. *(CARMEN goes toward
the rear door.)*

AUNT CAROLINA   Wait! *(CARMEN turns around near*

the door.) Gerard, I think you should have a cup of tea.

UNCLE GERARD (*accommodating but preoccupied with his strange little machine.*) Fine.

AUNT CAROLINA I'm so nervous. (*To* CARMEN.) Ask in the kitchen for a cup of tea for my husband.

CARMEN Very well, madam. (*She exits right rear.* UNCLE GERARD *sits down.*)

UNCLE GERARD (*calmly, still manipulating the little apparatus.*) What's the matter with you?

AUNT CAROLINA Beatriz has gone to the airport.

UNCLE GERARD (*undisturbed.*) Oh. To wait for her husband.

AUNT CAROLINA That's not the worst part.

UNCLE GERARD (*interested in the apparatus.*) What's the worst part?

AUNT CAROLINA She took the car.

UNCLE GERARD (*calmly.*) Ah. . . .

AUNT CAROLINA I can't get used to her driving alone.

UNCLE GERARD (*unperturbed.*) She's been driving for fifteen years now.

AUNT CAROLINA Yes, but I can't get used to it. Something could happen to her.

UNCLE GERARD (*without losing his calm, still interested in his manipulation.*) That's true.

AUNT CAROLINA A collision—an accident. . . .

UNCLE GERARD Of course, of course. . . .

AUNT CAROLINA Just read the newspapers—more pedestrians every day. And they're planting more trees. (*Interested in the apparatus.*) What's that?

UNCLE GERARD (*concerned.*) I don't know. It came this morning—I can't imagine what it's good for.

AUNT CAROLINA Isn't there a brochure with an explanation?

UNCLE GERARD Yes, but it's written in Swedish.

AUNT CAROLINA Well, my boy, you can tear it up.

UNCLE GERARD Why do that? We can invite the Swedish ambassador to lunch on some pretext or other.

AUNT CAROLINA Do we know him?

UNCLE GERARD No, but I can stage a meeting . . . one day when the weather is cold.

AUNT CAROLINA (*concerned now, like a good house-wife.*) What do Swedes eat?

UNCLE GERARD Hors d'oeuvres.

AUNT CAROLINA (*relieved.*) Ah, then it's simple.

EMILIA *enters from rear right with a cup of tea on a tray, with sugar bowl, napkin, teaspoon, etc.*

EMILIA Tea for Madam. (*Without waiting she goes over to* UNCLE GERARD. *He puts the apparatus on the sofa, takes the cup, and sweetens the tea patiently.*)

AUNT CAROLINA You don't know how grateful I am that you drink tea when I'm nervous. I can't stand it—and it calms me so much to see you so calm.

UNCLE GERARD Have you ever seen me nervous?

AUNT CAROLINA I should say I have—the day we got married, for example!

UNCLE GERARD That was a while back.

AUNT CAROLINA You don't remember?

UNCLE GERARD No. There may have been some reason.

AUNT CAROLINA (*pointedly.*) Perhaps it was because you were getting married.

UNCLE GERARD No, I knew that was going to happen

the day I met your mother. (*He's drunk his tea and returned the cup to* EMILIA.) Thank you.

EMILIA   Don't mention it, sir. There's a gentleman here who's come about the advertisement in the newspaper.

UNCLE GERARD (*very excited.*)   Ah. . . .

AUNT CAROLINA   What did you advertise today?

UNCLE GERARD   The vase in the entrance hall.

AUNT CAROLINA (*with a gesture of doubt.*)   It's an imitation.

UNCLE GERARD   Yes, but such a bad one.

AUNT CAROLINA   You can see him in here. I'm going to put on my costume before Beatriz returns.

UNCLE GERARD   Who are you playing today?

AUNT CAROLINA   Lady Agatha Bresford. But I assure you, I don't feel at all English today.

UNCLE GERARD   Well, don't worry. As soon as you change clothes . . .

AUNT CAROLINA (*with a gesture of boredom.*)   I have everything ready. (*To* EMILIA.) Have the gentleman come in.

EMILIA   Yes, madam. (*Exits through the rear left.*)

AUNT CAROLINA   Let's see if you can keep him until lunch time.

UNCLE GERARD   We'll see.

AUNT CAROLINA *exits through the left.* UNCLE GERARD *remains several moments toying with his little apparatus. Shortly,* EMILIA *returns bringing in* THE BUYER. THE BUYER *is a man also well along in years. He's wearing a light raincoat and in his hand, his hat and a folded newspaper. He is a neat and well-mannered man.*

EMILIA (*indicating* THE BUYER.)   The gentleman. . . .

THE BUYER Good day.

UNCLE GERARD (*standing up and leaving the apparatus on the sofa.*) Ah, come in, come in.

THE BUYER I read in the paper this morning——

UNCLE GERARD (*going over to him and extending his hand affectionately.*) How are you?

THE BUYER (*a bit disconcerted by all that effusion.*) Fine, and you?

UNCLE GERARD (*confiding.*) So-so.

THE BUYER Ah. . . .

UNCLE GERARD My blood pressure.

THE BUYER High?

UNCLE GERARD Ooh!

THE BUYER Mine, too.

UNCLE GERARD Over two hundred.

THE BUYER A hundred and ninety.

UNCLE GERARD (*satisfied with his score.*) Ah. . . .

THE BUYER Well, I came about——

UNCLE GERARD (*very graciously.*) Please sit down.

THE BUYER It's just that——

UNCLE GERARD (*knowing that he now has him.*) And take off your coat—you'll be more comfortable.

THE BUYER (*resisting weakly.*) No, if it's——

UNCLE GERARD (*to* EMILIA, *who has remained near the door.*) Emilia, take the gentleman's coat. . . . (EMILIA *advances.* THE BUYER *doesn't have a chance to refuse and begins to take off his coat, aided by* UNCLE GERARD.) And bring some glasses. . . .

THE BUYER No, no—don't bother.

UNCLE GERARD What have they forbidden you to drink?

THE BUYER Cognac, rum—but——

UNCLE GERARD   The same ones I can't touch. (*To*
EMILIA *who has taken* THE BUYER'*s coat.*) A bottle
of that old rum that they sent us from Cuba.

EMILIA   Yes, sir.

THE BUYER   (*to* EMILIA.) No—wait! (*To* UNCLE
GERARD.) You haven't understood—it would be
suicide.

UNCLE GERARD   Exactly. There's nothing better than
committing suicide a little every day. It takes all
those ideas about suicide right out of your head
completely. (*To* EMILIA *firmly.*) A bottle and two
glasses. (EMILIA *goes toward the door at stage
rear. To* THE BUYER.) Because the world, the way
things are going—or maybe you're satisfied with
the way the world's going?

THE BUYER   (*who had never thought about this prob-
lem, has some doubts.*) Sir, I don't know. Of
course, when you think about it . . .

UNCLE GERARD   Then you'll probably want some
cookies, too. (EMILIA *stops near the door, turning
around.*)

THE BUYER   No, not for me, thank you.

UNCLE GERARD   Surely you don't subscribe to that
fallacy of most men who think the moment their
beard begins to sprout that cigarettes take the
place of cookies. Cookies are the fountain of
youth. (*To* EMILIA.) Some of those imported ones.
(EMILIA *nods assent and exits left rear. To* THE
BUYER.) But do sit down. No, over here. (THE
BUYER *gives in. Stopping him.*) Wait—be careful
that you don't hurt yourself with this. (*He takes
the apparatus from the sofa.*)

THE BUYER   (*perplexed.*)   What is it?

UNCLE GERARD   (*leaving the apparatus on the table.*)

I really don't know. But it's kept me amused all
morning. Later we'll play with it a bit. What
were we talking about? (*They have sat down.*)

THE BUYER (*happy to be able to say something.*)
Well, I——

UNCLE GERARD (*interrupting him.*) Ah, yes . . .
about the world situation. (*Satisfied.*) An ample
subject. I don't know why they meet so much
when they never agree about anything. Now just
consider the pavement on the street which is a
thing really close to home. It's been this way a
whole year. I've written all the major powers
about the matter.

THE BUYER Russia, too?

UNCLE GERARD Yes, but at the post office nobody
could tell me how much postage the letter needed.
It seems that there've been no precedents.

THE BUYER (*thinking that he can now get a word
in edgewise.*) Well, I've come about——

UNCLE GERARD Are you in a big hurry?

THE BUYER No, but you should understand the object of my visit.

UNCLE GERARD (*crestfallen.*) If there's no other
way—the newspaper advertisement, right?

THE BUYER That's right. I read this morning in
the paper . . . (*He's kept the paper in his hand
and now unfolds it.*) . . . in the classified ads——

UNCLE GERARD (*bored.*) Yes, yes, I know.

THE BUYER (*reads after putting on his glasses.*) "For
sale. Chinese porcelain vase. Ming Dynasty." And
the telephone number. I called early this morning and they gave me your address.

UNCLE GERARD (*with resignation.*) And now you
want to see the vase.

THE BUYER (*again disconcerted.*) I . . . but, of course. . . .

UNCLE GERARD (*pensive.*) But of course. . . .

THE BUYER How much are you asking for it?

UNCLE GERARD Seventy thousand pesetas.

THE BUYER A little expensive—but if it's authentic Ming Dynasty . . .

UNCLE GERARD My good fellow, do you know a lot about these things?

THE BUYER Enough. And especially about that period.

UNCLE GERARD (*sincerely regretting it.*) That's too bad. Didn't you see it when you came in?

THE BUYER (*almost offended.*) You're not going to tell me it's the one in the entrance hall?

UNCLE GERARD (*sadly.*) Yes, I was going to tell you that. But now . . .

THE BUYER (*gravely.*) My good sir . . .

UNCLE GERARD (*admitting softly.*) It's not authentic.

THE BUYER (*implacable.*) You don't need to insist.

UNCLE GERARD (*timidly.*) It does have a dragon.

THE BUYER That's the least one could expect.

UNCLE GERARD And since it's been here so long . . .

THE BUYER How long?

UNCLE GERARD (*encouraged a bit.*) Just imagine— since my niece's wedding. Some . . . uh . . .

THE BUYER Four centuries?

UNCLE GERARD No, no—I think not. (*Thinks to make sure.*) No, I gave the bride away . . . myself.

THE BUYER The Ming Dynasty began in the fourteenth century of our era.

UNCLE GERARD (*convinced.*) Then, no.

THE BUYER   It's not even Chinese! At two hundred pesetas it would be robbery.

UNCLE GERARD   I'm not going to sell it for two hundred pesetas.

THE BUYER   You will want the seventy thousand?

UNCLE GERARD (*defeated.*)   No. I don't want anything. I can't sell it. (THE BUYER *looks at him amazed.*) I've already told you. It was a wedding gift from some cousins of ours. Those gifts from relatives, you know, must be borne with stoicism —because they drop in for a visit when one least expects them. (*Wearily.*) And they are eternal. Look at it there, in the way and right on the edge.

THE BUYER (*with the spirit of cooperation.*)   With a small, unintentional push . . .

UNCLE GERARD (*looking at him with understanding.*) Don't think that hasn't occurred to us. (*He sighs.*) Imitations are unbreakable. I don't know what they make them of. Had it been authentic Ming, just looking at it . . . (*There is a dolorous silence.*)

THE BUYER   Tell them it got broken and . . .

UNCLE GERARD (*sadly.*)   We don't have the courage. They're so happy when they come and see it there. Every man who gives a gift looks at himself in the gift, as in a mirror—and finds himself quite flattered. (*Another short silence.* EMILIA *enters through the rear right with a tray on which there's a bottle of rum, two glasses, and a plate with cookies. She places it on the table in front of the sofa and starts to open the bottle. To* EMILIA.) Leave it. . . . I'll serve.

EMILIA   As the Master wishes. (EMILIA *starts toward the exit.*)

UNCLE GERARD (*to* EMILIA.) And tell Madam that she can join us if she wishes. Tell her we have a very nice buyer.

THE BUYER (*surprised.*) Why, thank you.

EMILIA (*dubious.*) She's dressed as——

UNCLE GERARD It doesn't matter. The gentleman will understand. (EMILIA *exits rear right.* UNCLE GERARD *takes the bottle and removes the cork.*) Let's give blood pressure a chance. We'll see who's the best man. (*He fills the glasses.* THE BUYER *is silent and pensive.*) What are you thinking?

THE BUYER May I take the liberty of asking a question?

UNCLE GERARD (*looking at his watch.*) You may take the liberty of asking a dozen questions. Then I'll ask a question. How does that strike you? And so . . . (THE BUYER *looks at him without knowing what to answer.*) Let's drink first. (*He offers him a glass.*)

THE BUYER (*resigned to everything, takes the glass.*) So be it. If it's my time—but it's going to prove fatal.

UNCLE GERARD You can stretch out a while afterwards, if you want to. (*He raises his glass in a silent toast.* THE BUYER *repeats the gesture. They drink.*) What do you think?

THE BUYER Excellent! (*He sighs.*)

UNCLE GERARD Fine. Now what was your question?

THE BUYER (*remembering.*) Ah . . . well . . . if you don't intend to sell the vase why did you put the ad in the newspaper?

UNCLE GERARD (*a little sad.*) It's like this. . . . I'm getting along in years. I don't go out much. I while away a lot of hours at home. I run ads in the papers—two or three a week—paintings, antiques, crystal, thirteenth-century chests. People come to examine them . . . and we chat a while.

THE BUYER About what?

UNCLE GERARD Once they're convinced the sale is completely out of the question, people are very pleasant. You notice that I'm careful to indicate individual buyers only. The professionals are always in a hurry. A person who is of a mind to buy a sculpture by Alonso Cano or a Saxony centerpiece has money to spend. And the person who has money to spend also has time to spend. There are mornings when this attracts quite a bit of interest—and we all end up playing cards.

THE BUYER (*looking around.*) Well, as far as today is concerned . . .

UNCLE GERARD Yes, I've made a mistake. I thought that China could count on a larger following. Possibly it's because of political prejudices. The day I advertised a first edition of *La Tauromaquia* of Goya was stupendous. I thought it was my birthday. We even danced a bit. (*A short silence.*) In addition, I take advantage of the visits to collect autographs. (*He gets up and goes to the* secrétaire *from which he takes an autograph album bound in leather. He returns to* THE BUYER'*s side.*) Would you like to sign here? (*He hands him the open album.*)

THE BUYER (*surprised.*) I? But I'm no one important. . . .

UNCLE GERARD Well, certainly not. That's the reason—to possess autographs of people who are more or less famous is in the reach of anyone. I

collect unknowns. Just look—there's even a José
López . . . and an Antonio García. Do you realize not a single one of them has ever been heard
of? Nor have they ever been written up in the
papers. Nobody has autographs of any of them.

THE BUYER (*almost convinced, leafing through the
album.*) That's true.

UNCLE GERARD (*taking out a pen which he offers to
THE BUYER.*) Sign. (THE BUYER *can't refuse. He
takes the pen and signs. From the left* AUNT CARO-
LINA *has appeared. She is wearing the same dress
but has put on a hat full of artificial violets, a
feather boa, and some long gloves. She is carrying
a parasol and a purse that is out of style. She
stops in the doorway.* UNCLE GERARD *takes the
album out of* THE BUYER'S *hands.*) Thank you so
much. (*He notices the presence of* AUNT CAROLINA.)
Ah. (*He leaves the album and the pen on the
table. To* THE BUYER.) Let me present . . . (THE
BUYER *turns his head and stands up.* UNCLE GERARD
goes toward AUNT CAROLINA *and takes her by the
hand.*) . . . Lady Agatha Bresford. (THE BUYER
looks at AUNT CAROLINA *with amazement.*) The
gentleman of the Chinese vase.

THE BUYER   How do you do? I'm a great admirer
of England.

AUNT CAROLINA   What's he talking about?

UNCLE GERARD   He thinks you're English.

AUNT CAROLINA   Haven't you told him?

UNCLE GERARD   Well, you see . . . time passed so
quickly. (*To* THE BUYER.) Didn't it?

THE BUYER   Yes.

AUNT CAROLINA (*with a certain foreboding, to* THE

BUYER.)   You're not going to take the vase . . . ?

UNCLE GERARD   Do you think he's a fool?

THE BUYER (*to* AUNT CAROLINA.)   No, madam. I already know that you don't sell things.

AUNT CAROLINA   We have a lot of money, you know. We can't rid ourselves of a single horrible object. It would cause talk. People would say that we were ruined. Stocks would go down in the businesses in which we have controlling interest. As you will see, our niece——

UNCLE GERARD (*pointing to the bottle.*)   Another small drink?

THE BUYER   No, no. . . .

UNCLE GERARD (*offering him the plate.*)   You will have a cookie.

CARMEN *crosses in the background from right to left.*

THE BUYER (*taking a cookie.*)   Very well. . . . (*To* AUNT CAROLINA.) You were saying, madam?

AUNT CAROLINA   That Beatriz, our niece——

UNCLE GERARD (*who hears steps.*)   Careful, Carolina —I think she's here.

AUNT CAROLINA (*to* THE BUYER.)   She went to the airport to meet her husband on the flight from Barcelona.

THE BUYER   Ah. . . .

BEATRIZ *enters from the left. She is over thirty and she is well dressed, wearing a hat and light coat. Her movements are confident and gay.* CARMEN *follows her.* BEATRIZ *hands her the purse and hat which she takes off on entering.*

BEATRIZ (*to* CARMEN.)   Will you leave these in my room?

CARMEN   Yes, madam. (CARMEN *starts to leave.*

BEATRIZ, *who has been looking at her while handing over the purse and hat, stops her.*)

BEATRIZ   Wait. (CARMEN *stops*. BEATRIZ *passes a
finger over her cheek and looks at it afterwards.*)
When the coal vendor returns, tell him that the
last load he brought us was full of rocks painted
black. Quite well painted, I don't deny. I
shouldn't want to deprive him of his artistic due.
But we would prefer something combustible.

CARMEN   (*a bit embarrassed.*)   Yes, ma'am. (*Starts
to leave.*)

BEATRIZ   (*stopping her with her voice.*)   Newsflash!
The coal vendor is married and has four children
—three by his wife and one by a girl who was
upstairs maid. You couldn't, by any chance, have
made a date with him to go riding this Sunday,
to the mountains?

CARMEN   (*righteously.*)   No, ma'am.

BEATRIZ   Thank goodness.

CARMEN   This isn't my Sunday off. . . .

BEATRIZ   But something was said about a trip to
the mountains.

CARMEN   (*righteously.*)   No, ma'am. I never would
have agreed to that. He said we'd ride out to see
the countryside.

BEATRIZ   Ah . . . he's changing landscapes. Be on
your guard—just in case. . . . Well, you can take
those things now.

CARMEN   Yes, ma'am. (*Exits at right rear.*)

BEATRIZ *goes to the* secrétaire *and takes the phone
without having noticed apparently the presence of
the other characters. She dials a number. When we
suppose someone has answered, she speaks.*

BEATRIZ   (*on the phone.*)   Let me speak to Julia,

please. . . . Oh, is that you? How are you, darling? . . . I'm fine. . . . Yes, I went out. I went to the airport to meet Eugene. He was supposed to arrive today. . . . Yes, from Barcelona. . . . No, he didn't come—he'll be here tomorrow. . . . Yes, I'll go meet him then. And your husband—has he made up with his girl friend? . . . Do tell! That's a relief. You must feel better. . . . Yes, love. Men who have no affairs become terribly tedious. . . . Of course, they get bored. . . . Ah, yes. He did follow me again. . . . No, no—he didn't say anything to me. Well, yes he did—he asked me what time it was in the airport. . . . No, I didn't answer him because you never ask that question of a respectable woman. And after all, we were standing beside that large clock. That will give you some idea of his intentions. . . . How old? Oh—you know—the age when they can look ten years younger than what they are. . . . Yes, dear—I don't know how they do it. What we go through —and they achieve it without even putting on false eyelashes. If they did, who knows where we'd be? . . . Exactly! . . . Interesting? A lot depends on where you meet a man. On an ocean liner, he'd be sensational. In the air terminal—not so suitable. All types travel by plane these days. . . . No, darling, he didn't plan to give up his trip for me. It's such a long trip. . . . No, I didn't know where he was going, but by his appearance, it was something international. Further than Lisbon. . . . I don't know. . . . How was he dressed? Inconspicuously—I'd say. That in itself means that he dresses well. . . . Yes, he has a

car—how do you think he'd follow me if he didn't,
silly? A small car. . . . An ideal man? Hardly.
For a married woman—a very slight danger. For
a single one of seventeen or thirty-nine—irresist-
ible. . . . Yes, yes—he smokes. Much less than a
woman, of course. . . . Don't even think it! I'm
not going to introduce him to you because I'm
not going to meet him. You know very well that
I'm faithful to Eugene—and it's a pity, because
he'd go well at your canasta parties. . . . No,
no—I tell you I don't even intend to let on that
I've noticed him. If he asks me what time it is
again, I'll put him in his place. . . . Oh, well,
dear—let him learn. They've developed bad
habits in the bars—just ask the time of day and
things begin. Well, darling, I'll leave you. You
must have things to do. . . . The cook's salary?
I can't help you with that—you'll have to fight
that battle for yourself. . . . Yes, I'll call you
later. I don't know yet what I'm going to do.
Good-bye, treasure . . . good-bye. (*She hangs up.*
AUNT CAROLINA, UNCLE GERARD, *and* THE BUYER
*followed the whole telephone conversation in
silence.* AUNT CAROLINA *and* UNCLE GERARD *have
exchanged glances at certain points but are very
calm.* THE BUYER *understands nothing.* BEATRIZ
*turns around and for the first time appears to be
aware of the presence of the other characters. She
feigns surprise and goes to* AUNT CAROLINA.) Oh,
but were you here? Lady Agatha, darling, how are
you? (*Kisses her.*)

AUNT CAROLINA   Fine.

BEATRIZ   And your castle in Scotland?

AUNT CAROLINA   Full of ghosts, as always.

BEATRIZ Haven't you discovered some magic powders to exterminate them?

AUNT CAROLINA Yes, but they proved harmful only to living persons and there were some casualties among the servants. So naturally, there were several new ghosts to worry about. So it's a never-ending affair. . . .

BEATRIZ (*to* UNCLE GERARD.) And how are you, Uncle?

UNCLE GERARD The same.

BEATRIZ Do I know this gentleman?

UNCLE GERARD No.

AUNT CAROLINA He's today's caller.

BEATRIZ Is he staying for lunch?

THE BUYER No, no. . . .

UNCLE GERARD Of course you are. He's staying!

AUNT CAROLINA (*to* THE BUYER.) Do you like paella?

THE BUYER (*incapable of a lie.*) Yes, madam.

UNCLE GERARD (*without admitting discussion.*) Then it's settled.

AUNT CAROLINA We put prizes in the casserole, you see.

UNCLE GERARD Just like the Christmas cake. You might even find a watch or a cigarette lighter.

AUNT CAROLINA No, not that—it leaves a bad taste.

THE BUYER I think the chicken would be adequate.

BEATRIZ You can't imagine how dull chicken becomes. Do you remember, Lady Agatha, when I got the silver fox piece?

THE BUYER In the paella?

BEATRIZ No, in such cases they put in a certificate all folded up and you exchange it for the prize. Then I'll see you at lunch—I'm going to change.

AUNT CAROLINA   Are you going out before eating?

BEATRIZ   (*going toward the door at left.*)   I don't know. It depends. I'll see how the weather is.

AUNT CAROLINA   To whom were you talking on the phone?

BEATRIZ   (*already at the door.*)   I? Oh, with nobody —someone dialed a wrong number.

She leaves resolutely by the left. There is, among those who remain, a little silence. THE BUYER *doesn't know what to say.* AUNT CAROLINA *and* UNCLE GERARD *note his perplexity.*

AUNT CAROLINA   (*explaining to* THE BUYER.)   Of course she hasn't talked with anybody.

THE BUYER   But if . . .

AUNT CAROLINA   Julia doesn't exist.

UNCLE GERARD   She just dials any number . . . and talks.

AUNT CAROLINA   And says everything she doesn't want to say to us. . . .

UNCLE GERARD   But what she wants us to be aware of.

AUNT CAROLINA   (*with emotion.*)   She has no secrets from us.

THE BUYER   But if she dials a number, they must answer. . . .

UNCLE GERARD   Of course.

AUNT CAROLINA   They suppose it's a wrong number —and when they get tired they hang up. It all probably seems quite extraordinary to you.

THE BUYER   (*wanting to appear educated.*)   No, no. . . .

AUNT CAROLINA   Well, my good man, there's certainly nothing ordinary about it.

UNCLE GERARD   Do you know why our niece went to the airport this morning?

THE BUYER   (*delighted to be sure about something.*) That is the only thing I know. To meet her husband.

AUNT CAROLINA   And what happened?

THE BUYER   He didn't arrive.

UNCLE GERARD   But . . .

THE BUYER   . . . he will arrive tomorrow. . . .

AUNT CAROLINA   Do people still say "nix"? I go out so seldom.

THE BUYER   Well, not as much as they used to. . . .

AUNT CAROLINA   But you do know what it means?

THE BUYER   Nix? Yes, of course. . . .

AUNT CAROLINA   Well—nix! (THE BUYER *finds himself lost.* UNCLE GERARD *kindly comes to his aid.*)

UNCLE GERARD   Our niece goes to the airport every day.

AUNT CAROLINA   At the same hour.

UNCLE GERARD   They all know her.

THE BUYER   But isn't she going to meet her husband?

UNCLE GERARD   Yes, indeed.

AUNT CAROLINA   For ten years now, without fail.

THE BUYER   Ten years?

UNCLE GERARD   Since the morning he was supposed to arrive . . .

AUNT CAROLINA   . . . and didn't arrive.

UNCLE GERARD   She thought he had missed the plane and went back the next day . . .

AUNT CAROLINA   . . . and the next.

UNCLE GERARD   And on Thursday, and Friday, and Saturday . . .

AUNT CAROLINA . . . and in May, and June, and July . . .

UNCLE GERARD . . . and August with all the heat. . . .

AUNT CAROLINA In 1955 and 1956. . . .

UNCLE GERARD They extended the runways which had gotten too short for the planes.

AUNT CAROLINA Always more people arriving. . . .

UNCLE GERARD Tourists. . . .

AUNT CAROLINA Bullfighters—from Mexico.

UNCLE GERARD Bishops—from Rome.

AUNT CAROLINA Ava Gardner. . . .

UNCLE GERARD Everybody, except her husband.

THE BUYER What had happened to him?

UNCLE GERARD He had run off to Mallorca with a model.

THE BUYER Was he a painter?

AUNT CAROLINA Don't be silly, man. Painters don't use models any more. Everything is abstract.

UNCLE GERARD A fashion model.

THE BUYER (*catching on.*) Oh. . . . (*For something more to say.*) To Mallorca, eh?

AUNT CAROLINA Just imagine.

THE BUYER Fine—but people do come back from Mallorca. There are planes there, too.

UNCLE GERARD If one wants to come back, of course.

AUNT CAROLINA There's something final about Mallorca.

UNCLE GERARD Yes, and as small as it is, too.

AUNT CAROLINA Newlyweds go there to clinch their happiness. . . .

THE BUYER You went there?

AUNT CAROLINA No, when we were married, Mallorca hadn't been invented yet.

UNCLE GERARD Everything seems planned for love. . . .

AUNT CAROLINA The beaches. . . .

UNCLE GERARD The grottoes. . . . If he had gone off with a model to some other place, there might have been room for hope.

AUNT CAROLINA But Mallorca caught them with an incredible force. . . .

UNCLE GERARD They went off for only a week-end. . . .

AUNT CAROLINA And from there to Paris—which isn't lacking in charm, either.

UNCLE GERARD There we lost track of them.

AUNT CAROLINA The man who discovers Paris with a woman, whether native or imported, is irremissibly lost to the Castilian plateau. . . .

THE BUYER Ten years—and since then . . .

AUNT CAROLINA You've seen her. . . .

UNCLE GERARD She doesn't realize that time has passed.

AUNT CAROLINA For her, only the fashions change.

UNCLE GERARD She always has her husband's room ready.

AUNT CAROLINA Next to hers.

UNCLE GERARD Because she always believes that he's going to arrive.

THE BUYER (*impressed.*) It's awful.

UNCLE GERARD (*calmly.*) Yes, awful.

AUNT CAROLINA But we've gotten used to it. (*There is a short silence. The story seems to have had a great effect on* THE BUYER.) I suppose you understand now why I've dressed up today as Lady Agatha Bresford—and other days as an opera contralto, or an international spy. . . .

UNCLE GERARD   Or a girl from the chorus of *The Student Prince*.

AUNT CAROLINA (*clarifying.*)   On Thursdays. Usually they're characters I take from novels.

UNCLE GERARD   And it explains why I sell antiques, collect noodles for soup, and have six fishing harpoons.

THE BUYER (*confused.*)   Well, actually, I don't see the connection. . . .

UNCLE GERARD (*to* THE BUYER.)   Don't you know what complexes are?

AUNT CAROLINA (*explaining to him.*)   What we used to call having a screw loose. (*To* UNCLE GERARD.) You explain it all. You tell it better then I do. I'll probably interrupt you from time to time.

UNCLE GERARD   Do I start at the usual place?

AUNT CAROLINA   Well, more or less.

UNCLE GERARD (*getting ready to tell his story.*) Well, you see—another cookie?

THE BUYER (*interested.*)   No, no . . . go on.

AUNT CAROLINA (*to* UNCLE GERARD.)   Forget the cookies now—when you're getting ready to relate a drama. (*To* THE BUYER.) Because it is a tremendous drama. (*To* UNCLE GERARD.) Well, go on.

UNCLE GERARD   When our niece was five years old——

AUNT CAROLINA   Aren't you going to set the scene? It was a beautiful morning in spring. . . .

UNCLE GERARD   No. It's not a very effective line.

AUNT CAROLINA   Well, I like it!

UNCLE GERARD (*to* THE BUYER.)   At the age of five as I was saying, our niece lost her father——

AUNT CAROLINA In a shipwreck.

UNCLE GERARD Three months later, her mother
called us to Bilbao urgently. When we arrived,
we found poor Sophia in bed.

THE BUYER Seriously ill?

AUNT CAROLINA Seriously dead.

THE BUYER Oh, I'm sorry.

AUNT CAROLINA We appreciate your sympathy.

UNCLE GERARD The poor child was an orphan with
nowhere to go.

THE BUYER (*thinking he's caught on.*) And in the
greatest need. . . .

UNCLE GERARD Well, not so great—you see, she
was going to inherit eight million pesetas. Someone had to take charge of the child. All the
relatives fought to be her guardian. We won.

AUNT CAROLINA Because we had more money than
the rest. . . .

THE BUYER You mean she was put up for auction?

AUNT CAROLINA No, indeed. The family council
decided that we were not motivated by any desire
for profit.

UNCLE GERARD And since we had no children of our
own, our fortune would end up in Beatriz's
hands.

AUNT CAROLINA Which is not at all stupid, you
may well believe.

THE BUYER Well, I suppose——

AUNT CAROLINA My husband has a few million
pesetas of his own. I didn't go to the altar exactly
barefoot. . . .

UNCLE GERARD The child lived from then on at our
side.

AUNT CAROLINA We took pleasure in her laughter —which was like the sound of little golden bells.

THE BUYER (*moved.*) Of course.

AUNT CAROLINA (*to* THE BUYER.) Did you like that line, really? (*To* UNCLE GERARD.) You see? I don't know why you don't like the line. It had this gentleman on the verge of tears.

UNCLE GERARD (*to* AUNT CAROLINA.) It's not the line—it's the situation. (*To* THE BUYER.) I'll spare you the chicken pox, the whooping cough . . .

AUNT CAROLINA . . . the nights we watched beside her cradle. . . .

UNCLE GERARD (*to* AUNT CAROLINA.) That's a bad line, too. I've already told you that.

AUNT CAROLINA But isn't it true?

UNCLE GERARD Yes. But it's completely out of fashion.

AUNT CAROLINA (*to* THE BUYER.) Well, how about you? What do you think?

THE BUYER Well, I didn't see anything wrong with it. . . .

AUNT CAROLINA (*triumphant, to* UNCLE GERARD.) See? If sentiments are real, there's no reason to be ashamed of them. Let the people who use them for commercial ends be ashamed.

UNCLE GERARD (*trying to go on with the story.*) Several wars occurred.

AUNT CAROLINA The usual ones.

UNCLE GERARD And one day she got married.

THE BUYER And she left you?

AUNT CAROLINA No, indeed! You never get one right, do you?

UNCLE GERARD Do you think we could resign ourselves to living without her?

AUNT CAROLINA It's a very big apartment—it goes all the way to the street at back.

UNCLE GERARD They lived here. Apparently very happy.

AUNT CAROLINA Until one day . . .

UNCLE GERARD . . . he went off to Barcelona. He said that he was coming back on Monday.

AUNT CAROLINA He's missing the part about our own manias—but he doesn't dare to ask us about it. This friend of yours is very circumspect.

From the left BEATRIZ *enters. She's wearing a suit and hat and appears ready to go out to the street.*

BEATRIZ Well, are you having a good time?

AUNT CAROLINA We're having a fabulous time.

BEATRIZ (*to* AUNT CAROLINA *for the benefit of* THE BUYER.) Have you told him about the time you lived in India with your husband?

AUNT CAROLINA Not yet. (THE BUYER *looks amazed at* UNCLE GERARD, *who clears things up.*)

UNCLE GERARD Lord Bresford—Second Regiment of the Bengal Lancers.

THE BUYER (*catching on.*) Ah, yes. From the movies.

AUNT CAROLINA (*to* BEATRIZ.) Are you going out?

BEATRIZ I think not. Why?

AUNT CAROLINA No reason.

THE BUYER (*to* UNCLE GERARD *in a low voice.*) Then why has she put on her hat?

UNCLE GERARD Oh, she's very sensible today. Some days she puts on anything that comes into her mind.

BEATRIZ (*to* AUNT CAROLINA.) Hasn't Julia called me?

AUNT CAROLINA Yes, a moment ago.

BEATRIZ   Did you tell her to meet me for cocktails?

AUNT CAROLINA   I did.

BEATRIZ   The same place?

AUNT CAROLINA   Yes, the usual place.

BEATRIZ   Well, I'm off. If I'm late she gets furious. Shall I bring you something for dessert?

AUNT CAROLINA   No, I've already ordered something.

BEATRIZ   (*to* THE BUYER.)   How about you?

THE BUYER   Oh, don't go to any trouble for me.

BEATRIZ   But I'd love to. . . . Good-bye, until later.

THE BUYER   (*very kindly.*)   Good-bye. (BEATRIZ *exits. The three remain an instant in silence.*)

UNCLE GERARD   (*to* THE BUYER.)   Julia didn't call. You can testify to that.

THE BUYER   Indeed I can.

AUNT CAROLINA   But I said yes because——

UNCLE GERARD   We don't know if it was the mental shock, or what, but she began to have strange ideas.

AUNT CAROLINA   The first was this business of going every day to meet Eugene—as if nothing had happened. Oh, it hurt us terribly. (*To* UNCLE GERARD.) It hurt us terribly, although you've insisted that I should never confess it.

UNCLE GERARD   We didn't have the heart to tell her the truth.

AUNT CAROLINA   Especially when it would have served no purpose.

UNCLE GERARD   We decided to go along with her— in this mania and in others.

AUNT CAROLINA   Each one was like a knife cutting into our hearts.

UNCLE GERARD (*emphatically to his wife.*) You should never watch another serial on television! (*To* THE BUYER.) It seemed to us that the best thing would be to start doing a few crazy things ourselves.

AUNT CAROLINA If she was so happy with her extravagances, the best thing would be to go along with her.

UNCLE GERARD And that way she would feel that she had companionship.

THE BUYER (*serious.*) I understand.

AUNT CAROLINA Good for you.

UNCLE GERARD It didn't take too much effort for us.

AUNT CAROLINA Perhaps, because we already had a certain disposition. . . .

UNCLE GERARD Sometimes it's easier to do whatever comes into your mind than to stop doing it.

AUNT CAROLINA People began to avoid us.

UNCLE GERARD But people didn't matter too much to us.

AUNT CAROLINA (*simply.*) She was what mattered.

UNCLE GERARD (*to* AUNT CAROLINA.) That's the right tone. (*To* THE BUYER.) Almost no one visits us.

THE BUYER But with other people you didn't have to pretend. . . .

UNCLE GERARD Look: it's very difficult to have two lives. To go—and to return. To lose one's sense of proportion, to stop, then to start again. . . .

AUNT CAROLINA When one chooses a road like this one, you have to follow it with resolution, come what may.

UNCLE GERARD   And with all the problems.

AUNT CAROLINA   And the unquestionable advantages. We enjoy life.

UNCLE GERARD   Yes, indeed. (*To* THE BUYER.) You don't know what you're missing.

BEATRIZ *enters hurriedly from the left.*

AUNT CAROLINA (*on seeing her.*)   Back already?

BEATRIZ (*radiant.*)   I'll bet you don't know who I found downstairs on the sidewalk.

UNCLE GERARD   Who?

BEATRIZ   See if you can guess!

UNCLE GERARD (*calmly.*)   Very well. (*To* THE BUYER.) Do you want to play, too? (*To* BEATRIZ.) European?

BEATRIZ   Don't be silly, Uncle. (*To* AUNT CAROLINA.) I'll bet you know.

AUNT CAROLINA (*fearing the worst; serious.*)   Well, I don't know.

BEATRIZ   But you do know! I can read it in your eyes. He was closing his car door. And I had gone to the airport to wait for him today.

UNCLE GERARD (*to* THE BUYER.)   Today?

BEATRIZ   And it turns out, without telling me anything, he's come by car. (*The others don't know what to say.*) Yes, yes—Eugene!

UNCLE GERARD (*alarmed.*)   Eugene?

BEATRIZ   It seems strange to me that he didn't arrive on the day he said. He's always been so punctual. He's there—in the hallway. I'll go get him. (*She exits left.* AUNT CAROLINA *and* UNCLE GERARD *look at each other in amazement.* THE BUYER *is very interested.*)

UNCLE GERARD (*flabbergasted.*)   Eugene!

AUNT CAROLINA (*firmly.*)   He's going to have a word from me.

UNCLE GERARD (*calming her.*)   No, woman. For the moment, nothing. He said that he was arriving today, and here he is.

AUNT CAROLINA   Just like that?

UNCLE GERARD   We don't know anything. (*To* THE BUYER.) Isn't that the prudent thing?

THE BUYER (*sincere.*)   I think so.

AUNT CAROLINA (*nervous.*)   Of course. You might just as well be watching a movie! . . .

From the left, BEATRIZ *enters leading* VILLALBA *by the hand.* VILLALBA *is a man of about fifty. Well dressed. He is carrying a light coat and a hat. He enters in a somewhat hesitant manner.*

BEATRIZ (*gaily.*)   Here he is! (*There is a mortal silence.* AUNT CAROLINA *and* UNCLE GERARD *look at* VILLALBA *even more surprised than before.*) Well, aren't you going to say anything to each other? (*To* VILLALBA.) Say hello to Lady Agatha. . . .

VILLALBA (*without understanding.*)   Lady Agatha?

BEATRIZ   It's true that you don't know that she's a little——

AUNT CAROLINA (*nervously.*)   Me?

BEATRIZ (*to* AUNT CAROLINA.)   Come now, you act as if you're seeing a ghost! (*Taking the hat and coat from* VILLALBA.) Let me have those. Now give her a hug! (VILLALBA, *obliged by* BEATRIZ, *embraces* AUNT CAROLINA, *who receives the attention coldly.*)

THE BUYER (*softly to* UNCLE GERARD.)   It seems to me that she's exaggerating the note of coldness.

UNCLE GERARD (*nervous.*) Will you be quiet!

THE BUYER (*intimidated.*) I . . .

BEATRIZ And now it's Uncle Gerard's turn. (VILLALBA *looks at* UNCLE GERARD *and then at* THE BUYER *with uncertainty.* UNCLE GERARD *resolves the matter by stepping forward.*)

UNCLE GERARD How are you, my boy? (*He embraces him.*)

VILLALBA Fine. And how are you, sir?

BEATRIZ Sir! Sir! You'd think you hadn't seen each other for ten years!

VILLALBA (*to* UNCLE GERARD.) It's true, Uncle. How are things?

UNCLE GERARD Bad, as always. . . .

BEATRIZ (*indicating* THE BUYER.) And this is today's caller. (VILLALBA *starts to embrace him too.*)

THE BUYER (*timidly.*) Oh, don't bother about me.

BEATRIZ Why not? You're practically a member of the family.

THE BUYER Very well. How have you been, my boy? (*He embraces him.*)

VILLALBA Fine, thank you.

THE BUYER How's the weather in Barcelona?

VILLALBA (*surprised.*) In Barcelona?

BEATRIZ Yes, love, in Barcelona. That's what they always ask. And the answer is: "Better than here, though a bit more humid." . . . Well, I'll go see if your room is ready. You'll want to freshen up before eating. . . .

VILLALBA (*uncertain.*) Well . . .

BEATRIZ Do you want to take a shower?

AUNT CAROLINA (*quickly.*) No! Not that!

BEATRIZ Aunt, he's been driving all night!

AUNT CAROLINA (*energetically.*) I don't care if he has!

UNCLE GERARD (*intervening; to* AUNT CAROLINA.) Why not, woman?

BEATRIZ Everything's ready. But I'll take a look, just in case.

She exits left. The four characters stand looking at each other for a moment. AUNT CAROLINA *weakens first and breaks the silence with an accusing cry.*

AUNT CAROLINA (*to* VILLALBA.) You're not Eugene!

VILLALBA (*simply.*) No, madam.

THE BUYER (*very surprised; to* UNCLE GERARD.) Oh! He's not Eugene?

UNCLE GERARD (*exasperated; to* THE BUYER.) Will you be quiet! (*To* VILLALBA.) Who are you?

VILLALBA (*who has recovered his calm.*) Germán Villalba, architect, at your service. (*To* UNCLE GERARD.) Haven't you seen the new block of apartments going up on Serrano Street?

UNCLE GERARD (*surprised.*) Oh! Are you in charge of that?

AUNT CAROLINA (*very nervous.*) Gerard! We're not in the least interested in houses that only Americans can afford. (*To* VILLALBA, *catching on.*) You're the one from the airport!

VILLALBA The one from the airport? (*Understanding.*) Well, yes.

UNCLE GERARD What are you doing here?

VILLALBA Well, if I must tell the truth, I don't know. . . . I was standing on the street beside my car——

AUNT CAROLINA (*in a tone of accusation.*) Because you followed her! Don't deny it!

VILLALBA (*calmly.*) I don't deny it.

AUNT CAROLINA And you waited on the street to see if she'd come down again!

VILLALBA Now you're getting rather personal.

AUNT CAROLINA (*furious.*) It is personal! (*To* UNCLE GERARD.) Did you hear him?

UNCLE GERARD (*calmer.*) She has taken you for her husband.

VILLALBA Ah! I didn't know that. . . .

THE BUYER But does he resemble him so much?

AUNT CAROLINA (*indignant.*) There's not the slightest resemblance!

UNCLE GERARD And you've come up with her. . . .

VILLALBA She had me come up. I couldn't refuse.

AUNT CAROLINA You didn't want to refuse!

VILLALBA True.

UNCLE GERARD And you've had the nerve to present yourself to us!

VILLALBA I wasn't expecting to find you.

AUNT CAROLINA (*scandalized; to* UNCLE GERARD.) Did you hear that? He's a cynic besides. . . .

VILLALBA Besides what?

AUNT CAROLINA Besides not being Eugene!

VILLALBA For that I'm not to blame.

VOICE OF BEATRIZ Eugene, the bathroom's ready now.

VILLALBA I'll be right there!

AUNT CAROLINA (*overwhelmed, almost pleading.*) You're not going to take a shower!

VILLALBA Why not?

AUNT CAROLINA (*to* UNCLE GERARD.) Aren't you concerned about him catching a cold? (*To* VILLALBA.) It's a shared bathroom. . . . And has a door that connects with her bedroom. . . .

VILLALBA (*without losing his calm.*) Ah, yes. . . .

UNCLE GERARD If you're a gentleman!

THE BUYER (*joining the plea.*) Since you really aren't Eugene! . . .

BEATRIZ *appears in the doorway at left with a towel in her hand.*

BEATRIZ (*to* VILLALBA.) Aren't you coming, love?

VILLALBA (*his mind made up, he goes toward her.*) Yes.

AUNT CAROLINA (*in a quandary.*) Close the door! . . . And lock it! . . .

BEATRIZ (*to* VILLALBA.) What nonsense! (*To* AUNT CAROLINA.) Lady Agatha, you English women are too puritanical. . . . (*To* VILLALBA.) Don't pay her any mind. As if we hadn't been married a whole year!

She leads VILLALBA *off by the arm while the curtain falls.*

In the same room as the previous act, the morning of the following day. When the curtain rises, CARMEN *is onstage finishing her cleaning.* THE BUYER *appears at right. He is wearing a wool bathrobe and he has a newspaper in his hand.*

CARMEN Good morning, sir.

THE BUYER Hello there. Good morning.

He goes to one of the armchairs, sits down, opens the newspaper, and reads. CARMEN *finishes her task and exits at right. In a few moments* UNCLE GERARD *enters from left. He's wearing an ordinary suit without the smoking jacket of the first act. He is carrying several small boxes.*

UNCLE GERARD Here you are. . . . (*He spreads the boxes out on the table.*) There are some that are electric and there are some that are run by animal traction. And here's one—I can't figure out how it's run. Which do you prefer for shaving?

THE BUYER I shave with an ordinary razor.

UNCLE GERARD (*dejected.*) Well, I can't offer you an ordinary razor. We're mechanized here. (*Sincerely lamenting it.*) But man, who would have thought it? It's as if you'd asked me for an oil lamp or matches or an hourglass.

THE BUYER   Don't worry about it—I'll try one of these.

UNCLE GERARD   You may cut yourself if you're not used to them. You've probably seen some shaving lotion in the bathroom for afterwards. Each bottle contains, concentrated, one pine tree from Canada. As for the fluorescent toothpaste, I don't think you'll have any complaint. People can see you laugh in the dark.

THE BUYER   Laugh? At what?

UNCLE GERARD   At anything at all. The prospectus doesn't say. And the toothbrush is radioactive. The only drawback is that it stops your wristwatch. That's why I use this one—it's Swiss. It runs with the movement of your arm.

THE BUYER   You probably have to do push-ups to get it started.

UNCLE GERARD   I do push-ups every day to keep myself old.

AUNT CAROLINA *enters from the right. She hasn't put on her disguise of the day yet.*

AUNT CAROLINA   Good morning. For heaven's sake, don't get up. (THE BUYER *starts to sit down.*)

UNCLE GERARD   Yes, do get up. So we can see how the robe suits you. (THE BUYER *stands up.*) Let's see. . . . Turn around. . . . (THE BUYER *obeys meekly. Consulting with* AUNT CAROLINA.) Very fine, don't you think?

AUNT CAROLINA   Well, I don't know why you've never wanted to wear it. It's lovely.

UNCLE GERARD   It's just that it suits this gentleman's type of good looks better than mine.

AUNT CAROLINA   And it's a marvelous wool. I bought it in——

THE BUYER   Australia?

AUNT CAROLINA   In Barcelona.

UNCLE GERARD   Yes, indeed! When our national products are good, we buy them enthusiastically. In this house, for example, the *banderillas* are of Spanish make.

AUNT CAROLINA   We seldom use them—but they're good ones. And the orange juice that you had this morning when you woke up——

THE BUYER   Excellent.

AUNT CAROLINA   Well, you see—it's from Valencia. We also buy our firecrackers there.

THE BUYER   It was superb.

UNCLE GERARD   Made with the Turmix. In a few seconds, the whole orange—hull, seeds, and wrapping paper—not a single Vitamin C is lost.

AUNT CAROLINA   Now you can go in to breakfast. Whatever you prefer—tea, coffee, chocolate.

UNCLE GERARD   Or something more substantial.

THE BUYER   No, no. A little tea.

AUNT CAROLINA   Toast and butter?

THE BUYER   Fine.

AUNT CAROLINA   The butter is guaranteed.

UNCLE GERARD   Made at home.

AUNT CAROLINA   Later we'll take you out to see the cow. I got her for Christmas two years ago.

THE BUYER   (*timidly.*) I'd like to telephone my house so that they'll know that I'm all right. Since you insisted that I spend the night here.

AUNT CAROLINA   We weren't going to let you leave so late.

UNCLE GERARD   And with this weather so unpredictable.

THE BUYER   I live close by.

UNCLE GERARD Exactly! One of our cousins died from that.

THE BUYER From living close by?

AUNT CAROLINA Yes, indeed!

UNCLE GERARD Since he lived only a few blocks up the street, he didn't wait for the bus or call a taxi.

AUNT CAROLINA And he started walking, so sure of himself.

UNCLE GERARD On the second corner, pneumonia was waiting for him.

AUNT CAROLINA Double! My conscience would have troubled me if I'd let you go out after the great favor you did for us yesterday.

THE BUYER (*modestly.*) Oh, it was nothing.

UNCLE GERARD What do you mean nothing? Your idea was magnificent! And it solved everything.

AUNT CAROLINA At least for the moment.

UNCLE GERARD And what courage you showed—to go into the bathroom while that man was showering!

AUNT CAROLINA Running the risk of getting splattered.

UNCLE GERARD And the eloquence you used to get him to accept our bargain.

THE BUYER (*overcome by the praise.*) I only did my duty. . . . (*Timidly.*) Can I telephone now?

AUNT CAROLINA Why, of course. (THE BUYER *goes to the telephone.*)

UNCLE GERARD Can we stay and listen?

THE BUYER (*turning around, surprised.*) Yes, of course. Make yourself at home.

UNCLE GERARD That's what I mean.

AUNT CAROLINA We hear very few conversations

that don't interest us. (THE BUYER *takes the telephone. He dials a number. He waits a moment.*)
THE BUYER (*on the telephone.*)   Hello? Is my wife there? Tell her to come to the phone, please. . . . Yes, yes. (*He waits a moment.*) Hello. Matilde? How have you been since last night? Did you sleep well? . . . Me? Wonderfully. And the children? . . . I'm glad. Who did Pablo's arithmetic for him last night? . . . Oh, the cook. Fine. Because you know how hard they are in engineering school. And Juanita? Did she have her piano lesson? . . . Nothing new? Any mail? . . . Yes, I think so. This afternoon, I imagine. . . . No, no, I haven't had breakfast yet. A glass of orange juice. . . . No, don't worry. I'll stay on my diet. . . . Well, if I can't, I'll have them change it. . . . No, don't worry. Give the children a kiss. Good-bye. . . . Yes, another one for you. Good-bye. (*He hangs up.* AUNT CAROLINA *and* UNCLE GERARD *have been hanging on to every word, exchanging glances.*) It was my wife.
AUNT CAROLINA   She seems very nice.
THE BUYER   Oh, did you hear her?
AUNT CAROLINA   No, but we could tell from what you were saying.
UNCLE GERARD   Well, shall we have breakfast?
AUNT CAROLINA   Whenever you wish.
UNCLE GERARD (*to* THE BUYER.)   Shall we go?
He points to the door at right. He starts toward it and BEATRIZ *appears at left. She is wearing a simple but elegant dress as always. Repeating the game of not seeing the other characters, she walks resolutely to the telephone. She takes it and dials a number and waits.* THE BUYER *stops when he sees that* UNCLE

GERARD *is not following him. He looks at* THE
COUPLE. UNCLE GERARD *makes a sign to him to wait.*
AUNT CAROLINA Let's listen to the conversation.
BEATRIZ (*on the phone.*) Hello, Julia darling. How
 are you? . . . I couldn't have a drink with you
 because Eugene suddenly showed up. When I
 least expected him. . . . Yes, he'd come by car.
 . . . Very well, yes. But you don't know what an
 annoyance. He had to go away after lunch to
 Arenas de San Pedro. On an urgent business matter about some lumber. . . . Oh, he didn't remember it. But a gentleman that we've had here
 on a visit since yesterday reminded him. Aunt
 and Uncle insisted that he not let such an important matter out of his hands. You know how
 interested they are. . . . Eugene? Oh, he didn't
 have the slightest desire to go. . . . Of course
 not. Away from me for eight days. The first time
 since we've been married. . . . Well, what did
 you expect him to do? It was a business matter.
 . . . Yes, I told you. He left during the afternoon. (AUNT CAROLINA *and* UNCLE GERARD *look at
 each other satisfied.*) But he's coming back today. . . . (THE COUPLE *and* THE BUYER *look at
 each other surprised.*) Yes, he called me last night
 —at one thirty. . . . Yes, I suppose it was from
 Arenas de San Pedro because you could hear
 voices and an orchestra and Josephine Baker was
 singing. . . . Well, dear, the usual. He said he
 can't live without me. Poor thing. And as soon as
 he buys those pine trees, he's coming back here.
 I hold him not to buy them. Where do you think
 we're going to put six hundred tons of wood in
 this house—with the guest room occupied? And

I hope our gentleman visitor doesn't invent any more business matters for him to attend to outside Madrid—because I'm not going to let him leave. . . . (AUNT CAROLINA, UNCLE GERARD, *and* THE BUYER *look at each other again, amazed*.) Yes, darling. Since he's come back from Barcelona, I'm happier than ever. These eight days have seemed like ten years to me. . . . Who? . . . What man? I never told you that any man followed me. . . . No, dear. You must be mistaken. It must have been Victoria—who has that mania. No man ever followed me! Except one. When I was in school. There's only one man for me and that's Eugene. There'll never be another. Happiness only occurs once in life. . . . You ask how I know it's happiness. Well, for the fact that it would be all the same to me even if he weren't my husband. If he were yours, for example. Well, dear, maybe not yours—I never liked him. But some other friend's. You see how lucky I am— to love a man madly and also be married to him. . . . No, dear—that only happens in novels. If they end happily, they don't give them literary prizes. . . . Yes, I mean it. Without him, I'd die or do something insane because, although madness doesn't go very well with my personality, I'm sure I would be capable of something very spectacular if I lost him. Well, I'll let you go. I have no idea what time he'll be back from Arenas de San Pedro. I'm terribly impatient. Good-bye, Julia. . . . What's that? . . . I'll call you then. . . . (*She hangs up. She turns toward* AUNT CAROLINA, UNCLE GERARD, *and* THE BUYER.) Oh, good morning. (*To* THE BUYER.) Did you rest well?

THE BUYER   Yes, indeed.

BEATRIZ   Did Eugene's pajamas fit you?

THE BUYER   Fine.

BEATRIZ   You didn't get cold?

THE BUYER   Far from it.

BEATRIZ   (*as if reproaching him.*) And my poor darling—so near the mountains. And all that dangerous wildlife. . . . I've cancelled my appointment with the dressmaker this morning since I'm going to wait for Eugene.

AUNT CAROLINA   But is he coming back today?

BEATRIZ   Why, of course. He's not going to spend his life out there acting silly. I have to fix up a room for him here, so that he can work close to me.

AUNT CAROLINA   Eugene?

BEATRIZ   Oh, you didn't know? He wanted to give me a surprise.

UNCLE GERARD   Another one?

BEATRIZ   He's become an architect in the eight days he was in Barcelona.

THE BUYER   In eight days?

BEATRIZ   You don't know him. He's terribly clever. And since he didn't go out of the hotel at night . . . (*To* UNCLE GERARD.) Do you remember when he fixed the office door that was stuck? We were still going together. And that was what caused you to give your consent.

UNCLE GERARD   And where have you thought about making room for him?

BEATRIZ   In your office.

UNCLE GERARD   (*alarmed.*) In my office?

BEATRIZ   Yes—throwing out everything that's in the way.

UNCLE GERARD (*indignant.*) There's nothing in the way!

AUNT CAROLINA (*intervening.*) Well, just until he starts to get commissions.

BEATRIZ   But he already has I don't know how many. People must have found out and all at once . . . even a movie theatre. . . . We can have free admission. We can say we're the family of the architect. (*To* THE BUYER.) Whenever you'd like to go, just let us know.

THE BUYER (*with little enthusiasm.*) It depends on the picture.

BEATRIZ (*to* UNCLE GERARD.) A few things can go in the closet, and some more in the attic. (*Before* UNCLE GERARD *can protest.*) It's decided. I don't want him to be away from me a moment.

AUNT CAROLINA   But he'll have to go out to see the construction!

BEATRIZ   I'll go with him.

AUNT CAROLINA   You might get lost.

UNCLE GERARD   To the movie theatre, too?

BEATRIZ   There, especially. Those Hollywood stars are very clever. They'll probably try to get him away from me. Just let them try it. Metro-Goldwyn-Mayer will have to pass over my body.

AUNT CAROLINA (*frightened.*) No, for heaven's sake. Not that. They have a lion.

BEATRIZ (*embracing* AUNT CAROLINA.) Oh, Aunt, how happy I am. More than ever.

AUNT CAROLINA   Really, my dear?

BEATRIZ   So much that it frightens me. At times I think it might not be real.

UNCLE GERARD Oh, don't worry about that.

BEATRIZ (*to* AUNT CAROLINA.) Aren't you dressing up today?

AUNT CAROLINA Yes, I was just on my way.

BEATRIZ Who is it to be?

AUNT CAROLINA The international spy.

BEATRIZ (*to* THE BUYER.) Marvelous. Don't miss this one. (*To* AUNT CAROLINA.) I'll warn Eugene about you.

AUNT CAROLINA If I can get a little secret out of him . . .

BEATRIZ You just be careful. Don't do him any damage when you're getting it out of him. (*She exits at left, as if everything were perfectly normal. The other characters stand for a moment without being able to utter a word.*)

AUNT CAROLINA (*to* UNCLE GERARD.) Did you hear that?

UNCLE GERARD Yes, I heard everything she said. She's happier than ever.

AUNT CAROLINA Even happiness has a limit. She's taken over your office.

UNCLE GERARD (*with a motion.*) My office must not be an obstacle.

AUNT CAROLINA But, don't you realize that she plans to keep that man here?

UNCLE GERARD (*concerned.*) Yes. What could we do?

THE BUYER (*suggesting timidly.*) Perhaps start with breakfast.

UNCLE GERARD You're right. These problems can be handled best with a napkin in hand. Let's go.

They exit at right. AUNT CAROLINA *remains silent a few moments, worried. Then* EMILIA *enters at left.*

She is bringing a hat which is out of style with a veil, a silk scarf, and a large purse.

EMILIA This is for Madam, from Miss Beatriz.

AUNT CAROLINA (*returning to reality.*) Oh yes, thank you. (*She takes the purse from* EMILIA's *hands. Before slinging it over her shoulder she asks.*) Is everything inside?

EMILIA I wouldn't know, madam.

AUNT CAROLINA (*opens the purse and takes from it several objects which she places upon the table.*) Cigarette holder, secret codes . . . the revolver . . . the camera . . .

EMILIA My, it's awfully tiny.

AUNT CAROLINA Microfilm . . . for the documents, the maps, the formulas . . . (*She looks for something in the purse which she does not find.*) The narcotic is missing. . . .

EMILIA Doesn't Madam remember that she used it up last week? When she put the postman to sleep . . . to find out what was in a certified letter that he was bringing for the people on the second floor.

AUNT CAROLINA (*worried.*) That's true. I don't know how I'm going to work without a narcotic. . . . (*She places everything in the purse again.*)

EMILIA Does Madam wish something more?

AUNT CAROLINA Nothing else, thank you. (EMILIA *exits left.* AUNT CAROLINA *without the slightest desire to put on her disguise, behaving like a person who is undertaking a difficult duty, takes the hat and puts it on in front of the mirror. She puts the scarf over her shoulders and takes the bag. She looks at herself in the mirror. She decides that everything is correct. She sighs. From*

the left CARMEN *enters through the rear doorway,
bringing two suitcases covered with stickers from
steamships and hotels. She crosses the stage and*
AUNT CAROLINA *turns around when she hears her
pass by.*) Where are you going with those?

CARMEN (*stopping.*) To Master Eugene's room.

AUNT CAROLINA Master who?

CARMEN Master Eugene—they're his suitcases.

AUNT CAROLINA Who brought them?

CARMEN He, himself. He says that now he is coming up with the rest. (*She continues toward the
door at left.*)

AUNT CAROLINA (*in an outburst.*) Put down those
suitcases!

CARMEN (*frightened.*) Where?

AUNT CAROLINA (*in the same tone.*) Right there!

CARMEN But, Miss Beatriz told me that when he
arrived——

AUNT CAROLINA Don't pay any attention. (CARMEN
*has no choice but to put the suitcases down on
the floor.*)

CARMEN They're going to be in the way here. . . .

AUNT CAROLINA Don't worry about that. . . .
They won't be there that long!

CARMEN (*obeying.*) Very well, madam. (*She turns
toward the door at rear and stops when she gets
there, looking toward the left.*) Master Eugene
is here. Shall I wait just in case?

AUNT CAROLINA (*with the resolution of a matador
who has just challenged the bull.*) Everybody
out!

CARMEN *without understanding completely but impressed by* AUNT CAROLINA'*s tone awaits the arrival
of* VILLALBA. VILLALBA *comes in without a coat and*

*without a hat. He is carrying a briefcase of docu-
ments and a large box of drawing instruments. Under his arm a long roll of drafting paper and rulers.*

VILLALBA (*to* CARMEN.)　Will you tell your mistress
that I'm here?

AUNT CAROLINA (*to* CARMEN.)　You won't tell your
mistress anything!

VILLALBA (*who now realizes that* AUNT CAROLINA *is
there, and speaks very cordially.*)　Ah, good
morning, Lady Agatha. . . . Then I'll go tell
her. (*He starts to the door at left.*)

AUNT CAROLINA (*dryly, to* VILLALBA.)　I'm not Lady
Agatha, and that is not the way. . . . (*To* CAR-
MEN, *indicating with a gesture that she leave.*)
And you . . .

CARMEN　Yes, madam. (*She exits, upstage right.*)

VILLALBA (*to* AUNT CAROLINA, *smiling.*)　I beg your
pardon. But since I see you like this . . .

AUNT CAROLINA (*clearing things up without the
slightest suggestion of humor.*)　International
spy.

VILLALBA (*gaily.*)　Ah, then I should be very careful of what I say. . . .

AUNT CAROLINA (*with a warning tone.*)　And even
more careful about what you do.

VILLALBA (*noticing his baggage.*)　Are my suitcases
still there?

AUNT CAROLINA　I was going to throw them over
the balcony when you got here—I didn't have
time.

VILLALBA (*looking for a place to put down what he's
carrying.*)　With your permission.

AUNT CAROLINA　Don't unload, because you're leaving right now.

VILLALBA Me? To the country again?

AUNT CAROLINA *(indicating the door at left.)* Any direction you want, except that one.

VILLALBA Without speaking to Beatriz?

AUNT CAROLINA Without even seeing her.

VILLALBA Is that her desire?

AUNT CAROLINA No, it's my desire. And I think it's sufficiently clear.

VILLALBA Beatriz is an adult, isn't she?

AUNT CAROLINA For a long time as far as her identity card is concerned. But in life—it's not the same, do you understand?

VILLALBA Partly.

AUNT CAROLINA *(with determination.)* Shall we speak man-to-man?

VILLALBA Standing up?

AUNT CAROLINA It's better, since you're going down those steps.

VILLALBA Head over heels?

AUNT CAROLINA If we were in the war of 1914, I'd say no. I still hadn't participated in sports then.

VILLALBA What war are we in now?

AUNT CAROLINA The war of nerves.

VILLALBA *(willing to listen.)* Go ahead.

AUNT CAROLINA I shall. *(She opens her purse, takes out a long cigarette holder, places it between her teeth, and keeps on searching. Finally, she finds a cigarette, which she puts in the holder. VILLALBA takes a lighter from his pocket and offers her a light.)* Don't bother. It's plastic and full of menthol. The real ones give me a cough. *(She handles the cigarette holder with the air of a femme fatale.)* Well, let's get down to business. Because you're in a hurry.

VILLALBA   Yes, but not to go. . . .

AUNT CAROLINA   Look here, my good man. . . . Unlike you and me, my niece, Beatriz, is not in her right mind. . . . (*She plays with the cigarette holder as if she were smoking.* VILLALBA, *when he looks at her, cannot repress a smile.*) Don't look at me that way 'cause I'm not crazy. . . . It's the effect of the role I'm playing. Don't believe that I'm out of my head just because you see me going around dressed up like a grotesque thing.

VILLALBA   I haven't said anything.

AUNT CAROLINA   No, you haven't said anything because one can see from those stickers that you've traveled a great deal and travel educates. But I, this way, or as an ancient Greek, am in complete command of my faculties. So we can speak frankly. How much?

VILLALBA (*amazed.*)   How much what? (AUNT CAROLINA *rubs her index finger and thumb together indicating money.*) What's that? Do you think that I've come for your niece's money?

AUNT CAROLINA   No, but I do think you'll leave for mine. You're not going to tell me that you cannot live without Beatriz?

VILLALBA   Up to this point, it appears that I can't live with her.

AUNT CAROLINA   That is what I am determined to sustain. And I can, if it's necessary, count on reinforcements.

VILLALBA   Is yesterday's gentleman still here?

AUNT CAROLINA   Nobody has deserted. You'll see. Ten years ago, my niece went out of her head and somebody has to think for her.

VILLALBA   About what?

AUNT CAROLINA   About being a married woman.

VILLALBA   She hasn't left any doubt about that. And furthermore, she's madly in love with her husband.

AUNT CAROLINA   Madly! That's the serious part. It can't seem right to you.

VILLALBA   Why not?

AUNT CAROLINA   Because you're not her husband.

VILLALBA   It amounts to the same thing.

AUNT CAROLINA   To what thing?

VILLALBA   I mean, that as long as she believes that I'm her husband . . .

AUNT CAROLINA   You came in a car, didn't you?

VILLALBA   She's the one who——

AUNT CAROLINA   Yes, I know—the usual story. In these affairs, you men try to make yourselves look innocent. But be careful, for we women know how to type now. Well, I don't, but some of them do. You surely can't have any illusions about my niece's love? It's not directed to you.

VILLALBA   Madam, when a man at my age finds himself an object of love he doesn't stop to think if it's really directed to him or not.

AUNT CAROLINA   One day she's going to realize that you aren't Eugene.

VILLALBA   That day I'll stop being Eugene automatically. . . . I'll say that I got off at the wrong floor.

AUNT CAROLINA   Beatriz has a blindfold over her eyes. It keeps her from seeing clearly.

VILLALBA   That blindfold can also be love.

AUNT CAROLINA   Don't be so vulgar. You're simply taking advantage of her condition.

VILLALBA   I'm not taking advantage of anything.

She says that I'm her husband—I'm only going along with her.

AUNT CAROLINA   You're going along with her madness.

VILLALBA   As you will. Neither more nor less than you're doing. Or perhaps you would be dressed up that way even if she weren't . . . ? (AUNT CAROLINA *is silent.*) Aren't you all playing at the same game?

AUNT CAROLINA   No, my good man. Your game is much more dangerous. . . . Of course, since you have nothing to lose.

VILLALBA   Who says not? How about the day when the blindfold falls from her eyes?

AUNT CAROLINA   Are you in love with Beatriz?

VILLALBA   (*sincerely.*)   I don't know.

AUNT CAROLINA   Ah. . . .

VILLALBA   I don't know, yet. . . .

AUNT CAROLINA   For you it is only an adventure. . . .

VILLALBA   If I told you that yesterday, when I came up to this apartment for the first time, I was considering anything else, I would be lying. . . . But since then I've done a lot of thinking.

AUNT CAROLINA   Last night?

VILLALBA   Yes.

AUNT CAROLINA   (*with scorn.*)   In a cabaret?

VILLALBA   Did you see me?

AUNT CAROLINA   Sir! . . .

VILLALBA   Did you send your husband?

AUNT CAROLINA   I never send my husband anywhere except occasionally to the Bank of Spain.

VILLALBA   I went because I was alone.

AUNT CAROLINA A good place to find companionship. You probably go every night.

VILLALBA Last night may have been the last. Do
you understand?

AUNT CAROLINA (*resisting his sincere words.*) No,
I don't want to understand. Ten years have not
passed for this. You must not deceive her.

VILLALBA Then do you want me to tell her the
truth?

AUNT CAROLINA I want you to leave right now.

VILLALBA Without fearing the consequences?
(AUNT CAROLINA *is silent again.*) She thinks she's
found Eugene again. What would happen after
I leave? What would her fancy lead her to next?
Only to an innocent trip to the airport every
morning? (AUNT CAROLINA *remains silent.*) You
wouldn't have enough disguises then. (*There's a
short silence, which* BEATRIZ's *voice breaks.*)

BEATRIZ (*from within.*) Eugene?

AUNT CAROLINA (*begging.*) Please?

VILLALBA (*decided.*) No. Not now. (BEATRIZ *enters
at left.*)

BEATRIZ Eugene. Why didn't you come in to see
me the very moment you got back from that
town?

VILLALBA It was only a moment ago.

BEATRIZ (*for* AUNT CAROLINA's *benefit.*) Be careful
with that one—she'll try to rob you of your plans.
Give them to me to keep. (*She takes the roll of
paper and the rulers from* VILLALBA.) And this,
too, just in case. Your study is all ready. (*She
notices the suitcases that are on the floor.*) Well,
what is your baggage doing here? (*She goes to*

the doorway and calls.) Carmen, come get these bags. (*She begins to look at the suitcases.*) All those stickers. Did we go to so many places on our honeymoon? (CARMEN *appears in the doorway at rear.*) Carmen, carry these suitcases to my husband's bedroom. (*To* VILLALBA.) Is there nothing more?

CARMEN   One large suitcase.

VILLALBA (*explaining.*)   With some suits. . . .

AUNT CAROLINA (*to* VILLALBA.)   Did you bring your summer clothing?

BEATRIZ (*to* CARMEN.)   Hang them in the wardrobe.

CARMEN   All the space is taken.

BEATRIZ   Well, take out the other suits. (*To* VILLALBA.) You're not going to wear them, are you? (*To* CARMEN.) Put the new ones in their place.

AUNT CAROLINA   Wait, my dear. What hurry is there?

BEATRIZ   Why not?

AUNT CAROLINA   He may need them at any moment.

BEATRIZ   In the wardrobe they won't get wrinkled. (*To* CARMEN.) Go on. (*For* AUNT CAROLINA's *benefit.*) And don't let that woman get close to you. She may try sabotage. (CARMEN *takes the suitcases and exits with them at left. To* VILLALBA *for* AUNT CAROLINA's *benefit.*) She must have had some ulterior motive for keeping you here. Say no to everything she asks. (*To* AUNT CAROLINA.) Listen, madam, why don't you go spy on the people in the dining room for a while? (*Since* AUNT CAROLINA *resists a little, she insists.*) Go on, darling.

AUNT CAROLINA (*giving in.*) I'm going.

BEATRIZ (*taking the briefcase from* VILLALBA's *hand.*)
Here, you look as if you're just on a visit. (*She
goes to the table to leave the briefcase.* AUNT
CAROLINA *takes advantage of this to speak in a
low voice to* VILLALBA *before leaving.*)

AUNT CAROLINA Don't think that I'm a woman
who's alone and helpless or that we've remained
behind in the arms race. (*She exits with dignity
at right.*)

BEATRIZ What was she saying to you?

VILLALBA Nothing.

BEATRIZ I can imagine. Don't pay any attention
to her. Don't pay any attention to anyone. In
this house, everybody's crazy, you know. That's
why I wanted you to come back so badly . . .
so that you and I could go far away together.
Another honeymoon like the first one. (*Tenderly.*)
Do you remember?

VILLALBA (*who can't remember.*) Yes.

BEATRIZ (*dreaming.*)   The canals . . .

VILLALBA (*taking advantage of the opportunity.*)
Venice!

BEATRIZ The snow . . .

VILLALBA (*trying again.*)   Switzerland.

BEATRIZ (*correcting him.*)   The Pyrenees, love.

VILLALBA Ah, yes. That's right.

BEATRIZ The coast . . .

VILLALBA (*about to say the Riviera.*) Uh, yes . . .
the coast.

BEATRIZ You don't remember anything.

VILLALBA But I do, dear. It's just that . . .

BEATRIZ It doesn't matter. People live on memories when they're not really living at all. Now

everything is going to be new. As if we'd only just met each other yesterday. What matters is that each new hour begins, and we have life before us. I'll bet that you haven't even thought of me the last few days.

VILLALBA Rather than thinking of you, I was dreaming of you.

BEATRIZ That's even better. I also dreamed of you in order not to stop loving you. So that while still being the same man you would seem like another to me. Even the same kiss grows tiring. It ends up being mechanical, don't you think?

VILLALBA (*succumbing.*) I shall always have a new one invented just for you.

BEATRIZ It doesn't matter that you took those lines from the movies. But don't stop. I've always forgotten you every night just to find you anew each morning. Do you know what we're going to do?

VILLALBA Tell me.

BEATRIZ Go right this minute to a travel agency. I want exactly the same itinerary we had a year ago. As a challenge to the landscapes, to the cathedrals, to the hotel clerks, to the airline hostesses. (*As if she were seeing it all.*) Did you think that we wouldn't come back, like the others? That our love was going to get lukewarm when we'd written the final postcards, when we had exchanged the francs that were left over? (*As if she were in the lobby of the hotel.*) The same room, please, if possible. So that the mirrors will learn . . . so that the chambermaid will remember when she puts out our clothes at night which side I prefer to sleep on—with my

head on your heart. . . . The same gondola—
the gondolier was named Scarpa. (*As if she were
speaking with the gondolier.*) Do you see how
we've come back? Did you really think that one
day I'd come back alone, like an old English
spinster? Go ahead and sing if you wish. It
doesn't matter if your song is ordinary. We need
very little to make us think of love. (*She takes*
VILLALBA'*s hands but goes on talking to the
gondolier.*) Don't look. You already know. (*She
looks at* VILLALBA *tenderly.*) You see, I did the
right thing to tear up all the snapshots while
you were away—even the memories of happy
hours grow old if we don't renew them. You
wouldn't love me now with that hat which
seemed to be eternal at the time. Now, although
it's the same bridge, although it's the same Patio
of the Lions, although it's the same pigeon that
we fed in the Plaza of St. Mark . . . (*With a
sudden doubt.*) How many years do pigeons live?

VILLALBA   Like the swallows of the balcony of
Verona . . . like the nightingales in Andalucia
. . . like all the birds who are witnesses of love,
they are eternal.

BEATRIZ   Where did you read all that?

VILLALBA   In your eyes.

BEATRIZ (*enchanted.*) Barcelona agreed with you.
You lie much better than you did.

VILLALBA   You think I'm lying?

BEATRIZ   No, I believe you. I'm certain. And it
pleases me. Rest assured. Everything that doesn't
mean "I love you" is merely polite talk for passing the evening.

VILLALBA   Do you want me to say that to you?

BEATRIZ   No, not now. I want you to see your study. I really hated to take out the wedding photograph of Uncle Gerard with the spy, so I left it. Don't look at it when you're making your plans because you may turn out another Spanish church. Come along. (*She takes him by the hand.*) I've left a few feminine touches because I intend to go there during the afternoons to knit you a yellow sweater.

VILLALBA (*alarmed.*)   Yellow?

BEATRIZ   Of course. The color of one of those fevers. . . .

She leads him off through the door at left. There's no one onstage for a moment, then AUNT CAROLINA *peeps in at right. On making sure there is no one there, she enters. She goes to the door at left, where she listens. She turns around and when she reaches the center of the stage, she puts two fingers in her mouth and gives a strident whistle. A moment later from the right* UNCLE GERARD *and* THE BUYER *appear smoking some magnificent cigars.*

UNCLE GERARD   All clear?

AUNT CAROLINA   I hope so.

UNCLE GERARD   Where are they?

AUNT CAROLINA   In the ruins of your office.

UNCLE GERARD (*calmed.*)   Things could be worse.

AUNT CAROLINA   Yes, but I'm still uneasy. (*To* THE BUYER.) You are, too, aren't you?

THE BUYER (*sincerely.*)   Well, to tell the truth, I am. When I tell all this to my wife!

UNCLE GERARD   You think there's imminent danger?

AUNT CAROLINA   Anything can happen. I told you that this architect doesn't listen to reason.

UNCLE GERARD I don't think he'd dare go too far.

AUNT CAROLINA And what about her? Are we sure about her?

THE BUYER (*convinced.*) Of course, of course.

AUNT CAROLINA (*nervous; to* THE BUYER.) Don't agree with everything. Take the opposite opinion sometime.

THE BUYER Why?

AUNT CAROLINA Because that always adds variety. You know, I can't get the bathroom out of my mind.

UNCLE GERARD (*concerned.*) Yes, it is a danger zone.

THE BUYER (*in order to disagree for a change.*) Oh, I don't think so. . . .

AUNT CAROLINA (*correcting him.*) Oh, but it is, man. . . . Come, now.

UNCLE GERARD (*worried.*) He takes a shower at the slightest provocation.

AUNT CAROLINA He must be from a seaport. (*Thinking.*) If we could do something to the water pipes.

UNCLE GERARD How?

AUNT CAROLINA This friend of yours could say that he's a plumber and carry off all the faucets to fix them at his place. . . .

THE BUYER (*doubting.*) But what would I do without the right costume?

UNCLE GERARD And without the tools?

THE BUYER And without a boy apprentice?

AUNT CAROLINA The boy wouldn't be too difficult . . . and the tools. Didn't you buy some once?

UNCLE GERARD Those were for something else.

AUNT CAROLINA   What would she know about it?

THE BUYER (*doubting.*)   Do you think she's going to believe that I——

AUNT CAROLINA   Of course she would. The good thing about her condition is that you can tell her it's daytime and she doesn't object.

THE BUYER   But it is daytime.

UNCLE GERARD   But what about him?

AUNT CAROLINA   Oh, I think he has reasons to be circumspect.

EMILIA *enters upstage left.*

EMILIA   Madam?

AUNT CAROLINA   Yes, what is it?

EMILIA (*announcing.*)   Miss Julia.

UNCLE GERARD (*alarmed.*)   What's that?

AUNT CAROLINA   What Miss Julia?

EMILIA   The friend of your niece. (AUNT CAROLINA *and* UNCLE GERARD *look at each other, amazed.*)

AUNT CAROLINA (*trying to be calm.*)   Emilia, I raised your salary to three hundred and fifty pesetas on the condition that whatever you saw in this house, you would not start acting the way we do.

UNCLE GERARD (*clearing things up for* THE BUYER.*)   Julia doesn't exist. She's an imaginary character.

EMILIA   Well, she's wearing a fur coat.

UNCLE GERARD   Do you see what a hallucination can be? A fur coat on a day like this!

AUNT CAROLINA   Don't be silly, Gerard. This makes me suspect that we're really dealing with a woman of flesh and blood.

EMILIA   There's no doubt of that, madam.

AUNT CAROLINA (*to* EMILIA.*)   Have her come in.

EMILIA Yes, madam. (EMILIA *exits upstage left.*)

AUNT CAROLINA Well, we'll see.

UNCLE GERARD Maybe, she's coming to see Beatriz.

AUNT CAROLINA That's what we're going to see right now. (*To* THE BUYER.) And no back talk from you!

THE BUYER Madam, you make it difficult for a person.

EMILIA *appears at left and shows* HENRIETTA *in. She is a woman who is under thirty, according to her mathematics. She's quite good-looking, but rather overdressed. She's wearing a stupendous fur coat.*

HENRIETTA (*coming in.*) Good morning.

AUNT CAROLINA Do come in. (EMILIA *exits upstage right.*)

HENRIETTA (*resolutely.*) You must be Aunt Carolina. (AUNT CAROLINA, *taken aback, doesn't answer.*)

UNCLE GERARD (*intervening kindly.*) None other.

HENRIETTA (*turning to* UNCLE GERARD.) And you're Uncle Gerard.

AUNT CAROLINA (*dryly.*) Yes.

HENRIETTA And this gentleman?

UNCLE GERARD A good friend—we still don't know what his name is.

AUNT CAROLINA Because he hasn't told us.

THE BUYER (*ready to remedy his oversight.*) Well——

UNCLE GERARD (*to* THE BUYER.) Leave it for now. What difference does it make? We're not going to squabble over that.

AUNT CAROLINA (*not so cordially.*) Well, now that you know who we are, we still don't have——

UNCLE GERARD (*trying to be more courteous.*)   Ah, we should like . . .

AUNT CAROLINA   . . . to know who you are.

HENRIETTA   Well, I . . . I'm Julia.

AUNT CAROLINA (*distrustful.*)   Look me in the eye.

UNCLE GERARD   Carolina!

AUNT CAROLINA   I mean it! These days you don't know what to believe.

UNCLE GERARD (*to* HENRIETTA, *gently.*)   Your name can't be Julia.

HENRIETTA (*smiling.*)   No, sir.

AUNT CAROLINA   Ah, at last.

THE BUYER (*naively.*)   In this house, nobody's name is what he says it is anyway. . . .

AUNT CAROLINA (*severely.*)   Would you be quiet?

HENRIETTA   My name is . . . Henrietta.

UNCLE GERARD   Oh, that's not so bad.

HENRIETTA   But you can call me Julia. Which is what Beatriz calls me. (*These words produce a painful silence.*)

UNCLE GERARD (*resolving the situation.*)   Do sit down, for heaven's sake.

HENRIETTA   Just for a minute. . . . (*She sits down, still wrapped in her fur coat.*)

UNCLE GERARD   Don't you want to take off your coat? It seems that . . .

HENRIETTA   No, thank you.

AUNT CAROLINA   Can we turn up the heat?

UNCLE GERARD (*intervening.*)   You just said that Beatriz . . .

HENRIETTA   Yes, she telephones me every day.

UNCLE GERARD   Well, uh . . . we know that.

AUNT CAROLINA   But, do you answer?

HENRIETTA   No, I don't.

UNCLE GERARD   Then what do you do?

HENRIETTA   I listen. Doesn't that seem to you sufficient?

THE BUYER   Without talking?

HENRIETTA   Does that surprise you?

THE BUYER   Well, yes—that a woman could be happy just listening to another woman.

AUNT CAROLINA   (*fearfully.*) And you've found out . . .

HENRIETTA   Everything. You see how I recognized you the moment I came in. I can even draw you a plan of the apartment.

AUNT CAROLINA   We already have one.

HENRIETTA   (*smiling.*) I'm not surprised. With an architect in the house! (AUNT CAROLINA *and* UNCLE GERARD *look at each other.*)

AUNT CAROLINA   (*very nervous.*) Well, madam. Make your choice. Either you speak straightforward or I shall throw some kind of fit.

HENRIETTA   Oh, I'll speak. Just be comfortable. (*A pause.*) One day they called me to the phone —I always have a phone handy to take care of my clientele.

AUNT CAROLINA   (*with a sudden suspicion.*) What clientele?

HENRIETTA   (*smiling.*) I have a beauty salon.

AUNT CAROLINA   Oh, forgive me.

HENRIETTA   Why don't you come by one day? How about tomorrow?

AUNT CAROLINA   (*alarmed.*) Do you think it's a desperate case? A matter of life or death?

UNCLE GERARD   (*interested.*) Go on, please.

THE BUYER   Yes, don't pay her any attention.

HENRIETTA   Well, I picked up the receiver . . .

and a woman's voice, after calling me Julia, began to speak. I was about to tell her that she'd gotten a wrong number but the plot was already beginning to interest me. I didn't even breathe. She paused occasionally and answered things that I hadn't even said. And the story was very moving. She must have found such a discreet telephone number very convenient. One that didn't interrupt her at all. One that didn't hang up silently. So she called again. And I listened again. And so it went on for months.

AUNT CAROLINA   Do you think that's nice?

HENRIETTA   What?

AUNT CAROLINA   Listening in on a private life. It's not proper. The first thing you should have thought about was that you were dealing with an abnormal person.

HENRIETTA   Yes, it was the first thing I thought, naturally. Because it was the easiest. But if you knew what a desire there was in that voice to confess—a desire to empty her soul. . . . It was like a shipwrecked person—one of those who throws a message into the sea in a bottle without knowing whose hands it's going to reach. After all, why shouldn't I be Julia, the confidante, the silent friend for her words . . . ?

UNCLE GERARD   (*at the short silence, he speaks to* THE BUYER.)   Beautiful, isn't it?

THE BUYER   Yes. But I would have stopped at the sentence about the bottle. More effective.

AUNT CAROLINA   And then?

HENRIETTA   The story was being filled out every day. People were taking form. So I came to know all of you.

UNCLE GERARD Ah.

HENRIETTA You seemed so likable.

UNCLE GERARD You're very kind. (*To* AUNT CARO-LINA.) Why don't you thank her, dear?

AUNT CAROLINA Just wait a moment. Don't get so friendly with this woman—I know you!

UNCLE GERARD (*embarrassed.*) Oh, for heaven's sake, Carolina. What will Julia think?

AUNT CAROLINA It doesn't matter what she thinks. And don't call her Julia.

UNCLE GERARD (*to* THE BUYER.) Do you hear that?

THE BUYER Sure, sure.

AUNT CAROLINA Don't look for aid from your chum, for I've noticed that he seems to like the lady a little himself. (*To* HENRIETTA.) All men are revolting when in the presence of a woman who isn't . . .

HENRIETTA (*still smiling.*) Well, thank you.

AUNT CAROLINA Don't mention it. Things are the way they are. Now tell me—did you limit yourself just to listening? Or did you make some investigations of your own?

HENRIETTA (*smiling.*) I see that the feminine heart has no secrets for you. . . .

AUNT CAROLINA No, madam. I've taken after my father.

HENRIETTA I did find out a few things. Once I got the telephone number and address, the other was simple. Madrid is really very small. And in a beauty salon, women talk.

AUNT CAROLINA In order not to waste their time completely.

HENRIETTA I reconstructed the story with all its details—and that's why I've come.

AUNT CAROLINA   With a bill in hand.

HENRIETTA   I don't understand.

AUNT CAROLINA   I mean that you plan to black-mail us.

UNCLE GERARD (*embarrassed.*)   Woman, you're impossible today.

AUNT CAROLINA   I know what I'm talking about.

HENRIETTA (*still smiling.*)   Nothing like that, madam.

AUNT CAROLINA   Then you've come for curiosity's sake—to meet Beatriz's husband.

HENRIETTA   Wrong again. I know that he isn't her husband.

THE BUYER (*amazed.*)   Well, now.

AUNT CAROLINA (*a bit disconcerted.*)   Then have you come for the pleasure of telling us that you know as much as we know?

HENRIETTA (*calmly.*)   For the pleasure of telling you I know something you *don't* know.

THE BUYER   My goodness!

AUNT CAROLINA   More than we? Why I'll bet you don't know all the names of the Kings of Spain.

HENRIETTA (*without losing her calm.*)   Not all of them. (*With a doubt.*) Just by chance, was one of them called Eugene? (*The name Eugene has the immediate virtue of putting* AUNT CAROLINA *on guard, and of making* THE BUYER *more interested.*)

AUNT CAROLINA   Eugene?

THE BUYER (*delighted.*)   This is just like being in a theatre.

AUNT CAROLINA (*turning to him.*)   Can you see all right or shall I take off my hat?

HENRIETTA   Does that name sound familiar?

AUNT CAROLINA   It sounds unpleasant.

HENRIETTA   I know where Eugene is.

AUNT CAROLINA   Very far?

HENRIETTA   It depends on how you look at it. These days there are no distances.

UNCLE GERARD   Well do tell us, Henrietta.

AUNT CAROLINA (*to* UNCLE GERARD.)   Don't call her Henrietta in front of me.

UNCLE GERARD   I can't use that name either?

AUNT CAROLINA (*to* HENRIETTA.)   Is he abroad?

HENRIETTA   In Madrid!

AUNT CAROLINA   Ah. . . .

UNCLE GERARD   Is he well?

HENRIETTA   He's managing.

AUNT CAROLINA   How?

HENRIETTA   Not too well.

AUNT CAROLINA (*feeling the sleeve of* HENRIETTA's *coat to determine its quality.*)   Well, apparently you aren't doing too badly. In business of course.

HENRIETTA   No, I can't complain. I have a capitalist backer.

UNCLE GERARD   Who is very generous. . . .

HENRIETTA   Well, most of the time.

UNCLE GERARD   How is it that we haven't heard from Eugene?

HENRIETTA   He hasn't dared—the poor thing.

AUNT CAROLINA   The poor thing!

HENRIETTA   Furthermore, he's not well.

AUNT CAROLINA   You don't say. Thank goodness.

UNCLE GERARD (*to* HENRIETTA.)   What's wrong with him?

HENRIETTA   A very strange malady—he swallows air.

THE BUYER (*explaining.*)   Aerophagia.

UNCLE GERARD (*to* AUNT CAROLINA.)   Have you noticed he understands everything?

AUNT CAROLINA   Yes. (*To* THE BUYER.)   Do you know something that will take away the stains that stain removers leave on clothes?

UNCLE GERARD (*to* HENRIETTA.)   Do you know him?

HENRIETTA   Eugene? For a long time. I was a friend of Marichu's.

AUNT CAROLINA   Who's Marichu?

UNCLE GERARD (*to* AUNT CAROLINA.)   The model.

THE BUYER (*interested.*)   The one that went to Mallorca?

HENRIETTA   Yes. We used to work together for a designer.

AUNT CAROLINA   Are they still together?

HENRIETTA   No, she left him. She was aiming for something higher. She went off with a bullfighter.

AUNT CAROLINA   A minor one, of course.

HENRIETTA   It was several years ago.

AUNT CAROLINA (*with a sudden decision, to* HENRIETTA.)   How long will it take you to bring him here?

UNCLE GERARD (*alarmed.*)   Carolina!

AUNT CAROLINA   But don't you realize that the architect is still in there making his plans? (*To* HENRIETTA, *urgently.*) How long?

HENRIETTA   Well . . . not very long. I have a taxi downstairs.

AUNT CAROLINA   It's on us. Ten minutes?

HENRIETTA (*doubting.*)   I don't know. If he's dressed.

AUNT CAROLINA   Let him come as he is. Well, provided he doesn't attract too much attention.

UNCLE GERARD (*worried.*) It seems slightly mad to me.

AUNT CAROLINA Well, one thing more won't matter. (*To* HENRIETTA.) Will you, please?

HENRIETTA (*standing up.*) Yes, I'll go.

AUNT CAROLINA (*detaining her.*) Wait! (*She goes to a bell that is beside the doorway at rear. She rings and waits.*)

UNCLE GERARD I'm afraid of what you're up to, Carolina.

AUNT CAROLINA (*returning to center stage.*) Oh, I know.

CARMEN *appears in the doorway at rear.*

CARMEN Did Madam call?

AUNT CAROLINA Yes. Tell my niece to please come here for a moment.

CARMEN Yes, madam. (CARMEN *exits left.*)

AUNT CAROLINA Our friend Julia isn't going before she sees her. (*She takes off the hat and all the articles of her spy's disguise and throws them upon a chair.*)

UNCLE GERARD What are you doing?

AUNT CAROLINA Nothing. It's just that the Carnival of Rio de Janeiro has just ended. (*To* THE BUYER *who looks at her amazed.*) Is there something wrong?

THE BUYER (*frightened.*) No. But . . .

BEATRIZ *appears at left.*

BEATRIZ (*to* AUNT CAROLINA.) What do you want? (*Seeing there is someone in the room whom she doesn't know.*) Good morning.

AUNT CAROLINA Well, nothing. But your friend . . .

BEATRIZ What friend?

AUNT CAROLINA   Who do you suppose? Julia. Your dearest friend.

BEATRIZ (*going toward* HENRIETTA.)   But of course. Julia! It's just that in the dim light . . . How are you, darling? (*She kisses her affectionately.*)

HENRIETTA (*letting herself be kissed.*)   Fine, and you? (*After the kiss,* BEATRIZ *stands looking at* HENRIETTA *pensively.*)

BEATRIZ   My dearest friend. And the fact is . . . I've seen your face, some place. (*To* HENRIETTA, *very politely.*) Are you going to spend a few days?

HENRIETTA   I'm going right now.

BEATRIZ   But so soon?

AUNT CAROLINA   She had an urgent message. (*To* HENRIETTA.) Well, my dear, let's not keep her waiting.

BEATRIZ   Are you coming back?

HENRIETTA   Maybe. (*To the others.*) I'll see you shortly.

BEATRIZ   I'll go with you.

HENRIETTA   Don't bother.

BEATRIZ   The very idea—you're my dearest friend!

AUNT CAROLINA (*to* HENRIETTA.)   Good luck.

UNCLE GERARD   Yes, good luck. (*The two exit upstage left. To* AUNT CAROLINA.) I think we're going too far.

AUNT CAROLINA   It doesn't matter. You heard her say that she has a taxi.

UNCLE GERARD   But that man—in this house.

AUNT CAROLINA   It's better to have him in this place than the other one.

BEATRIZ *enters upstage left, trying to remember.*

BEATRIZ   Where did I know this intimate friend? (*To the rest.*) She's very nice, isn't she?

AUNT CAROLINA Yes, we were always eager to see her sometime.

BEATRIZ So was I. (*She starts to the door at left.*)

AUNT CAROLINA Listen, Beatriz . . . (BEATRIZ *stops.*) Will you listen to a few words?

BEATRIZ If they're not too long. Eugene is waiting for me to put ink on his drawing pen. (*To the others.*) He can't make a line without me.

AUNT CAROLINA (*persuasive and maternal.*) Look, my dear. There are times when we women suffer some strange hallucinations. I used to think it was because of the corsets. Now it must be the tobacco. The fact is, we sometimes confuse certain people with others.

BEATRIZ (*very interested.*) Oh, yes?

AUNT CAROLINA Take me, for example. One summer when I was a girl I got it into my head that my husband was an agent from the stock exchange who lived in front of our house. But, of course, when your uncle showed up——

BEATRIZ With a cane . . .

AUNT CAROLINA I realized my error at once. . . . Well, you might say that the blindfold fell from my eyes. . . .

BEATRIZ (*calmly.*) How fortunate. The man from the stock exchange could use it.

AUNT CAROLINA The same thing could happen to you just any day without your realizing it.

BEATRIZ (*without losing her calmness.*) Don't worry, Aunt. Those fantasies only happen to you. You've always been a little scatterbrained. . . . Forgive me, but . . . he's waiting for me. He says that if I don't give him a hand——

AUNT CAROLINA Be careful that he doesn't twist it.

BEATRIZ   He just drew a tower that was a little off scale but I told him not to worry because there's that one in Pisa which people like so much. (*She exits with the greatest naturalness through the door at left. The others watch her go, concerned.*)

UNCLE GERARD (*timidly.*)   I insist that it seems to me——

AUNT CAROLINA (*recognizing it.*)   Yes, it's dangerous, but there's no other way. The moment has come for heroic actions.

UNCLE GERARD   Are you sure she's going to recognize Eugene?

AUNT CAROLINA   Oh, my boy—how should I know?

THE BUYER   He'll probably be very changed.

AUNT CAROLINA   What nonsense. However much a man changes, he can't fool us completely after we've seen him in his undershirt.

UNCLE GERARD   And in case she does recognize him —after ten years, do you think she's going to throw her arms around his neck?

AUNT CAROLINA   Undoubtedly. Although it might possibly be to strangle him. But just in case, we'll be watching.

UNCLE GERARD   And Eugene? Will he come?

AUNT CAROLINA   Don't you suppose he sent that woman from the beauty salon to explore the terrain?

THE BUYER   Very clever.

AUNT CAROLINA (*extending her hand.*)   Thank you, my fellow.

EMILIA *enters upstage left.*

EMILIA   Madam?

AUNT CAROLINA   What is it?

EMILIA The woman who was here before has come back—with a gentleman.

AUNT CAROLINA (*eagerly.*)   Have them come in.

EMILIA If they can—because something seems to have happened to the gentleman in the elevator.

AUNT CAROLINA (*to* THE BUYER.) Please—you go. Because you're only an observer.

THE BUYER (*helpfully.*) Yes, madam, I'll go. (*He goes to the door at rear and exits at left.*)

EMILIA Maybe someone insulted him.

AUNT CAROLINA Impossible! Why we haven't even begun. Go and see if they need help. And get him here—even if it takes several trips.

EMILIA Yes, yes. . . . (*She exits left.* AUNT CAROLINA *and* UNCLE GERARD *look at each other nervously.*)

AUNT CAROLINA Courage, Gerard.

UNCLE GERARD Courage, Carolina.

They take each other's hand, ready to offer a united front. From the left, HENRIETTA, THE BUYER, *and* EMILIA *literally carry in* QUINTANA. *He is a man of less than forty years but old-looking and sick.*

THE BUYER (*directing the operation.*) Careful around this curve.

AUNT CAROLINA (*withdrawing from* UNCLE GERARD *and getting a chair ready.*) Here, bring him over here.

HENRIETTA (*leading* QUINTANA *to the chair, aided by* EMILIA *and* AUNT CAROLINA.) The occasion has been too much for him. When he gets excited, he loses his breath. (*They seat* QUINTANA *in the chair.*)

QUINTANA (*almost without voice.*) Thank you. (*With difficulty, he takes from his pocket a small glass bottle. He uncorks it and breathes deeply. The others stand around in suspense. He pulls himself together a bit. He looks around and notices* AUNT CAROLINA *and* UNCLE GERARD. *He keeps the bottle in his hand.*) Thank you very much.

UNCLE GERARD   Not at all, my boy.

AUNT CAROLINA   Do you feel better? (*Affirmative gesture from* QUINTANA, *but not very convincing.*)

HENRIETTA   It's just that there's too much smoke here.

AUNT CAROLINA (*to* UNCLE GERARD *and* THE BUYER.) Put out those cigars!

UNCLE GERARD (*rebelling.*)   No. He's been away for ten years living his own life and the day that I take a notion to light up a Havana . . . (*To* THE BUYER.) Stand firm.

AUNT CAROLINA   (*pleading.*)   Please . . . (UNCLE GERARD *and* THE BUYER *give in reluctantly. They put out their cigars in an ashtray.*)

UNCLE GERARD (*lamenting.*)   And after I'd nursed it so carefully.

From the left, BEATRIZ *and* VILLALBA *enter. General expectation.*

BEATRIZ   Well, we're off. (QUINTANA *who has sat up on seeing* BEATRIZ *come in feels bad again and almost passes out.*) What is wrong with this visitor? Is he sick? (*They all look at* BEATRIZ. HENRIETTA *has taken the bottle from* QUINTANA'S *hand and holds it to his nose.*)

HENRIETTA   But of course. . . . Now we have this——

BEATRIZ   Why my dear friend is here, too. (*To* HENRIETTA.) Is this your husband?

HENRIETTA No, woman. (*She wants to say, "He's yours."*)

BEATRIZ Forgive me. I thought . . . (*To* QUINTANA.) Are you feeling any better?

QUINTANA (*almost without voice.*) Yes.

BEATRIZ Well, I'm glad! Then we won't tire you any more. We're going, before the stationery store closes. Eugene needs an eraser. I told him that with a piece of bread he could erase wonderfully . . . but he says it has to be with rubber. So I'll go with him. So he won't have a pretext for going off with another woman and leaving me alone for ten years. (*To* VILLALBA, *taking him by the arm.*) Come along, handsome. (*To* QUINTANA.) I hope it's nothing serious. (*She leads* VILLALBA *toward the door at rear. The others are stupefied. To* VILLALBA, *along the way.*) Let's see if the travel agency is open. . . . (*Holding* VILLALBA's *arm, she turns around in the doorway and speaks to* AUNT CAROLINA.) We won't forget to buy you something while we're taking care of our affairs in Paris. (*She exits with* VILLALBA *upstage left. The others are unable to say a word.*) A very rapid curtain.

Act Three

In the same room, during the early hours of the afternoon. The scene has not changed at all. Even the articles that AUNT CAROLINA *left on the chair are still there. For a few moments there is no one onstage; then* UNCLE GERARD *and* THE BUYER *appear at right.* THE BUYER *is dressed as in the first act. They sit down on the sofa.* EMILIA *enters upstage right with a cup of something warm in her hand. She stirs it with a spoon as she moves toward the door at right.*

UNCLE GERARD (*to* EMILIA.) You can serve our coffee here.

EMILIA (*stopping.*) Madam says that there'll be no coffee today; that there are enough nerves already in this house and that if the gentleman wants to have coffee, let him go down to the bar on the corner and send us the bill. (EMILIA *exits at right.*)

UNCLE GERARD (*to* THE BUYER.) I don't advise it. Their coffee is detestable. The only strong thing about it is the price. But if you wish——

THE BUYER No, no. Thank you very much. (*With little enthusiasm.*) Just going out and crossing the street—it's so much trouble, isn't it? It's so comfortable here in the house.

UNCLE GERARD   You're a man after my own heart. People without imaginations are the ones who need to travel. I can imagine everything right here. I'm sure that as on postcards, one never sees the truth of things. Reality can be very uncomfortable. You have to see almost everything on foot and without a hat. And if it's ancient, it's certain to have a draft. And, of course, they always arrange for you to arrive in bad weather. I'm fed up with people saying the moment I've set foot in a city, "If only you'd come last week." (AUNT CAROLINA *and* HENRIETTA *enter at right; on seeing them come in.*) Well, do we have our man?

AUNT CAROLINA   We have two. That's the serious thing about it. The poor girl. Ten years without a husband—and now a pair of them.

THE BUYER   Yes. The world is very disorganized.

AUNT CAROLINA   Well, we have done everything possible to prevent this. Our play was very well worked out but it's like the theatre. When the author turns his back, the actors do what they please. (*To* UNCLE GERARD.) Have you had any news?

UNCLE GERARD   No, not since they called to tell us that it was a lovely afternoon and that they were stopping at a village inn to eat.

AUNT CAROLINA   (*to* THE BUYER.)   You can't tell me that a village inn isn't full of temptations.

UNCLE GERARD   (*to* THE BUYER.)   Don't disagree with her because we'll never hear the end of it. (*To* HENRIETTA.) Aren't you going to sit down?

HENRIETTA   Thank you, but I must leave.

UNCLE GERARD   So soon?

HENRIETTA   My establishment opens at four.

AUNT CAROLINA   So you're going off leaving us with the goods.

HENRIETTA   What goods? (*Understanding.*) Well, you asked me to bring him here.

AUNT CAROLINA   Yes, but . . .

HENRIETTA   Or did you expect me just to bring him by and then carry him back?

UNCLE GERARD   No, of course not—uh . . . you've done exactly what we asked.

AUNT CAROLINA   But just look at the fix you've put us in.

UNCLE GERARD   (*to* AUNT CAROLINA.) It was your idea. . . .

AUNT CAROLINA   Yes, I know that. But who would have supposed that when she found the man whose pictures line her room . . . No matter how worn out he's become—heavens! She was mad about him before they married and afterwards—well, who could describe it?

UNCLE GERARD   Well, now you see. She believes she's having lunch with him at a country inn and she's quite happy.

AUNT CAROLINA   (*pensive.*) Well, something will have to be done to revive her memory. Heaven knows you can't erase things just like that. (*To* UNCLE GERARD.) Do you think if we dressed Eugene up in tails? There are some costumes that are unforgettable.

UNCLE GERARD   Please, Carolina. . . . You're capable of inviting all your friends to another marriage breakfast.

HENRIETTA   (*saying good-bye.*) Well, you can tell me how things turn out. . . .

UNCLE GERARD Yes.

HENRIETTA I have an idea that she's not going to call me again on the phone. . . . (*She gives her hand to* UNCLE GERARD.)

UNCLE GERARD Good-bye, Henrietta. . . .

HENRIETTA (*to* THE BUYER.) It's been a pleasure.

THE BUYER (*giving her his hand.*) You know where you have a friend. . . .

HENRIETTA (*to* AUNT CAROLINA.) And you——

AUNT CAROLINA I'll go with you to the door. . . .

HENRIETTA Don't bother.

AUNT CAROLINA I'll come by some afternoon to see you and have my hair fixed. And if you can do something for wrinkles . . .

HENRIETTA That's easy enough.

AUNT CAROLINA Well, mine have got set in their ways. . . . (*They exit upstage left.*)

UNCLE GERARD (*who hasn't taken his eyes off* HENRIETTA.) Well, you know what they say: "It's an ill wind that blows no good."

THE BUYER They say what?

UNCLE GERARD I mean this beauty operator is quite a specimen.

THE BUYER Surely you aren't thinking . . . ?

UNCLE GERARD Indeed I am. I'm not much of a man for action any more—but when it comes to thinking, I can keep up with anybody. . . .

AUNT CAROLINA *returns and speaks to* THE BUYER.

AUNT CAROLINA We're awfully grateful to you for giving up your bed so that Eugene could rest a little.

THE BUYER (*modestly denying the importance of his good deed.*) Oh, don't mention it. Is he better?

AUNT CAROLINA   He's pulled himself together a bit. But I wouldn't put any money on him in the condition he's in now.

UNCLE GERARD   (*worried, to* THE BUYER.) And what if Eugene can't get up? Where are you going to sleep tonight?

THE BUYER   (*complying readily.*) Oh, any place at all. On the sofa. . . .

UNCLE GERARD   I won't hear of it.

THE BUYER   It's only for a night.

AUNT CAROLINA   (*pensive.*)   But if things get more complicated and . . .

CARMEN *walks by upstage from right to left.*

UNCLE GERARD   (*to* AUNT CAROLINA.)   You could move to Beatriz's room and then we could use your bed. . . .

THE BUYER   Nothing doing.

AUNT CAROLINA   (*thinking.*)   I don't know if Beatriz . . . (*To* THE BUYER.) At any rate, you're here. As a final resort, I can go to the Castellana Hilton. . . .

THE BUYER   I hear it's very nice. But I couldn't permit that. I can be comfortable anywhere—just with a blanket.

CARMEN *enters upstage left.*

AUNT CAROLINA   (*to* CARMEN *before she can say anything.*)   Are they back?

CARMEN   No, but a lady is asking for Mr. Requena.

AUNT CAROLINA   Did you tell her he's not here?

CARMEN   No, madam. Since there are so many new people around, one never knows.

UNCLE GERARD   Tell her to try another floor.

AUNT CAROLINA   Or if she has a parachute . . . (CARMEN *is about to leave.*)

UNCLE GERARD Wait. It just occurred to me that she might be looking for Eugene. (*To* THE BUYER.) Don't you think so?

THE BUYER Anything is possible in this house.

AUNT CAROLINA But if she's asking for . . .

UNCLE GERARD It may be a pseudonym that he uses with women. . . .

AUNT CAROLINA (*with hopeful anticipation.*) Maybe he'll turn out to be a bigamist.

UNCLE GERARD (*frightened.*) Carolina!

AUNT CAROLINA Or a trigamist. Nothing would amaze me. No woman could do a man in so much if she didn't have help.

UNCLE GERARD (*considering.*) Anything can be expected from a man who gives a false name.

AUNT CAROLINA And such a strange one, too. (*To* CARMEN) What name did you say?

CARMEN Requena.

THE BUYER (*calmly.*) Maybe it's a relative of mine.

UNCLE GERARD Why?

THE BUYER Because my name is Requena.

AUNT CAROLINA Well, that woman knows it. (*Catching on.*) But of course, she's come for you.

THE BUYER (*amazed.*) A woman? No. I'm a married man.

AUNT CAROLINA That's who it is.

THE BUYER Who?

AUNT CAROLINA Your wife!

THE BUYER (*surprised.*) You think so?

AUNT CAROLINA (*to* CARMEN.) Have her come in.

THE BUYER No, hold on a minute. . . . I'll go see. (*He exits upstage left, followed by* CARMEN.)

UNCLE GERARD Why did you think it was his wife? It never occurred to him.

AUNT CAROLINA　You men are always ready to break with the past.

THE BUYER *returns, leading in* MATILDE. MATILDE *is a woman of about sixty and well preserved.*

THE BUYER　Come in, come in, Matilde.

MATILDE　Good afternoon.

AUNT CAROLINA (*to* THE BUYER.)　It really is your wife.

MATILDE　What do you mean, really? (*To* THE BUYER.) Was there some doubt?

THE BUYER　No, dear. Let me present you to my friends.

MATILDE　Yes, how are you?

AUNT CAROLINA　Fine, and you? (*They shake hands.*)

UNCLE GERARD　Delighted to meet you. Do sit down.

MATILDE (*sitting down.*)　Thank you. Philip told me over the phone how nice you've been to him.

UNCLE GERARD　Philip?

AUNT CAROLINA　What Philip?

MATILDE　This one. (*Indicating* THE BUYER.)

AUNT CAROLINA　Ah, that's a relief. Today one can't keep up with the surprises.

UNCLE GERARD (*to* THE BUYER.)　You certainly kept quiet about it.

MATILDE　You'll have to forgive him. At times he's very shy. (*To* THE BUYER.) Are you all right?

THE BUYER　Fine.

MATILDE　You stayed on your diet?

THE BUYER　No.

UNCLE GERARD　Emphatically no! He's eaten a little bit of everything.

AUNT CAROLINA　And his table manners are excellent.

MATILDE You have no idea what a high opinion he has of you.

AUNT CAROLINA Yes we do. We've heard everything.

UNCLE GERARD He's a very fine man.

THE BUYER (*to* MATILDE.) I told you you'd like them when you got to know them.

MATILDE Well, it must be something extraordinary to get him to spend a night away from home.

AUNT CAROLINA You were probably dying of curiosity.

MATILDE Oh, not really. Acquiring a man is not like buying a watch. You get the certificate of guarantee after you've had him a few years.

AUNT CAROLINA At any rate, you did come to make sure.

MATILDE No, I came to get him.

AUNT CAROLINA (*alarmed.*) You're not going to take him away from us?

UNCLE GERARD So soon?

MATILDE (*to* THE BUYER.) Haven't you remembered that today is Egglebert's birthday and that they're expecting us for dinner?

UNCLE GERARD What a bore.

THE BUYER (*convinced.*) Indeed.

MATILDE (*explaining.*) They're relatives of ours. (*To* THE BUYER.) I've already sent the cake we send each year. (*To* AUNT CAROLINA.) They have a charming little house in the suburbs.

UNCLE GERARD Will it last very long?

MATILDE No, we usually leave at nine.

UNCLE GERARD Then you can drop him off on the way back.

MATILDE Me?

AUNT CAROLINA   Or send him back to us with the maid.

THE BUYER   Oh, no. I can come back alone.

MATILDE   But Philip, don't you realize? You have a home! Children!

THE BUYER   It's just that these friends . . .

MATILDE   I see.

THE BUYER   . . . are having a difficult time just now. I can't desert them.

AUNT CAROLINA   (*impressed.*)   How thoughtful.

MATILDE   (*confidentially to* AUNT CAROLINA.)   He really is a marvelous man. And with the children, he's a saint.

AUNT CAROLINA   Isn't that going too far?

MATILDE   I mean . . .

UNCLE GERARD   (*sadly.*)   It's just that without him . . .

AUNT CAROLINA   . . . the roof will fall on our heads.

MATILDE   Is there some danger?

UNCLE GERARD   We were referring to our loneliness.

MATILDE   I don't understand.

AUNT CAROLINA   We've come to consider him as one of us.

MATILDE   But the children—at their age they ask questions. They won't understand.

AUNT CAROLINA   The poor little darlings.

MATILDE   And I've always remembered that I am a mother first of all . . . in the best sense of the word, you may be sure. . . .

BEATRIZ *and* VILLALBA *enter upstage left. They're dressed as at the end of the second act.* BEATRIZ *is carrying an armful of wild flowers.*

BEATRIZ   (*radiant.*)   Here we are.

VILLALBA   Good afternoon.

MATILDE (*to* THE BUYER.) Which one is he? The real one?

THE BUYER No, woman. The phony one.

MATILDE What a pity.

BEATRIZ (*very politely, to* THE BUYER.) Is this your wife?

THE BUYER Yes.

BEATRIZ (*affectionately, to* MATILDE.) Congratulations. You don't know what a jewel of a husband you have. Sincere, faithful, hard-working, tidy.

MATILDE Yes, I've met him—we have three children.

BEATRIZ Only three? With a man like this?

UNCLE GERARD (*calling her to order.*) Beatriz!

BEATRIZ (*turning to him.*) Hello, Uncle. Thinking pure thoughts as always. . . .

UNCLE GERARD (*stung a little.*) Don't believe it. With all that's happened today.

BEATRIZ Well, let's not complain. You've got your health and you'll probably bury all of us.

UNCLE GERARD (*doubting it.*) I'd like to but . . .

BEATRIZ (*to* AUNT CAROLINA.) Oh, Aunt, you don't know what a time we've had. We've been out in the country. We cut these flowers for you. A policeman gave us a ticket. You should have seen it! We were like two lovers. (*She hands her the flowers. She turns to* THE BUYER *and* MATILDE.) You're not going to leave, are you? I'll be back in a moment. (*She exits left. The others remain a moment in silence and then they look at* VILLALBA.)

AUNT CAROLINA (*to* VILLALBA.) Do you think you've done the right thing?

VILLALBA What are you talking about, madam?

AUNT CAROLINA   Running around like that through
the countryside.

UNCLE GERARD   You must be exhausted.

AUNT CAROLINA   I shouldn't think you're accustomed to long hikes.

VILLALBA   (*sincerely.*)   You're quite right.

AUNT CAROLINA   I thought so.

VILLALBA   We went too far. . . .

THE BUYER   Farther than the village?

MATILDE   (*to* THE BUYER.)   Don't get involved in
this.

THE BUYER   (*to* MATILDE.)   You're permitted to ask
questions here. You can try if you wish.

VILLALBA   Too far . . . and now it's time to return. As soon as possible—to reality. If that man
had not come back to this house it would have
all been a kind of dream. Now . . .

AUNT CAROLINA   Yes, and now it's time to wake up.

VILLALBA   So I'm leaving.

MATILDE   (*deciding to ask her question.*)   So soon?
(*She looks at* THE BUYER. *He shows her with a
gesture that everything is all right.*)

VILLALBA   One of us doesn't belong here.

UNCLE GERARD   Wait. We still don't know which
one it is.

VILLALBA   For the time being, I'm the one. Because
I don't know if it's my kiss or the other man's
kiss that's going to awaken the sleeping
beauty. . . .

AUNT CAROLINA   (*with a new uneasiness.*)   But if
Beatriz asks me . . . what shall I say to her?

VILLALBA   Tell her whatever you wish—except the
truth. It might hurt her. . . . (QUINTANA *appears*

*at the doorway at right. It is obvious that he can
hardly stand up.* VILLALBA *looks at him for a
moment, makes up his mind, and turns to the
others.*) Good-bye. (*He exits upstage left.* QUIN-
TANA *is about to follow him.* AUNT CAROLINA *comes
between them.*)

AUNT CAROLINA Where are you going?

QUINTANA Leave me alone.

AUNT CAROLINA Indeed I won't. What more do
you expect? He's left the field open to you.
(BEATRIZ *appears in the doorway at left, in time
to catch the end of the scene.*)

BEATRIZ What's going on? Oh, it's our sick guest.
Are you feeling better?

QUINTANA (*controlling himself.*) Yes.

BEATRIZ (*to* AUNT CAROLINA.) And Eugene?

AUNT CAROLINA (*uncertain.*) Eugene?

BEATRIZ Yes. Where is he? (*There's a moment of
silence.*)

AUNT CAROLINA (*vaguely.*) He's gone out. . . .

UNCLE GERARD (*without knowing what to say.*) He's
not far away, he . . .

QUINTANA Beatriz . . .

BEATRIZ (*turning to him.*) I beg your pardon, sir.
. . . (QUINTANA, *taken aback, does not dare to
speak. There is new silence.*)

THE BUYER (*understanding the situation.*) We were
just leaving, too.

MATILDE (*to* THE BUYER.) Without knowing how
it turns out? (THE BUYER *silences her with a
glance.*)

AUNT CAROLINA (*to* MATILDE.) I'd like to show you
the apartment before you leave. (*She points to-*

ward the door upstage. UNCLE GERARD *does not move. He's very interested.*) Come along, Gerard.

UNCLE GERARD   I've already seen the apartment.

AUNT CAROLINA (*with authority.*) Come on. (*To* MATILDE, *pointing.*) This way.

THE BUYER (*to* MATILDE.)   You'll like it. It doesn't seem as large as it really is.

MATILDE (*to* AUNT CAROLINA *as they leave.*) They don't build houses like this any more. (AUNT CAROLINA *and* MATILDE *exit upstage left.*)

UNCLE GERARD (*to* THE BUYER *as they follow.*) You will both come back to see us sometime?

THE BUYER   Well, of course I will. (*They exit arm in arm upstage left.* BEATRIZ *and* QUINTANA *remain looking at each other in silence.*)

QUINTANA   Beatriz . . . don't you recognize me? (BEATRIZ *looks at him without speaking.*) Is it possible that you don't remember? All the hours we spent together? All our dreams?

BEATRIZ   What dreams? (BEATRIZ *is now a different woman. Her calmness is impressive. Without passion, without hate. Because she has said them to herself for so many years, her words are precise. Her resolution is clear. So we know that all she says is final.* QUINTANA *watches her.*) You don't need to say any more. I remember everything. I was not fortunate enough to lose my memory when I lost all the rest.

QUINTANA   I thought . . .

BEATRIZ   That I was crazy. . . .

QUINTANA   No.

BEATRIZ   Well, slightly mad . . . not enough to arouse pity in anyone. Something they could even smile about when they said: "She's that

way. She has a screw loose. A little bizarre."
What could I do after I went to meet you three,
four, five days believing that the delay had a
reason? That there must be an explanation. Can
you imagine what it was to return home and find
them looking at me and not daring to ask a
question? Improvising conversation about everything except your absence. . . . Do you know
how people whisper outside a sick man's room?
My friends gave me the sympathy no woman ever
wants. And no one but I dared to say your name.
And beside me, two old people like statues—
holding their breath. Expecting at any moment
a cry of anguish or a wild laugh that has no
cure. . . . The laugh that must be put behind
locked doors. So I kept on going to meet you, although I knew quite well that someone else was
sitting in your seat in the plane. That there was
no luggage that had my picture inside. . . . I
went back every day, from winter to winter. In
rain and sun, ignoring the titters behind my back.
Brazenly, I read you into my future. And yet
I knew where you were—and that you were dead
for me, forever.

QUINTANA There were other ways. . . .

BEATRIZ Yes. Two. Two extremes—abandoning
myself to a futile passion, or becoming a little
saint. But I felt no more passion, and I wasn't
meant to be a saint. So I chose a kind of limbo.
. . . My aunt and uncle were the only parents
I've ever known. They began to hope that there
would be a way . . . that time could stop at that
point. So they adapted their lives to the rhythm
of mine. They went along with me at the risk

of losing their own sanity. We made our own private world—to our own specifications. A world in which you also lived.

QUINTANA Because you were waiting for me. . . .

BEATRIZ Not for you. Your physical presence was beginning to grow dim in my mind. Only the idea of you remained—a kind of myth. Now everything depended on your not coming back. Because my illusion was based on your absence. You really shouldn't have come back, should you? You shouldn't have come back. Why did you come back?

QUINTANA (*without knowing what to say.*) I'm your husband. . . .

BEATRIZ It's a fine time to remember that. Weren't you my husband then, more than ever? Weren't you my husband when there was still time to forgive you? When you still existed as a real person in my mind . . . in my heart? Why didn't you come back if you knew that simply by returning you would find forgiveness?

QUINTANA I couldn't, Beatriz. I had a child.

BEATRIZ (*rebelling.*) With that woman?

QUINTANA (*with bowed head.*) Yes.

BEATRIZ (*with rancor, for the first time.*) That was my child. That was the child I should have had—you stole him from me to give him to her. (*With a moment of involuntary tenderness.*) Where is he?

QUINTANA He died.

BEATRIZ (*bitterly.*) You even deprived me of sorrow. His death was mine, too. You made a life empty, sterile, and useless. (*She controls herself and after a short silence she speaks with a firm tone.*) Leave now, Eugene.

QUINTANA (*seeking another way.*) There is a law, Beatriz. And a vow. You swore before the altar. You signed your name—and it can't be erased.

BEATRIZ I know that. But I swore for love and companionship. And my share of happiness . . . and my share of pain. But together. I did not sign my name for loneliness.

QUINTANA (*seeking her compassion.*) Beatriz, look at me now. I'm a sick man.

BEATRIZ What does that matter? The contract gave me a young and healthy man. Your sickness is another deceit.

QUINTANA Marriage is also for sickness and old age.

BEATRIZ Women are made for compassion and care. But not from afar. We have the right to dissolve the first aspirin. And it's the same with old age. Going hand in hand. Not counting the days. But I'm not concerned with an illness that you bring now, from far off, suddenly. It's yours alone. . . .

QUINTANA Then . . .

BEATRIZ Go now, Eugene. . . .

QUINTANA (*bitterly.*) To die. . . .

BEATRIZ Your death is your own affair.

QUINTANA You wish it. . . .

BEATRIZ No. Because I don't even have enough love left for you to hate you.

QUINTANA My death would mean your freedom. Then you'd marry that man.

BEATRIZ Most surely.

QUINTANA   And until then?

BEATRIZ   Until then, I'll hear again the music of
the words that I had forgotten long ago. The
words that another man said to me.

QUINTANA   Who?

BEATRIZ   You. You don't even remember them.

QUINTANA   Love is more than words.

BEATRIZ   You've come to tell me that?

QUINTANA   I'll not give my permission. The law is
on my side.

BEATRIZ   I've learned something about laws. I've
had a long time to read books. And when I
finished all the novels, I read some about law. I'm
separated from you, free from you, forever.

QUINTANA   Nothing permits you to belong to
another man.

BEATRIZ   You are stupid. There's no evidence. No
love letters. No clandestine meetings. Do you
think I would have held back all these years
if it was only to you and the law that I was
responsible? When all the opportunities were
there?

QUINTANA   But you can't go on pretending that
man is me.

BEATRIZ   Why not? You forget that I've been out
of my mind for ten years.

QUINTANA   But I know that you aren't crazy.

BEATRIZ   And the rest? What do they count for?
Try to prove it. I have ten years head start. And
the experience ought to be of some use to me.

QUINTANA   Insane people can be locked up.

BEATRIZ   I know that. But not husbands like you.
But I've tried to stay close to the edge. And don't
believe that I'm going to recognize you or even

call you the name that you have. You can leave
and take your accusations with you. . . .

QUINTANA *(defeated, after a short silence.)* Good-
bye, Beatriz.

BEATRIZ Good-bye . . . *(She was about to say
Eugene.)* Good-bye, sir. . . .

QUINTANA *waits a moment with a final hope and
then he exits upstage left.* BEATRIZ *remains alone
in silence. She cannot bear it any longer and she
puts her handkerchief to her eyes.* AUNT CAROLINA
comes in upstage left.

AUNT CAROLINA I saw him go out.

BEATRIZ *(drying her eyes.)* Yes.

AUNT CAROLINA *(frightened on seeing her crying.)*
Child! Are you crying because of him?

BEATRIZ *(trying to soften everything with a smile.)*
Isn't crying permitted?

AUNT CAROLINA In this house it's prohibited by
the Treaty of 1956. What's wrong?

BEATRIZ I was saying good-bye to youth.

AUNT CAROLINA What youth?

BEATRIZ To mine, what else? Didn't you say good-
bye to your youth?

AUNT CAROLINA My youth just disappeared. I can't
imagine where it went.

BEATRIZ You didn't feel it because you weren't
alone. Because someone went with you every
step. For growing old, one needs piano accompaniment. I have no one to defeat loneliness with.

AUNT CAROLINA Dear, don't say that.

BEATRIZ Why shouldn't I say it? It's easier than
keeping silent, as we've kept silent for ten years.

AUNT CAROLINA Why do you have to remember
now?

BEATRIZ   So I'll know what awaits me. So there will
be no doubt. To be sure that in the future each
hour is going to have sixty minutes. Not one
less. . . . And each day twenty-four hours, without compassion . . . and each year three hundred sixty-five days all the same.

AUNT CAROLINA   Except leap years.

BEATRIZ   Yes, one day every four years to straighten
out the accounts. That extra day which ought to
be voluntary. A day for those who want it. For
those who are happy; for those who have hope;
for those who have love. I know what to expect.
There's nothing worse. I know what flowers do
not know when they open—what it is to wither
in a vase, stupidly . . . without the kiss of the
sun. Without even being touched by the bees.
I know what it is to be nothing. To turn gradually
into stone.

AUNT CAROLINA   You're not going to help things by
crying.

BEATRIZ   I know that. And I'm not even going to
cry. . . . Why try to hasten what's going to come
in its own inevitable way? You mustn't worry.
. . . You're not going to see me cry again. If I
cry it will be alone . . . as you have cried so
many times for me. (AUNT CAROLINA *no longer
can speak. With emotion she embraces her.* UNCLE
GERARD *enters upstage left.*)

UNCLE GERARD   (*surprised.*)   What's going on?

BEATRIZ   (*reacting, she smiles.*)   Nothing, Uncle.
Don't worry. Just some things between women.
(*She exits at left.* UNCLE GERARD *remains pensive.*)

UNCLE GERARD   Bad business. Things between
women are always about a man.

AUNT CAROLINA   Or two.

UNCLE GERARD   No, when there are two it starts being a thing concerning men.

AUNT CAROLINA (*serious.*)   She frightens me, Gerard.

UNCLE GERARD   She has always frightened you.

AUNT CAROLINA   Now more than ever. Now it's as if we were tied down. Before we weren't. Don't you understand? And it was easier. We can't follow our fancy any more.

UNCLE GERARD (*nostalgically.*)   And it was so pleasant to follow our fancy.

AUNT CAROLINA   But we were always in the air. What did we know about the ground?

UNCLE GERARD (*sighing.*)   I suppose we're lost.

AUNT CAROLINA   Even worse, Gerard. We've been caught up with. There's no escape.

A sad silence. Suddenly BEATRIZ *enters from the left. She marches to the telephone, without paying any attention to them. She takes it and dials a number.*

AUNT CAROLINA *and* UNCLE GERARD *watch her.*

BEATRIZ (*on the phone.*)   Hello . . . is that you Julia? . . . (*Surprise and keen interest from* AUNT CAROLINA *and* UNCLE GERARD.) I'm calling you to tell you not to count on me this afternoon. I'm going out with Germán. . . . Yes, dear. A boy—who studies architecture. We're going to the movies. Afterwards I'll come right back home—you know that my aunt and uncle don't like for me to stay out late. They say it's not proper for a single girl. . . . (*While she's been speaking the* AUNT *and* UNCLE *have exchanged a glance of surprise and another of understanding. With a gesture of happiness and hope and without saying a word to each other, as if obeying a signal, they react.* AUNT CAROLINA *goes to the chair where she left her articles and begins to get dressed again as a spy with great enthusiasm while* UNCLE GERARD *sits down and looks for something in his pockets, from which he takes some long strips of curled paper of all colors. Then he finds a toy on a string which, when he leaves it on the table, begins to move; and finally, a folded piece of paper which he places on the table. Then he starts to look for things in the inner pockets of his jacket. He takes out a harmonica, a small duster, and finally, his fountain pen. He writes rapidly, very satisfied with himself.* BEATRIZ *continues on the phone.*) What do you expect, dear? They have old-fashioned ideas. . . . When is he going to be invited to the apartment? Well, certainly not for some time. Not until he finishes his studies—he has two years more. And look at me. I still haven't gone out formally. I have time to think about it. . . . Yes. . . . Do I like him? Yes, I like him. But it's nothing serious. First let him have his future assured and then we can find an apartment. . . . No. On the Vespa. We're going dancing probably. Good-bye, dearest. Have fun. . . . I? All that I can. Good-bye. (*She hangs up, and she dials another number. She waits, smiling.*)

AUNT CAROLINA (*as a spy, to* UNCLE GERARD.) How are things?

UNCLE GERARD Stunning. What do you think of this? (*He reads the paper that he's written.*) "For sale to individuals. Authentic Gobelin tapestry. Fifteenth century."

AUNT CAROLINA (*with a slight fear.*) Put sixteenth, just in case.

UNCLE GERARD (*striking out what he has just written.*) That's better. "Apartment furnishings for sale." (*He writes.*)

BEATRIZ (*on the phone.*) Hello? Is that you, Germán? . . . Yes, of course, Germán. . . . Your name isn't Germán? Then what do you want me to call you? . . . What's that? Eugene? How silly. Eugene has just died. . . . (UNCLE GERARD *has taken the harmonica from the table. He raises it to his lips. He plays the scale on it. He smiles, delighted, and plays with much spirit an old American song: "Oh, Susanna."* BEATRIZ *continues on the phone.*) What do you mean, what is that noise? (UNCLE GERARD *plays the melody with all his might and* AUNT CAROLINA *beats time with her foot and accompanies him by clapping.* BEATRIZ *on the phone, enchanted.*) It's Uncle Gerard, and a very extraordinary lady who are providing the accompaniment for my happiness. *A very quick curtain.*

The Boat Without a Fisherman

By Alejandro Casona

La barca sin pescador
Translated by Richard Damar

La barca sin pescador was originally published in
Buenos Aires in 1951. Copyright is controlled
by the Casona estate.

TRANSLATION COPYRIGHT © 1970 BY RICHARD DAMAR

Characters

RICHARD JORDAN
HENRIETTE
JOHN
FIRST ADVISOR
SECOND ADVISOR
BANKER
THE GENTLEMAN IN BLACK
THE GRANDMOTHER
FRIDA
OLD MARK
ESTELA

"In the furthest confines of China lives an immensely rich Mandarin whom we've never seen and of whom we've never heard a word. If we could inherit his fortune, and to kill him we needed only to press a button, without anyone else knowing it, . . . which of us would not press that button?"
—CHATEAUBRIAND, *Génie du Christianisme*

"Afterwards a greater remorse assailed me. I began to think that the Mandarin must have had a sizeable family which, dispossessed of the inheritance that I was consuming on Sèvres plates, would suffer all the customary hells of human misery: days without food, body without clothing, charity denied . . ."
—EÇA DE QUEIROZ, *O Mandarim*

Act One

Office of financier RICHARD JORDAN. *Coldly expensive. On the table, ticker tape and telephones. On the walls, maps with tiny flags grouped together on the great financial centers and ribbons indicating communications. A great terrestrial globe on a tripod. Pendulum clock. Winter.*

HENRIETTE *is seated.* RICHARD, *in a bad humor, reaches for the telephone which has been ringing since the curtain went up. While he speaks, she is freshening her make-up.*

RICHARD   Hello! Long distance . . . ? Yes, yes, go ahead. . . . The same here: another four points in half an hour. But I repeat: there's no cause for alarm. No, never do that; my orders are final and apply to all exchanges. No matter what happens, buy! Nothing else! Thank you! (*He hangs up and examines the ticker tape for the quotation of the moment.*)

HENRIETTE   More bad news?

RICHARD   It looks that way.

HENRIETTE   Serious?

RICHARD   The worst yet, and I've had some storms to weather before. When you can see the blow coming, it's easier to parry it.

HENRIETTE   If you'd settle for that . . . But I know

you; you're not a man who's content just to parry a blow without giving one in turn.

RICHARD (*offering her a cigarette.*) It's what I've always done. Is there any reason to lose my courage now?

HENRIETTE It's figures that matter now; not courage. How much has the Canadian company's stock gone up today?

RICHARD Fourteen points more. The same that we've dropped.

HENRIETTE And how long can you stand the decline?

RICHARD The limit is of no importance to me since it's a drop that's been artificially triggered. The game is quite clear: either the Canadians or me. We'll see who laughs last.

HENRIETTE They can afford the luxury of losing indefinitely if they can ruin you. It's not just a business that's defending its own interests; there's a man involved who hates you: Joshua Mendel.

RICHARD Joshua Mendel. . . . An apprentice. The first shady dealings he made in his life were learned from me. I'll teach him to respect his master.

HENRIETTE But today he's a great power in banking and industry. He knows how to win people with a smile; and women admire him.

RICHARD So I see.

HENRIETTE Don't be sarcastic, Richard. It's a risky game. A lot of people could be ruined with you.

RICHARD I can't waste my time thinking of others. Are you frightened?

HENRIETTE For you. You are an impulsive man,

capable of risking your whole life on one card.
Mendel has cold eyes. He moves slowly . . . but
he always gets what he wants.

RICHARD   I never thought of you as a pessimist.
What are you suggesting that I do? Surrender?

HENRIETTE   Compromise.

RICHARD   With Mendel? Never. He wants war, so
we'll have war. But let's not discuss it any more,
please. It's not becoming to a woman like you.
Why didn't you call me last night?

HENRIETTE   After such an upsetting day I thought
you'd need rest. I was having dinner at the
Claridge . . . with some friends.

RICHARD   Isn't there a telephone at the Claridge?

HENRIETTE   I didn't want to wake you up.

RICHARD   How curious. . . . I've never liked the
Claridge. It's where Mendel's crowd usually
meets.

HENRIETTE   What are you insinuating . . . ?

RICHARD   Let's be open, Henriette. Until yesterday
you'd never seen that man. Where did you find
out that Mendel has cold eyes?

HENRIETTE   A display of jealousy now, Richard?

RICHARD   I'm sorry.

JOHN *enters with a tray; two glasses, a cocktail
shaker, and soda.*

JOHN   Pardon, sir.

RICHARD   Who ordered that?

JOHN   Since the Director has gone three nights
without sleeping, I took the liberty. . . . Try
it, sir, and you'll be glad you did; but with
caution. It's a formula for putting you to sleep on
your feet!

RICHARD   Thank you, John.

JOHN (*leaving the tray.*) The Bank Director and your advisors are waiting to see you.

RICHARD Calmly?

JOHN Palely. The Director has lighted three cigarettes in succession without smoking one of them.

RICHARD Have them come in. (JOHN *exits.*) You'd better leave if you don't want to witness a stormy session.

HENRIETTE Listen to what they have to say. At a time like this any advice could be useful. Why do you look at me that way?

RICHARD I don't know. I find you very strange. Too full of ideas. My dear, it must be that we're getting old. (*He kisses her coldly.*)

HENRIETTE Think it over carefully, Richard. Very carefully. (*She exits.*)

RICHARD *watches her go thoughtfully. He pours himself a drink.* JOHN *opens a sliding door upstage, admitting the* BANK DIRECTOR *and the two* ADVISORS.

RICHARD Come in, gentlemen. Anything new?

FIRST ADVISOR Too many things for such a short time. Have you seen the latest quotations? Yesterday we closed at one-eighty, and today we opened at one-seventy-five. Since then——

RICHARD I already know. We've dropped fourteen points more.

SECOND ADVISOR Pardon; eighteen as of this moment. Before closing time it will be twenty, maybe thirty.

BANKER I left the Exchange when they put up four thousand more shares. I saw the agents' confusion; the nervous little groups of a hundred small stockholders; the figures melting like butter on the blackboard.

RICHARD Nevertheless, I can assure you that it's a false alarm.

BANKER It's not an alarm. It's panic! they're howling like a pack of animals in terror and fighting to get rid of stocks that are plummeting.

FIRST ADVISOR An alarm can be cut off with one bold stroke. But there's no human force that can endure in the face of panic.

RICHARD There you have the word: endure. Endure! Whom does this panic favor? Mendel. That's why he's paying for it. When our stocks have hit bottom, he'll come along calmly to pick them up and take control of our companies. Only a stupid man would fail to see his game.

SECOND ADVISOR Do you mean that you still don't see in all this anything more than simple speculation?

RICHARD I've done it myself many times and I know the system: the press is bribed, saboteurs hired, rumors spread——

BANKER Unfortunately they're not all rumors: there are also some realities. The strike is spreading in the refineries and threatening total stoppage.

RICHARD The labor leaders have been bought. We'll double the price Mendel has offered them.

BANKER And our petroleum holdings across the border? The nationalist movement has seized the government and refuses to recognize foreign interests.

FIRST ADVISOR Our oil wells will be expropriated at the price they decide!

RICHARD   Political propaganda that no one would dare to carry out. Oil has no national boundaries!

SECOND ADVISOR   It's not just a threat. It's information confirmed by our investigators. Look at this cable.

BANKER   (*while* RICHARD *reads the cable.*) When this news is announced in the Exchange, the drop will turn into total collapse.

FIRST ADVISOR   We must save what we can, before it's too late.

RICHARD   In short: what is it you're suggesting I do? Surrender to Mendel?

FIRST ADVISOR   We still have time today to come to an agreement. Tomorrow he'll have us tied hand and foot.

RICHARD   Absolutely not! While I hold the directorship of the companies, my sole order is resist. And then, hold firmly.

BANKER   With what capital? Under these conditions my bank can't risk new credit.

RICHARD   Have you lost faith in me, too?

BANKER   And who could have faith when the cause of the panic came from this very office? Those four thousand shares dumped on the market this morning belonged to Henriette. Your own friend!

RICHARD   It isn't possible!

BANKER   Last night they saw her dining with Mendel. At the Claridge.

RICHARD   They lie! Who saw her?

FIRST ADVISOR   I did, Director.

SECOND ADVISOR   And I.

RICHARD   Then you were also there? Now I see the maneuver clearly. The boat is sinking and the rats are in a hurry to abandon it. Am I right? Well, gentlemen, not so fast. I'll find a way to set it afloat again. And if the company's money isn't enough I'll fight with my own, to the last cent. (*The ticker is heard again.*)

BANKER Consider it carefully. It could be your ruin.

FIRST ADVISOR (*who has run to watch the ticker.*) Look at these figures. It's a complete collapse!

SECOND ADVISOR The stockholders demand your resignation. It's the only thing that can save us all!

RICHARD Enough of this! Go kneel at Mendel's feet. For my part, I intend to keep on fighting; all or nothing. That's final.

BANKER All right. We'll have our say. Let's go! (*They exit.*)

RICHARD (*alone, murmuring between clenched teeth.*) Cowards. . . . Cowards. . . . And her . . . ! (*He collapses into a chair. He drinks again in silence.*)

Sound of rain. The lights dim perceptibly while we hear in the background a strange, obsessive music. The sliding door upstage slowly opens by itself, noiselessly, admitting THE GENTLEMAN IN BLACK. *It closes behind him mysteriously.* THE GENTLEMAN IN BLACK *is wearing a cutaway coat and carries a briefcase under his arm. Only the cold smile, the eager nostrils, and the pointed beard betray, under the commonplace appearance, his eternal personality. He advances silently and then speaks over* RICHARD's *shoulder with a kind of confidential solemnness.*

GENTLEMAN Don't give it any more thought, Richard Jordan. Your mistress has betrayed you.

Your friends, too. You're on the brink of ruin.
Perhaps you'll go to jail. Under such conditions,
I am the only one who can save you. (RICHARD
*looks around in surprise and then observes the
stranger as if he can't quite comprehend his
presence.*)

RICHARD (*getting up.*) Who are you?

GENTLEMAN An old friend. When you were a
child and had faith, you dreamed of me more than
once. Don't you remember me?

RICHARD I think I've seen that face before. . . . I
don't know where.

GENTLEMAN In a picture book your mother had,
where they spoke naively of heaven and hell.
Remember? Page eight. . . . On the left.

RICHARD (*looking at him fixedly.*) In a cloud of
smoke? With a red cape and a rooster feather?

GENTLEMAN It was attire of the period. It's been
necessary to change the scenery and wardrobe a
bit to keep in style.

RICHARD (*not wanting to believe.*) No!

GENTLEMAN Yes.

RICHARD (*rubs his eyes.*) Let's talk seriously, please.
. . . You're not going to try to make me believe
that I'm dealing with . . . with . . . ?

GENTLEMAN Say it without fear. With Satan in
person.

RICHARD The devil you say!

GENTLEMAN One and the same. All my names are
used as exclamations.

RICHARD (*trying to pull himself together.*) Stranger: I don't know what lunatic asylum you've
escaped from or what you're up to. But I warn
you that you've chosen a very bad moment.

GENTLEMAN Bad? Why? Weren't you a desperate man when I arrived?

RICHARD Indeed I was. I can swear to that.

GENTLEMAN Then . . . ? I always bring my propositions to men at that critical moment of no return—just as you do with women.

RICHARD But do you realize how absurd this situation is? You can't actually be standing there, even if I do think you are. The devil isn't a character of flesh and blood. He's an abstract idea.

GENTLEMAN And, nevertheless, here I am. From time to time even we abstract ideas need to stretch our legs.

RICHARD It can't be. An apparition in these times. . . . And with your appearance.

GENTLEMAN (offended, looking at himself.) Appearance?

RICHARD Pardon me. I mean with that provincial look of an ordinary middle-class citizen.

GENTLEMAN I'll explain that. In reality there are three different devils according to the classes of souls. There's one who's aristocratic and subtle, to tempt kings and saints. Another hot-blooded and earthy, for the use of poets and peasants. I'm the devil of the bourgeoisie.

RICHARD Now I understand the outfit; and even the briefcase. Doesn't it seem a bit too realistic for you?

GENTLEMAN Realism is always fine. Even for the supernatural. If I may. (He sits down calmly and pours himself a drink.)

RICHARD Enough of this nonsense. Either get out right now or I'll have you thrown out.

GENTLEMAN I think you'll be wasting your time. But try it. (*He serves himself soda. Drinks.* RICHARD *presses the buzzer in vain and then tries to use the telephone.* THE GENTLEMAN IN BLACK *comments without watching.*) It's useless. The buzzer won't work. Nor the telephone.

RICHARD (*shouting.*) John! John . . . !

GENTLEMAN Don't tire yourself out; while I'm here, no one will move or hear your voice. Time itself will remain asleep on the clocks. (RICHARD *looks at the clock. The pendulum has stopped.*)

RICHARD But then . . . it's true. I'm not dreaming?

GENTLEMAN You'll soon be completely convinced. Sit down quietly and let's talk like two good friends.

RICHARD Friends . . . ?

GENTLEMAN Don't be modest. Sit down.

RICHARD If there's no alternative . . . (*He sits down and takes out his cigarette case.*) Cigarette?

GENTLEMAN No, thank you; smoke bothers me.

RICHARD (*lighting his.*) Very well; now, can you tell me why you've come?

GENTLEMAN I was passing through the Stock Exchange—where I have so many clients! I saw your plight and I've come to propose a deal. A spiritual deal, naturally.

RICHARD Still the romantic!

GENTLEMAN Always; it's my destiny. While you worry only about material things and the economy, I keep on busying myself exclusively with the soul.

RICHARD Do you think that mine deserves the trouble?

GENTLEMAN   In this case, yes. It's an experiment I'm making.

RICHARD   I don't believe condemning my soul would take much effort; the poor thing must be sufficiently damned already.

GENTLEMAN   (*taking a file card from his briefcase.*) To be sure; according to the information I have, it's almost ripe for damnation. But it still needs a little push: the final one.

RICHARD   Things could be worse, I suppose.

GENTLEMAN   Your list is filled up with betrayals, bad deeds, scandals, and hurts. Human pain has never moved you, you've never kept your word, nor have you respected your neighbor's wife. As for coveting your neighbor's goods, I think it will be best not to talk of that—right?

RICHARD   Yes; it would really be a long story.

GENTLEMAN   In a word, all that the law commands you to respect you have defied; all that's prohibited to you, you've done. Until now you've stopped short of breaking only one commandment: "Thou shalt not kill."

RICHARD   (*standing up uneasily.*) Have you come to propose a murder to me?

GENTLEMAN   Precisely; the only thing that's missing on your list. Dare to complete it, and I'll return to your hands the reins of power and all the money you've just lost.

RICHARD   No, thank you. I've probably stooped very low, I don't deny it. But a murder is too much.

GENTLEMAN   Are you so certain that you haven't committed one already? There are bloodless crimes which aren't covered by laws.

RICHARD   For example?

GENTLEMAN   For example . . . (*He consults [the] card again.*) When you were living in povert[y] a child you used to haunt the docks looking [for] rotting bananas to satisfy your hunger. Thi[s] years later you caused hundreds of carloads [of] bananas to be thrown into the sea to make pric[es] go up. What would hungry children who stil[l] haunt the docks call that?

RICHARD   I can't be ruled by sentimentality. The heart is a bad business advisor.

GENTLEMAN   Agreed. So let's leave sentiments aside and go on to numbers, which are your strong point. (*He consults the card again.*) In your enterprises three thousand men work while breathing the gases of mines and the smoke of factories. According to the statistics, all of them will die five years before their time. Three thousand men times five years are one hundred fifty centuries of life cut off. Pretty figure, eh! The entire history of the world is not that long.

RICHARD   That's not my fault either. I didn't invent the system.

GENTLEMAN   But you do live comfortably from it. And all this without counting the young men who are already coughing thanks to you; and those prematurely old, and the mutilated ones.

RICHARD   We have the best hospitals in the nation.

GENTLEMAN   A familiar story: first you supply the sick men and then you build the hospitals.

RICHARD   Let's understand each other. Have you come to condemn my soul or to give me a lesson in morality?

GENTLEMAN I've never known how to do one without the other.

RICHARD Then you should feel ashamed. If you were a serious devil instead of a trite preacher, you'd be proud of me.

GENTLEMAN And who says I'm not? From my point of view everything you've done up till now is perfect.

RICHARD Ah! But those wrongs you accuse me of. I'm not the only man responsible. There are many of us. All men!

GENTLEMAN You have a point there. But using your terminology I'd say that they are "corporate crimes without personal liability."

RICHARD Exactly.

GENTLEMAN That's why I've come to propose one that will be exclusively yours; with complete responsibility.

RICHARD It's no use. I won't kill . . . ! I won't kill!

GENTLEMAN Just be calm. A man who craves to win as much as you won't reject a business deal without hearing the conditions.

RICHARD It doesn't matter how good they are. It's one thing to shrug when other men are dying, but quite a different matter to kill with your own hands.

GENTLEMAN And if hands weren't required?

RICHARD What do you mean?

GENTLEMAN That the material act doesn't matter to me. The moral intention is enough. Just will to murder and I'll take charge of the rest.

RICHARD I won't risk it. A deal that's so simple makes me suspicious.

GENTLEMAN   Ah, so it's beginning to seem simple to you now?

RICHARD   Why not? If the victim falls far away, without my having to see him, how can it matter to me?

GENTLEMAN   Just as I expected. To suffer another man's pain, the first thing needed is imagination; and you don't have any. You can be at ease about that part. It's a clean business transaction.

RICHARD   Bloodless?

GENTLEMAN   Bloodless. Accepted?

RICHARD   The proposition is tempting. But who's going to vouch for you?

GENTLEMAN   I've never gone back on any of my contracts. I promise you that no one will know about it, nor will there be a human law that can punish you. Are you still in doubt?

RICHARD   They say that criminals dream of their victims.

GENTLEMAN   Not you. You won't even need to meet him. You can choose any man in any place on earth. The further away the better. For example . . . (*He stands up, takes off a glove which he leaves on the table, and makes the globe spin. Then he stops it with a finger at random.*) Here. On the other side of the sea. A small fishing village in the North. Have you ever been in the North?

RICHARD   Never.

GENTLEMAN   Good; knowing a country is almost like knowing the man. Now make a mental effort and follow me. (*The light grows dimmer, leaving only the two figures visible beside the globe.*) Look, it's already night in the village. There's

Peter Anderson—an ordinary fisherman—climbing the hill to his house that faces the sea. A
strong wind is blowing. Do you hear it? (*We hear
the wind whistling—from far off at first and then
growing louder.*)

RICHARD I don't know. . . . It's like something
buzzing in my ears. . . .

GENTLEMAN Concentrate harder. Peter Anderson
has just bought a boat, and he's happy as he
climbs the hill singing an old song. . . . Can
you hear it? (*We hear the song far off, then
nearer. Accordion accompaniment in the background.*)

RICHARD I hear it coming closer. It's not my own
imagination?

GENTLEMAN No. The fact is your soul is there now.
Peter Anderson has had a drink or two. . . . The
cliff above the beach is dangerous . . . and the
wind is strong enough to knock a man off balance. Tomorrow, when they find him at the foot of
the cliff, everyone will think that it was the wind.
(*Pause. We hear the song and the sound of the
wind more clearly now.*) Why do you hesitate? A
simple effort of the will, and all your fortune
and power will return to you immediately. If
that's not enough, I can also offer you Mendel's
ruin. . . . What are you waiting for?

RICHARD I don't know. . . . I can't. . . .

GENTLEMAN It has to be now, before he reaches the
top! Close your eyes, Richard Jordan! It takes
only a moment.

RICHARD (*lowers his voice instinctively.*) What do
I have to do?

GENTLEMAN (*putting the contract on the table.*)

Your signature is enough. Here. (RICHARD *dips the pen in ink and hesitates. The sound of the wind and the song grow louder.* THE GENTLEMAN IN BLACK *shows his aesthetic appreciation as he listens.*) At the top of the hill there's a lighted window. . . . Peter is raising his hand to wave. . . . Sign now! This is the moment!

RICHARD *signs. Then, as if coming from the globe itself, we hear the heart-rending cry of a woman.*

CRY   Peter!

The song is cut off and the wind ceases suddenly. Absolute silence.

GENTLEMAN   Poor Peter Anderson. . . .

RICHARD   (*frightened and almost speechless.*) It's over . . . ?

GENTLEMAN   It's over. Do you see how simple it was? A gust of dark wind over the precipice, and one fisherman less in the village. It happens every day. (*He puts the document away.*) As for your business problems, you'll have good news soon. Congratulations. (*He starts to leave.*)

RICHARD   Wait. . . . Who cried out?

GENTLEMAN   What does that matter now?

RICHARD   Peter wasn't alone. I heard it clearly—it was a woman's scream!

GENTLEMAN   Don't ask questions. The less you know the better for you!

RICHARD   But the scream . . . If only I'd not heard that scream . . . !

GENTLEMAN   (*ironically.*) We're starting already . . . ? Don't think of it again. And above all, don't forget your own words: "The heart is a bad business advisor." (*He turns around near the door with an ambiguous smile.*) At any rate, poor

Peter Anderson. Right? He was singing like a man in love. . . . And he seemed so happy. (*He bows courteously.*) Many thanks.

The door opens silently by itself just as when he entered and closes again behind him. Normal light returns. RICHARD *stands gazing at "the scene of the crime" on the globe. Finally he reacts and rubs his eyes as if he were waking up. He looks at the clock. The pendulum is moving again.*

RICHARD   It can't be. Even though I saw it with my own eyes, it can't be! (*He hits the buzzer impatiently, calling at the same time.*) John . . . ! John . . . ! (JOHN *opens the door upstage.*) Stop that man! Bring him here again!

JOHN   Whom, sir?

RICHARD   You must have passed him. He just left through that very door!

JOHN   Impossible. I was sitting there, as always, in the vestibule.

RICHARD   And you didn't see him? A man dressed in black . . . with a briefcase. . . .

JOHN   I can swear that no one has entered or left this room.

RICHARD   Are you trying to make me believe I'm crazy? And the wind? You didn't hear that either?

JOHN   Wind? Not a leaf is stirring in the garden.

RICHARD   And a song? And that scream . . . a woman's scream, right there!

JOHN   (*looking suspiciously at the cocktail shaker.*) If the Director will permit me a word of advice, I think that he should go to bed. I cautioned him before that the cocktail formula was one that could put a man to sleep on his feet.

RICHARD　I wish that it had only been a dream. But I saw it so clearly. . . . (*Pause.*) Tell me, John, do you believe in the devil?

JOHN　(*gravely.*) I don't think the Director has the right to ask that question. Freedom of conscience is guaranteed in the Constitution.

RICHARD　Pardon me. I didn't mean to offend your convictions. (*Thoughtful.*) At any rate, it's strange . . . very strange. . . .

JOHN　Why should it be strange? The Director has gone three nights without sleep, his nerves are upset . . . and he's had two drinks.

RICHARD　Two . . . ? What makes you so sure that I was the one who drank both?

JOHN　(*with the glasses in his hand.*) The young lady would have left a lipstick mark on the edge. Although modest, I, too, have had experience.

RICHARD　The bad part is that I only remember drinking the first one.

JOHN　Don't worry; after the first nobody can remember the others.

RICHARD　You're right. Everything can be explained by natural laws. Furthermore, anything else would be too absurd—an anachronism. (*He breathes deeply with relief.*) Thank you, John. You don't know what a load you've taken off my mind.

JOHN　It's not necessary. It's all part of my job. (*He puts everything on the tray.* RICHARD *starts to light a cigarette.*) This black glove belongs to the Director?

RICHARD　(*alarmed again, he throws away the cigarette.*) A black glove? (*He takes it and looks at it fixedly.*) So! Finally a trace of reality. What do

you have to say now? When you dream of apple
trees, you don't find an apple when you wake
up, do you?

JOHN It's not customary.

RICHARD Well, here's the apple. If this glove that
we both see is real, it means that the hand was
real too . . . and the man.

JOHN (*uneasy.*) Is something wrong with the Director?

RICHARD Nothing that you can understand. What
has happened here is a mystery; and mysteries
aren't provided for in the Constitution. (*The
telephone rings.*) You can leave. (JOHN *exits,
shaking his head sympathetically.* RICHARD *answers the phone.*) Hello? Yes, speaking. Go
ahead. . . . Already? Yes, yes, I was expecting it;
but not so soon. Suspend all buying until further
orders. Thank you. (*He examines the tape from
the ticker, which is operating again. Then he sits
down heavily.* HENRIETTE *enters all smiles.*)

HENRIETTE Richard! I'm so glad to find you alone!
I came as fast as I could; I wanted to be the
first to give you the news——

RICHARD (*coldly.*) That I've won. If I didn't know
it already, just seeing you here would be sufficient.

HENRIETTE They've told you?

RICHARD Yes. There's been a complete reversal on
the Market and our shares are rising more
rapidly than they declined.

HENRIETTE You should have been there! It was
a moving spectacle. Suddenly—like a bolt of
lightning. It's enough to make me believe in
miracles!

RICHARD   Your happiness surprises me. If you were selling and I was buying, then it's bad news for you.

HENRIETTE   You're not going to scold me for being afraid. They made me believe that all was lost, and I tried to save something . . . thinking of the two of us.

RICHARD   Very generous of you. But which "two" are you talking about?

HENRIETTE   I swear I did it for your sake. Only for you!

RICHARD   Thank you, my dear. I didn't expect less. But next time don't be so impatient. It's best to be sure that the bear is dead before you start dividing his skin. You have your car downstairs; that's my final gift to you.

HENRIETTE   Am I to understand that you're putting me in the street?

RICHARD   I'm leaving you where I found you. My regards to Mendel.

FIRST ADVISOR *and* SECOND ADVISOR *appear at the same time through different doors. Then the* BANKER.

FIRST ADVISOR   Mister Jordan . . . !

SECOND ADVISOR   Mister Jordan . . . !

RICHARD   Not so fast, gentlemen. Great news, right?

FIRST ADVISOR   Splendid! Our oil wells in the South are safe!

SECOND ADVISOR   The trouble at the refineries has been settled. The strikers are withdrawing all their demands.

FIRST ADVISOR   There's a fantastic upsurge on the Market. The figures are rising like a fever!

RICHARD Nothing more? That's only the first part. Something more spectacular has yet to occur. (*The* BANKER *enters waving a cablegram triumphantly.*)

BANKER Sensational!

RICHARD Perhaps the news is here already.

BANKER An urgent cable. Mendel's oil wells are on fire!

FIRST ADVISOR Wonderful! We must make that information public immediately. Extra! Extra!

BANKER Permit me to congratulate you. Only a mind like yours could have organized such a move.

RICHARD Thank you, gentlemen, thank you. It was only what I expected. (*Without accepting the hand proffered by the* BANKER.) And now? Why are you here? To lend your heroism to the victor?

BANKER I always had faith in you.

FIRST ADVISOR We were only trying to give you good advice. . . .

RICHARD You shouldn't worry about your share. The wheel of fortune is turning and no one can stop it now. But: will there be enough money in the world to erase that drop of blood?

HENRIETTE Blood?

BANKER Where?

RICHARD Over there! On a beach in some town. Tomorrow a flock of seagulls will discover the spot . . . and some child will be the first to find him. . . . (*The others look at each other in confusion.*) I ask you, men who buy everything and sell everything: how much does it cost to take from your ears a woman's scream? What river of gold can return light to those blue eyes that gaze sightless at the stars?

HENRIETTE   Richard!

BANKER (*restraining her, in a low voice.*)   Quiet. It's his nerves.

RICHARD   Why are you still here? Don't you understand that what I need now is to be alone . . . ? Alone! . . . Alone!! (*The* BANKER *takes* HENRIETTE *by the arm. They all begin their exit. The wind is heard again.* RICHARD *makes the globe spin rapidly.*) That wind . . . ! That wind! If it would stop just for a moment . . . ! (*He sinks down in a chair. All around him obsessive voices are heard repeating a name in his ears.*)

VOICES   Peter Anderson . . . Peter . . . ! Peter . . . !

Again we hear the scream. The globe continues to spin.

Curtain.

Act Two

Some time later in the house of Peter Anderson. A humble fisherman's cottage on a northern coast. There is an oar nailed to the door and nets are hanging from the railings. On a shelf, small ship models, some half finished and others already assembled in bottles or glass jars. A rustic dining table, a sideboard with plates and tableware, an old iron stove or woodburning fireplace. On one side an entrance to the kitchen; on the other, the beginning of a stairway and an exit to the garden. Through a window and door at rear we see the cliff and further on the silhouette of the promontory above the sea. Afternoon light. THE GRAND-MOTHER, *alone, is setting the table while she ponders and grumbles aloud.*

GRANDMOTHER   A cloth for dinner, a cloth for supper. When the cloths are folded, it's time to turn back the sheets; and when the sheets are back in place, there's the tablecloth again. And silence. Now two plates. And two knives and forks. Yesterday there were two; and the day before that . . . and so it goes from day to day. When there were three of us, there were voices in the house and we talked of tomorrow. Tomorrow! Sometimes one of us spilt wine and we'd laugh and sprinkle some salt on it. Now that there's one plate less the table's too big. The man's plate is missing, and when the man's plate's missing, there's no laughter, or wine . . . or tomorrow. Two lonely women; there you have it: cold tablecloths, cold sheets, and silence. Damned be the houses of lonely women!

FRIDA, *who has appeared in the doorway a moment before, listens in surprise and then calls to her.*

FRIDA Grandmother.

GRANDMOTHER You? A sight for old eyes. I thought you'd forgotten the way to this house.

FRIDA I heard your voice from outside and I looked in. I thought someone was with you.

GRANDMOTHER All alone with myself, thank you. As you can see, I'm the only one who still puts up with me.

FRIDA When I heard you talking like that——

GRANDMOTHER And what do you want me to do with the words that are chafing me here? Swallow them? I'll free them to the wind, even if no one's listening. Things that aren't said rot inside you, and it's worse. (*She continues to arrange the table.* FRIDA *begins to help her.*) And your husband?

FRIDA At home; working.

GRANDMOTHER The less you leave him alone the better. Christian's been drinking too much. Keep an eye on him. And the boy?

FRIDA He's fine.

GRANDMOTHER He's fine, he's fine. . . . That's all you can think of to say about a son? He doesn't tie cans to the cat's tail? He doesn't scrape his shoes on the flagstones? He doesn't throw rocks at seagulls? Never! It's come to this! The sons

of my grandchildren are simply obedient, and
that's all!

FRIDA But Grandmother, you saw him only yesterday.

GRANDMOTHER It wasn't easy for me. I don't have
the legs for climbing hills any more, and if I
don't go up it won't occur to anybody to come
down. You could have brought him with you.

FRIDA I was just passing by. I didn't know I was
going to stop.

GRANDMOTHER It wouldn't be the first time I've
seen you come this way and then pass on with
your head down.

FRIDA It's not because of you.

GRANDMOTHER Then what is the reason? Your sister?

FRIDA Is she home?

GRANDMOTHER Pruning in the orchard. Shall I
call her?

FRIDA No, leave her in peace. I'd rather say it to
you alone.

GRANDMOTHER Anybody would guess that you
were afraid of her. Is it your sister who makes
you bow your head and pass by our door?

FRIDA Estela's not the same any more. Since Peter's
death she looks at all of us as enemies. As if
someone were to blame for her misfortune.

GRANDMOTHER We must always forgive those who
suffer. She's been left alone without anyone; you
have all that's needed to be happy. And there's
more than enough bread on your table.

FRIDA Do you believe that's all I need? I would
give her all my earthly goods, but she won't accept help from me.

GRANDMOTHER   From you or anybody else. A poor
man's pain is very proud.

FRIDA   Now do you understand why I've passed by
so many times without looking this way? It hurts
to see my sister sewing nets for others, or working in the fields like a man, and carving those
boats on winter nights.

GRANDMOTHER   She says it very well: the best way
to remember those who have gone is to fill their
place.

FRIDA   Why condemn yourselves to this loneliness?
My house is large; we could all live together
there.

GRANDMOTHER   Do you think she'd leave these
walls? It would have to be feet first. One day I
suggested renting the room that faces the sea.
There's always some foreign traveler who'd pay
well. But no indeed. She won't consent for any
stranger to look from the window that Peter
looked from.

FRIDA   And how long can she go on this way? A
woman doesn't have the strength to maintain
this house and keep a boat that never goes to
sea.

GRANDMOTHER   It's been almost two years; for better or worse we've survived.

FRIDA   Grandmother, you know as well as I: the
rent on the land is due. And the only thing you
have to put up is the boat. Are you going to let
her lose it?

GRANDMOTHER   Nobody will take that away from
her. We'll hold on to it with teeth and nails.

FRIDA   There's only one solution: to pay.

GRANDMOTHER Fifty kroner is too much for a house without a man.

FRIDA There's a man in my house who's healthy and strong. That's what I came to tell you. Peter's boat is saved.

GRANDMOTHER Christian paid? And you're hiding that from your sister?

FRIDA If she knew the money was ours, she might not accept it.

GRANDMOTHER Then . . . what are you two keeping from me? Has something happened between you?

FRIDA On my part, no. But she—I wish it was only my imagination. (*She steps closer to confide.*) Tell me, Grandmother, has Estela ever said anything to you?

GRANDMOTHER About what?

FRIDA I don't know—about me . . . about Christian. . . .

GRANDMOTHER About your husband? What does she have to do with your husband?

FRIDA He was Peter's companion; they were always together.

GRANDMOTHER Companions, yes; friends they never were. You know that quite well. Why are you remembering all that now?

FRIDA For no reason.

GRANDMOTHER For no reason. You were going to tell me something.

FRIDA (*steps away.*) I've forgotten. Sometimes we get strange ideas.

GRANDMOTHER So we do, my girl, so we do! If something is gnawing on your soul, keep silent

and let it turn sour inside. Like her. Like all the
rest. Silence. Always silence. And I'm in the midst
of it with my throat filling up with words and
no one to share them with.

FRIDA   I've already told you what I had to say. All
I'm asking is that Estela not find out.

GRANDMOTHER   And why shouldn't she as soon as
she steps through that door? I'm a fine one to go
around keeping secrets! I was born the way I am
and I'll stay that way. You've seen some children
who are afraid of the dark? Well, silence used
to scare me when I was a child. And how do we
know that silence and darkness aren't really the
same thing?

OLD MARK *appears in the doorway. He's an old fisherman who has become slow and clumsy. He is
carrying a small sailboat and some carvings in a
wicker basket.*

MARK   Afternoon.

GRANDMOTHER   The same to you. Was it good or
bad? You never say. I'll bet you haven't sold
anything.

MARK   You win the bet. Not a piece.

GRANDMOTHER   With all the people who arrived
on that ship today? And such people they were!
People from faraway places who travel just to be
traveling and have money in their pockets.

MARK   They look. They walk away. Sometimes
they take a second look. But those foreigners
come just to see.

GRANDMOTHER   And there you were, as still as a
post, watching them look and walk away. If mer-
chandise doesn't catch the eye, you have to start
to work on the ear.

MARK   Maybe I'm no good at that. People aren't all alike.

GRANDMOTHER   There's not one the likes of you.

MARK   You never stop, do you? What a person has to endure and endure and endure. . . . One day I'll just stop enduring and then you'll see what happens.

GRANDMOTHER   I'd like to. Better than seeing you in a daze with your arms folded. But what's the use! When they baptized you they put sugar on your tongue instead of salt.

FRIDA   (*taking the boat from him to place it on the shelf.*)   It's not his fault. Nobody buys these things any more. Nowadays they make them cheaper in factories and send them everywhere.

GRANDMOTHER   How much did you ask?

MARK   What I was told: ten kroner.

GRANDMOTHER   Even before they tried to bargain? Oh, if they'd let me do it! (*Takes the boat from* FRIDA's *hands.*) "How much is this model worth?" . . . "Fifteen kroner, sir. It's carved out of fir. You can still smell it!" . . . "Not bad." . . . "But you can have it for twelve." . . . "That's a lot." . . . "A lot? It takes twenty nights to carve one of these. Imagine a woman with cold hands for twenty nights!" . . . "I can't give you more than ten." . . . "Ten?" . . . "Ten." . . . "Very well, for ten it's yours!" And there you have it. (*She makes the motions of washing her hands of the affair and returns the boat to* FRIDA *who places it with the others.*)

MARK   (*after an effort at meditation.*)   Well, I don't see the difference. With a lot of words or a few words, the price is the same.

GRANDMOTHER So you think words don't have their use? If you'd gone to church on Sunday instead of getting drunk, you'd have heard what the pastor said. And how well that rascal speaks. . . . He was saying: "When Jesus of Galilee sent his disciples through the land, they were just poor fishermen like you. And do you think He gave them a sword or a horse to fight with? No! He gave them the word. And with the word alone they conquered the world."

MARK That's not the same thing. The apostles were men, and well He knew that they wouldn't abuse it.

GRANDMOTHER Insults from you, eh? Well, look what holding your tongue has got you.

MARK Sell I didn't, but speak I did.

GRANDMOTHER With whom?

MARK I don't know him. A passenger from the ship. He was down on the beach staring up at the cliff. He asked me: "Do you make those boats?" "Not I," I said; "Peter Anderson's wife." When he heard that name, he lost his color, and it even seemed to me that his lips trembled, just as if he was cold. Twice he mumbled: "Peter Anderson . . . Peter Anderson. . . ."

FRIDA How odd. . . . And then?

MARK Then he pointed this way, as if he knew the village, and said to me: "That's the house, at the end of the slope, isn't it?" . . . "Yes, sir; that's the one." Then he was silent again and just kept on gazing. . . . And that was all.

GRANDMOTHER And that was all? For heaven's sake. So a man who knew Peter arrives from another land and asks for his house . . . and you leave him there as if it happened every day. (*She calls loudly.*) Estela . . . ! Estela . . . !

FRIDA (*starting to leave in order to avoid meeting her sister.*) Good-bye, Grandmother. . . .

GRANDMOTHER Stay here! Why are you suddenly in such a hurry?

FRIDA It's late now. The boy may be by himself. . . .

GRANDMOTHER I told you to wait!

ESTELA *appears at the door leading to the garden. She detains her sister imperiously.*

ESTELA Were you going because I've come?

FRIDA I didn't realize how late it was.

GRANDMOTHER It's never too late for bringing things into the open. If you have something to say to each other, speak up, and let's set things straight.

FRIDA *steps back into the room.* ESTELA *puts her pruning hook down and lays an armful of green branches on the table.*

ESTELA Why did you call me that way?

GRANDMOTHER Uncle Mark's to blame. Can you believe that a friend of Peter's came to the harbor asking for this house? And here we stand not knowing who he is, or what he wants, or why he came, or where he's going.

ESTELA A friend . . . ?

MARK I didn't say he was a friend. I only said that he seemed to know Peter's name and this house.

ESTELA Where did he come from?

GRANDMOTHER Where would he come from? From the South. He arrived on the ship.

ESTELA The South isn't a place, Grandmother.

GRANDMOTHER (*to* MARK.) Is he tall and lean?

Does he have flaxen hair and blue eyes? I'll bet not.

MARK No.

GRANDMOTHER You see? From the South. Are you going to tell me what the South is!

ESTELA (*pensive.*) It could be. Peter sailed many seas; and people who met him loved him.

GRANDMOTHER Do you hear what she's saying? Why aren't you running to find that man?

MARK No one told me to. Should I go?

ESTELA Go. Peter Anderson's house was always open to his friends. (MARK *exits.*)

GRANDMOTHER (*fluttering with impatience.*) A friend! A friend who comes from God knows where and us with nothing to offer him. We must light the fire. Polish the pans! (*Hesitating before* FRIDA.) Wait. . . . What was it you wanted me not to tell your sister? Ah, yes; about the rent on the land. She paid the fifty kroner!

FRIDA Couldn't you be silent just once?

GRANDMOTHER Me be silent? Me keep quiet? No, daughter; there'll be time enough for that when I'm under six feet of earth. (*She exits toward the kitchen.*) Oh, if one could only sing and fly at the same time, like birds and bells!

ESTELA Why did you do it? I've told you a hundred times that I intend to support my house by myself.

FRIDA Wouldn't you do the same for me? Haven't you always helped me? Before we were married, it was never "yours" or "mine" with us.

ESTELA Now it's different. What there is in the house of a married woman is her husband's.

FRIDA   Christian doesn't know it. It's money I've saved.

ESTELA   You spent that money without telling him?

FRIDA   I was afraid that it might be humiliating for you.

ESTELA   I've never asked anybody for anything. I don't need it.

FRIDA   It's my money, and it's to save Peter's boat. You would offend me by giving it back?

ESTELA   No, Frida. I shall return it to you with the same love that made you bring it to me. That's all. Thank you. (*She takes down a net which she spreads over her knees and begins to mend it.*)

FRIDA   Do I bother you?

ESTELA   On the contrary; I'm grateful to you. It's been a long time since we've seen each other.

FRIDA   (*sitting down beside her to try to help.*) It's not my fault; but when I come I find you so different, so faraway. . . . I try to speak to you and you don't even hear me; as if you were in another world.

ESTELA   For me there is no other world. I'm always in the same.

FRIDA   Then why that desire to torment me? A lot of women in the village have gone through what you're going through now, and they've found a way to bear it. We must respect God's will.

ESTELA   They found a way to go on because they believed that. But God did not will Peter's death.

FRIDA   Who controls the wind?

ESTELA   It wasn't the wind that pushed him off the cliff. It was a man's hand.

FRIDA   Do you still think that someone is guilty?

ESTELA   I saw it from the window. But crying out to warn him was no use. It was too sudden, a shadow that struck like lightning. I saw it reach out at him, without warning, and then disappear in the night.

FRIDA   Why didn't you say that when the judge questioned you?

ESTELA   I couldn't swear who it was. And even if I could, I was afraid. You know how everyone loved Peter. If I accused a man, the whole town would rise up and fling him over that very cliff.

FRIDA   Maybe your eyes deceived you. Sometimes the fog rises up like ghosts and the wind makes the shadows of trees seem to dance.

ESTELA   It was a man; that's all I know. A man of flesh and blood. (*She stops her work and sits gazing into the distance.*) But who? When I sleep, they file by, one by one in my dreams, like a procession in the mist. Some of them fade away as they pass by. Always they move in silence with their eyes lowered and their hands hidden. I beg them for the truth, but no one answers me! No one takes pity on the sorrow of a lonely woman whose sleep is filled with unanswered questions. (*Pause. She begins her mending again.*)

FRIDA   I understand why you avoid people. But why me? It seems scarcely a hundred steps from your door to mine, but for you it might as well be a hundred leagues.

ESTELA   I want to live nailed here, like that oar. All that remains for me is in this house.

FRIDA   And I'm not a part of your life?

ESTELA   You don't need me. You have your husband and your son.

FRIDA   You say that with bitterness, as if it in-
creased your misfortune to see people happy.

ESTELA   Can you really think that of me? No,
Frida. I've never felt envy for another's happiness. And listen to me now, in case you've
doubted it: if it were in my power to lessen this
awful sorrow at your expense, I'd rather cut off
my hand than cause you harm.

FRIDA   If you have nothing against me, why do you
refuse to set foot in my house? (*She goes closer
to* ESTELA.) Is it because of Christian? (*There is
a tense pause.*) Answer.

ESTELA   (*controlling her voice.*) Will you un-
tangle the shuttle for me? My fingers are clumsy.

FRIDA   Don't try to change the subject. Answer! Is
it because of Christian?

ESTELA   (*with effort, avoiding her eyes.*) Christian is
another matter. Those who were not Peter's
friends can't be mine.

FRIDA   So . . . ! I thought the time for forgetting
old grudges had arrived.

ESTELA   Let's not speak of it any more. They're
things that are past.

FRIDA   No, Estela; though it may be difficult for
both of us, it's better to say these things once and
for all. You've always believed that my husband
hated yours.

ESTELA   Hate, I don't know; but there was rivalry.
Without their wanting it, life forced them to be
rivals more than once.

FRIDA   The first time it was because of you. Before

you chose Peter, Christian had eyes only for you.

ESTELA   Why are we remembering this?

FRIDA   If there was jealousy between them then, it doesn't matter now. The two of us married the same day, and after the wedding they were friends again as before.

ESTELA   But their rivalry kept coming up at any pretext. When they went to sea together, Peter was a better fisherman. When they sang in church or in the tavern, Peter's voice rang out louder.

FRIDA   (*standing up.*) It's not important. If they had hard feelings, they soon forgot. One day they would quarrel and the next they had their arms around each other.

ESTELA   There was the fight over the boat. Both of them dreamed of buying the same one; they worked day and night to get it. But the one who worked most got it, and he was the one who needed it most. That day they quarreled for the last time . . . but they didn't put their arms around each other again. . . . (*Deeply.*) It was the night Peter died.

FRIDA   And is a fight between our husbands enough to justify a separation like this? We've said it: first young men jealous for the same girl, and then two fishermen who yearn for the same boat. That was all. Can you blame Christian for anything more?

ESTELA   Have I ever blamed him?

FRIDA   I'm not asking what you are saying aloud; I want to know the thing gnawing inside you.

ESTELA   Don't be upset. I don't have anything against Christian, nothing. . . . (*Controlling her voice.*) If I did, just remembering you and your son would be enough to keep me silent.

FRIDA (*suddenly apprehensive, she looks at her intensely.*)   Estela! Do you realize what you've just said?

ESTELA (*anguished.*)   I've said nothing!

FRIDA   You've said a great deal, and now it's too late to turn back. (*Lifting* ESTELA's *face with her hand.*) Show me your face! Look at me! Why didn't you remember before that they quarreled the same night Peter died?

ESTELA (*desperate.*)   For the sake of what you love most, be quiet!

FRIDA   Who is the man who appears in your dreams? Is it Christian?

ESTELA   I haven't said that! I won't say it. (*She hides her face in her arms.*)

FRIDA (*rigid; repeating with disbelief.*)   It's Christian . . . It is! And is it my own sister who believes that? (*She sits down heavily with a strange look in her eyes.* ESTELA *kneels beside her and takes refuge in her lap.*)

ESTELA   Forgive me, Frida. I swear to you that I didn't want to believe it either; that I'd give my life not to believe it. But it's stronger than I am! A person can clench his fists and grit his teeth to put a chain around words, but no one can close out a thought. You don't know how I've struggled against an idea that burns my mind like fire, the cries I've stifled against my pillow, repeating: "It cannot be. Christian is good. You are an unhappy, bitter woman." But always I'd fall asleep again only to see Christian standing in my dream, like a black bolt of lightning against red blood on a cliff!

FRIDA (*motionless, without looking at her.*) You'll still expect me to be grateful for your silence. It would have been better for you to accuse him openly. He would have known how to defend himself.

ESTELA   I'd hoped I could convince myself of his innocence. I would be the happiest of women if one day I could forgive. But everything he did only raised new suspicions. Why, when Peter was laid out here, was Christian the only one who didn't come to pay his respects? Why does a man who never drank before drink so much now? Why has he never been able to sit down in my presence and smoke his pipe without his hands trembling?

FRIDA   That's enough! I won't listen to any more of this. (*She stands up.*) Perhaps you deserve pity more than I do; you've broken the bond that was between us.

ESTELA   Don't go off like that. Wait.

FRIDA   What's there to hope for now? When I walked out of my house, I left a man who had all my faith and whom I could kiss with laughter in my mouth. Now I must return with a sad silence that will chill our home. And you are the one who could cut off her hand before doing me harm? You've done me the worst harm you could, the most useless. You've not regained your own peace of mind but you have destroyed mine. That's what you've accomplished. Cut off your hand, Estela! Cut it off! (*She exits sobbing deeply.*)

Evening has fallen. ESTELA *is on her knees crying.
There is a long pause. From far off the church bells
toll for prayer.* ESTELA *gets up slowly and goes to
light the lamp.* THE GRANDMOTHER *returns from the
kitchen drying her hands.*

GRANDMOTHER Now the pottery and the copper
are sparkling like living coals. He may find us
poor, that's for sure, but clean as the sun on the
sea. Why don't you fix yourself up a little?
There's a fine silk kerchief and a bottle of co-
logne in the bottom of the chest.

ESTELA Who am I fixing myself for? Don't I look
all right this way?

GRANDMOTHER I didn't say that. As a woman, you
have no reason at all for envy. I wasn't any bet-
ter-looking myself when I was your age. But men
notice everything; especially foreigners, because
it's all new to them. (*She is cleaning and arrang-
ing everything she can put her hands on.*) Think
of the things he must have seen! All that traveling—the countries, the people coming and going.

ESTELA His visit has made you awfully nervous.

GRANDMOTHER Nervous isn't the word for it. Can't
you see that I'm tingling from head to toes?

ESTELA I see; indeed I do. But why?

GRANDMOTHER Almost no reason at all! After so
much loneliness, to think that a man from a faraway country is going to come through that door.
To hear a man's footsteps in the house again! To
hear a man's voice!

ESTELA Isn't my voice enough for you?

GRANDMOTHER What is a conversation between
two women worth? No more than the rain on the
sea. We can be as proud as we wish and even

avoid their eyes—because it's proper and because that's what we were taught. But a man is still a man. When you have him near, even the walls seem more secure. If they don't look at you, you don't even realize you're a woman! And the houses where men live have in them the strong smell of tobacco smoked quietly before sleep comes.

ESTELA Grandmother . . .

GRANDMOTHER (*listening nervously.*) Be quiet. . . . There he is. . . . There he is . . . ! (*Instinctively she tears off her apron and arranges her gray hair.* OLD MARK *enters leading* RICHARD.)

MARK Estela Anderson. . . . Her grandmother. . . . (*They acknowledge each other without words.*) I don't know what his name is.

RICHARD (*advances, embarrassed.*) Jordan. Richard Jordan. (*They look at each other in silence. Pause.* RICHARD *looks around the house with emotion.*)

MARK As you can see, the gentleman isn't much of a talker either. Well, I think that's all I'm supposed to do, isn't it?

ESTELA Thank you, Old Mark.

MARK Night. (*Turning to* THE GRANDMOTHER, *more loudly.*) Good night! (*Exits.*)

ESTELA Richard Jordan. . . . I don't remember having heard that name.

GRANDMOTHER It's not surprising. When Peter came back from his voyages, he would talk of ships and trees and tall chimneys. But of people, very little. He liked to talk of things more than people.

ESTELA Were you a friend of his?

RICHARD Friend is not the word. I met him for
only a moment, some time ago; he was singing
a song. But it was something so important in my
life that I shall never be able to forget it. That
memory is what brought me here.

ESTELA You made the trip for him? You didn't
know . . . ?

RICHARD Yes, I knew. But the desire to see his
village, the things that were his, the people that
he loved, was so strong.

ESTELA The things that he owned are few: these
four walls and a useless boat moored in the harbor. The people that he loved—the whole town,
and us.

GRANDMOTHER How can you remember him so
well if you met him for only a moment?

RICHARD There are moments that are worth a life;
that was one. My fortune or my undoing depended on a signature, and Peter Anderson decided it all. What I didn't imagine then is that
one's fortune and one's misfortune can be the
same thing.

ESTELA Did he know this?

RICHARD He had no way of knowing it. But one
thing is certain: what I have I owe to him. And
if it were possible, I would give it all to repay
that debt.

ESTELA Thank you for your kind memory of him.
But the thing that is missing in this house cannot be paid for with money.

RICHARD I feared that. A hundred times I was at
the point of making this trip, and always I hes-
itated through fear that it would be in vain.

GRANDMOTHER Not in vain. What did you come

seeking? A friend? Well, here you have two. Did you believe you owed us something? Well, you've more than paid us just by having come. You speak, Estela; you're the mistress of the house. What would Peter have said if he were here?

ESTELA   He had only one way of welcoming those who came to him: this is my table, this is my house. They are yours.

RICHARD   Don't be so quick to offer your hospitality. Have you asked yourself if I deserve it?

ESTELA   One doesn't ask questions when he gives to someone who comes from far away. That is what our fathers taught us.

RICHARD   (*moved by her words, he looks up at her with respect.*)   Thank you . . . dear lady.

GRANDMOTHER   You heard: lady . . . ! How well the people from the South know how to say "lady." (*Pushing a chair toward him.*) Sit down, please; standing there like that you look as if you're going to leave any minute. Aren't you tired from the trip?

RICHARD   I'm used to traveling.

GRANDMOTHER   When does the ship sail again?

RICHARD   Tomorrow, at dawn.

GRANDMOTHER   So soon? But tonight you'll eat with us, won't you? No, no; don't say no. Would you like something to drink? I can bring you a mug of beer.

RICHARD   Thank you, but I'm not thirsty.

GRANDMOTHER   Are you cold? Do you want me to light the fire?

RICHARD   Not cold either; don't bother.

GRANDMOTHER   (*almost angrily.*)   You're not tired, you're not thirsty, and you're not cold. . . . There must be something wrong with you. People always have a need for something.

ESTELA (*smiling.*) Don't misunderstand. Grandmother would like for everyone to be thirsty so that she could give them something to drink; or light the fire to warm them. It's her way of finding happiness.

GRANDMOTHER Supper will be ready before you can recite the Creed. Yes indeed, though there's nothing but herring, and plenty of that. But not the smoked kind you have over there. Fresh. Fresh from the sea to the frying pan. Do you like herring?

RICHARD Don't bother about me. With you to feed me I think I'd end up liking everything. Many thanks.

GRANDMOTHER You are thanking me? Me? I should have thanked you, man sent by God—although it may be for only one night. Set another plate, Estela. (*With a light tremor in her voice.*) You don't know what a table's like when there are only two plates . . . and one of those belongs to a grandmother. (*She exits happily.*) Three plates again. . . . Three plates!

RICHARD *watches her with fascination;* ESTELA *silently sets another plate on the table.*

RICHARD Remarkable. . . . What vigor at her age!

ESTELA She'll soon be seventy.

RICHARD And is she always this way?

ESTELA Always; in good weather and in bad. There are trees that never lose their leaves.

RICHARD You are a peaceful and strong people. I've seen girls on the farms doing a man's work and singing all the while. Their smiles were bright and they waved at me when I passed by. And they all had blue eyes.

ESTELA Just as the sea is so blue in this land. Do you like our country?

RICHARD I've just come but already I wish it were my home.

ESTELA That's kind of you.

RICHARD Old Mark told me that you work too.

ESTELA It's no curse. What would I do if I didn't?

RICHARD But it's more than those hands can stand. Even tilling the soil.

ESTELA Only a small orchard and a bit of land, just out there.

RICHARD Did you do that work before?

ESTELA It wasn't necessary before. When Peter was alive we planted roses. Afterwards I had to dig them up to grow food. The saddest thing about houses without a man is that we must turn gardens into fields.

RICHARD Would you refuse to accept my aid? With what I've spent in one night I could buy all that your land would produce in a hundred years.

ESTELA Your night was yours. My work is mine. And it helps me to remember.

RICHARD I hope my words haven't offended you.

ESTELA No. I understand that they are sincere and decent, and I'm grateful to you. (*Pause.*) It appears that you aren't very happy with your fortune.

RICHARD What good does it do me? I can't lessen a woman's burden with it, nor buy an hour of peaceful sleep.

ESTELA Do you have something you want to forget?

RICHARD   If I only could. . . .

ESTELA   Time will help you. And your travels. Will you be going far?

RICHARD   There's no one waiting for me anywhere. I'd like to miss that ship tomorrow and remain here until it returns.

ESTELA   Ours is a poor village. You wouldn't find life here to your taste.

RICHARD   What I need is so little . . . and so difficult to find.

ESTELA   Rest?

RICHARD   Rest. Perhaps here I could find the peace that I've been searching for.

ESTELA   (*looking at him thoughtfully.*)   How long will it be before the ship returns?

RICHARD   A couple of weeks.

ESTELA   (*avoiding his eyes.*)   If a table of pine and a window that looks out on the sea are enough for you . . . there is an empty room upstairs.

RICHARD   In this house? And is it you, Estela Anderson, who offers me the shelter of her home?

ESTELA   Always I try to do what he would have done. . . . Why do you lower your eyes?

RICHARD   I don't know. . . . I'm not accustomed to kindness. I come from a world where everything is done for money; even the most cowardly of crimes. There they look at every stranger as a possible enemy. But you have opened your door to me without asking who I am or where I come from. Do you understand why I lower my eyes? Thirty years of shame must show in my face.

ESTELA   Don't think of that now. I'm sorry that I have so little to offer you. Have you always been rich?

RICHARD   Not always. As a child I knew hunger
. . . and the memory of it has come back.

ESTELA   Then it will all be easier for you now.

RICHARD   But my poverty was not voluntary like
yours. I know that Peter's boat is the finest in the
village and that many fishermen would be eager
to buy it.

ESTELA   I'd rather beg my bread along the high-
ways than sell his boat. It would be like selling
a part of him.

RICHARD   I know the story. Peter bought it the day
he died.

ESTELA   How easy it is to say: he bought it. To describe it with a word or two. But how many days
of exhaustion and how many nights without
sleep before it was possible! When he couldn't
go to sea, he would work with his ax in the
forest. At night we would carve those boats together, using the wood that we needed for the
fire. And it took so long. One day he'd have to
do without wine; another day, tobacco. Seven
days of work were like one step forward. Slowly
it grew—that small pile of silver capable of
breaking a man and yet easily contained in a
handkerchief! (*She pauses for breath.*) Finally
the great day came. I don't know what the anxiety of a woman who expects a child must be,
but it couldn't be greater. Peter went down to
the harbor, happy, wearing his clean shirt. I had
filled his pipe and placed it beside his plate and
was waiting behind that window, with a terrible
joy that I could feel in my veins. From far off
I heard him coming; he was singing with that
full and manly voice of his. When he reached

the crest, he raised his hand to wave to me . . .
and suddenly, right there before my eyes . . .
(*Her voice breaks.*) No! It couldn't have been
God's will! God would not have chosen that
night! (*She manages to control herself.*) Forgive
me. I shouldn't have remembered those things.

GRANDMOTHER (*returning with a loaf of bread and
a platter of fish.*) To the table; it's getting cold!
I took a long time, didn't I? I don't know what's
wrong with me today, for everything slips out of
my hands. I would have liked to put a slice of
lemon on the fish—oh, yes, we've had lemons
here—but with two drops of vinegar and a leaf
of mint it's almost the same. The bread is wheat
and the freshest in the village. No ordinary bread
tonight. (*Indicating to* RICHARD *the place at the
head of the table.*) Here. This is the man's place.
That's right. (*The three of them sit down.*)

ESTELA (*handing the knife to* RICHARD.) Will you
cut it? Here it is the man who slices the bread
and blesses the table.

RICHARD Thank you. I shall divide the bread. But
as for the prayer, however much I might wish to
say it, I wouldn't know the words.

He cuts the bread which he offers first to THE
GRANDMOTHER *and then to* ESTELA. *From far off a
chorus of men's voices is heard singing Peter's song
with accordion accompaniment.* RICHARD *drops the
knife.* ESTELA *clenches her hand upon the tablecloth to retain control of herself.*

ESTELA The window, Grandmother . . . the window. . . . (THE GRANDMOTHER *closes the wooden
shutters. The song is still audible but fainter.*)

GRANDMOTHER They're boys making the rounds.

What do they know about the songs they sing.
. . . (*She sits down again.*)

ESTELA   Lord, bless the woodsman's ax in the forest. Bless the fisherman's nets upon the sea. Provide for us bread and fish on our table as your Son did on the mountain of miracles. Give us peace at work and in sleep. And if we have done harm to another, forgive us, Lord, as we ourselves have forgiven . . . (*She breathes deeply.*)
. . . as we have forgiven . . . (*She breaks into sobs and buries her head on the tablecloth.*) No! It's a lie! I have not forgiven. I cannot forgive . . . !

The fishermen's chorus grows louder as the curtain falls.

Act Three

The same place. Two weeks later. An afternoon bright with sunshine. OLD MARK *whistles as he mixes pigment and glue in a jar before testing it on a piece of wood.* THE GRANDMOTHER *enters from the garden with a basket of green vegetables.*

MARK Things to be picked already?

GRANDMOTHER The first spring peas, small and tender like drops of honey. It's a glory to watch them shoot up and twist around the poles, reaching out for the sun. The sun. . . . I'd climb up too, if I could reach it. (*She sits down and begins to shell the peas.* OLD MARK *slowly fills his pipe.*) To think that there are countries that have sunshine all year and still they complain.

MARK Fog isn't so bad either. It's more restful.

GRANDMOTHER Rest, rest. . . . Do you still want more of that? Seated you were born and seated you'll die. If I were as old as you, nobody would take from me this day of sunshine, with the sap rising in the forest, the trees atremble with birds, and all the roads bedecked with lovers! But with you it's always the seventh day.

MARK What seventh day?

GRANDMOTHER The day of rest!

MARK I'm not a man for celebrations. They raised

me this way and now it's late for turning back.
If I could live twice——

GRANDMOTHER　You'd do exactly the same again.
A cat has nine lives but he never stops chasing
rats.

MARK　Just keep it up! Don't pick a quarrel with
me, don't pick a quarrel——

GRANDMOTHER　It wouldn't be worth the trouble.
You'd only get tongue-tied, and I'd win! (*Pause.
She goes on shelling the peas.* OLD MARK *studies
an unfinished boat of light wood.*) Are you going to paint it?

MARK　No. Mr. Jordan began this one and he
wants to finish it himself before he says farewell
to us.

GRANDMOTHER　Don't talk to me about farewells.
The hour will come without you calling it. When
does his boat leave?

MARK　At nightfall.

GRANDMOTHER　So soon? And with the days as short
as they are here. Why did that blessed ship have
to come back?

MARK　It was scheduled to come today.

GRANDMOTHER　It could have been lost at sea. Or
passed on by.

MARK　You've taken a liking to our guest, haven't
you?

GRANDMOTHER　And who wouldn't? All the people
in the village are friends of his; he has a good
word for everybody. And when he sits on the
wall and talks with the old people, he seems one
of us.

MARK　As for making people like him, he does
have his way. And he knows how to be useful.

In two weeks he's learned to cast the nets like the best fishermen.

GRANDMOTHER Always good-humored; and so open with everyone. With the world he's seen and the things he knows!

MARK Stop there! On some things we don't see eye to eye. As a decent man and a friend, you couldn't ask more. But when it comes to common sense—he doesn't know anything.

GRANDMOTHER Are you going to give him lessons?

MARK It wouldn't be the first time. This morning, for example, when he saw the poppies budding in the moss on the roof, he asked me very seriously who took care of sowing flowers on the roof tops. "But who do you suppose, sir? The wind!"

GRANDMOTHER A fine thing! As if he had nothing more important to keep in his head.

MARK Sure, sure. A lot he's learned from schools and books. But the truth is he doesn't know how to tell an ash tree from a birch, or if there's going to be a storm by the flight of the seagulls, or how soon nightfall will come from the bending of the grass. To tell what time it is he has to look at the clock. And that's sense? The one who has sense is the clock.

GRANDMOTHER Those are things he learned where he came from. Each one knows the ways of his own land.

MARK I agree. But leave him alone at night in the forest and let's see if he's capable of finding his way out by the stars! Or is it that there are no stars in his land either?

GRANDMOTHER Probably there are other stars. . . .

MARK (*surprised.*) Other stars? But can there be other ones?

GRANDMOTHER I mean——

MARK Ah! That's fine. There may be other kinds of plants and other ways of talking, because that's the world down here; but there's no one who can change the stars. The one who fixed the North Star up there knew what fishermen needed.

ESTELA *arrives exhilarated from being outdoors. On her arm she is carrying a small basket covered with leaves.*

ESTELA After such a long wait, the sun almost stuns you with its rays when it comes down through the pine trees. . . .

GRANDMOTHER Are you alone . . . ?

ESTELA Richard is coming directly. He had to go down to the harbor.

GRANDMOTHER What do you have there?

ESTELA Wild berries. They're everywhere on the heath, but you have to search for them on your knees. They know how to hide between the leaves as if they understood fear.

GRANDMOTHER Does Richard like the taste of them?

ESTELA And when have you seen something he didn't like here? Why, he wants to shout out his thanks for the rising sap and the salt in the air. He's like a blind man who is beginning to discover the world. The first time he saw the northern lights he thought it was a miracle. When he was eating the berries—and the red juice dripping all over him—he laughed like a young boy. (*She puts the basket down and turns to* OLD

MARK.) Go down to the harbor with him; he
may need your help.

MARK   I'll go. . . . (*From the door.*) One question, Estela: Did Mr. Jordan know what the wild
berries were?

ESTELA   No. Why?

MARK (*looking satisfied at* THE GRANDMOTHER.)
No reason. Just curious. (*He exits.*)

GRANDMOTHER   Why did he go so soon?

ESTELA   To arrange his passage and say good-bye
to friends. Now the farewells are beginning.

GRANDMOTHER   Farewell! A curse on the man who
invented that word. People should always be arriving. They should never go away.

ESTELA   It had to be like this. You knew that from
the first day.

GRANDMOTHER   We know from the first day that a
person has to die, and that's no consolation when
the time comes.

ESTELA   You'll get used to things the way they
were. Two weeks isn't enough time to change a
life.

GRANDMOTHER   Time is measured by what goes on
inside; and these two weeks have been full. What
do you expect from me now? That I watch him
walk away without anything more than waving
a handkerchief and saying "Have a happy voyage," as if it were nothing out of the ordinary?

ESTELA   If you feel something more, you must keep
it to yourself. Men come and they go; we women
stay. It's our fate.

GRANDMOTHER   Are you going to tell me that you're
pleased about it?

ESTELA No. Ships that sail away always leave sadness behind.

GRANDMOTHER I've watched hundreds of them pass by and never have I felt what I feel today. It's my fault. One should never take a liking to anything but trees—those that don't move around —and you can always be sure of leaving before they do.

ESTELA (*nervously.*) That's enough, Grandmother! Richard's life is over there; ours here. It's the best thing for all of us.

GRANDMOTHER I don't say that he shouldn't go back. I already know that what can't be can't be. But when it comes to not feeling it . . . When he arrived, it was like new windows being opened all over the house. Even you were beginning to see with different eyes. And now . . . (*She goes over to* ESTELA *and looks at her face to face.*) Woman to woman, Estela. If you had the power to hold back that ship . . .

ESTELA (*firmly.*) I'd do nothing. Richard must leave; that is the only thing I know. If only he'd continued his voyage the night he came.

GRANDMOTHER Do you have something against him?

ESTELA I have something against myself, which is worse. Haven't you noticed it? Before, I at least knew what I wanted; and I knew that tomorrow I was going to want the same thing as the day before. But now I can no longer think calmly about anything or be at ease—as when someone is watching what you do over your shoulder. I don't want to go on this way! I need to be at peace with myself again—with an oar nailed to the door and sitting down to wait. That's all.

GRANDMOTHER Just imagination. You're blaming yourself for things that only pass through your head.

ESTELA I'm not the only one who feels this way. When we're together there's a kind of pretended happiness. But he's not at ease either; something is troubling him inside.

GRANDMOTHER You're not going to start thinking that he's hiding some evil intention? Richard is a decent man; a true friend to you.

ESTELA No, Grandmother; true friends speak to each other easily, face to face. We don't. Always there's something dark between us.

GRANDMOTHER You never told me that.

ESTELA This very day, when we were laughing and looking for berries on the heath, our hands met accidentally, and suddenly we were both silent, not able to look at each other. . . . It was like a stone thrown into a tree full of birds. I do know that I didn't dare raise my eyes. But he—why was he silent?

GRANDMOTHER If it's like that, perhaps you're right. Something that can't go on is better ended in time.

ESTELA Thank you. That's what I was waiting to hear from you. (*She sighs with relief. Pause.*) Are his clothes ready?

GRANDMOTHER Upstairs. Sprinkled with lavender water so that he'll carry with him the clean smell of this place.

ESTELA Did you close his suitcases?

GRANDMOTHER That's not my business. For open-

ing suitcases I'm more than willing. But for closing them I'm too old.

ESTELA (*starting toward the stairway.*) You were
always the youngest person in this house; and
the strongest. I hope you won't forget that at the
last moment. (*She goes up.*)

GRANDMOTHER   Don't worry. If I feel a pang, nobody is going to notice it. (*Alone. She mutters as
she gathers up the basket and the peas.*) And of
course I do. It would be good if I didn't. Is there
no way except farewell? I'll say "Have a good
voyage, friend . . . and keep going straight
ahead to see if it's true that the world is round."
Then a catch in the throat . . . and it will all
be the same again, now and forever. Amen!

RICHARD *enters followed by* OLD MARK.

RICHARD   Hello, Grandmother. Were you talking to
yourself?

GRANDMOTHER   I have to get used to it again. Not
everyone has your patience with me.

RICHARD   It's not patience. It delights me to listen
to you. Truly.

GRANDMOTHER   At least you pretend well enough.
And when all is said and done, what effort does it
take? Since I don't ask anyone to answer me. Or
even listen to me. It's enough to make me happy
that they look at me and move their heads from
time to time. Is that too much to ask?

RICHARD   You have a real fear of silence.

GRANDMOTHER   That's the word: fear. And rightly
so. When is the ocean silent? When there's going
to be a storm. When does the forest become
hushed? When men pass through with guns.
Whenever there is a great silence, there's danger

in the air. (*Evoking the past, intimately.*) I remember a time, when I was just a child. There
were nine of us—eight tall brothers and me. One
night something had happened at home; tears
were streaming down my mother's face; my father
was clenching his fists on the table; and all eight
of my brothers were pale, with their eyes fixed on
their plates. No one dared to move or scarcely
breathe. There was a silence so cold you could
feel it in your blood. All that I could hear was
water dripping from a jug—drip-drip . . . drip,
drip . . . drip-drip . . . ! Because of that I
didn't burst into tears. And look how it is with
me after seventy years—I no longer remember the
terrible thing that had happened in my house.
But what I shall never forget, in gratitude, is
that drip-drip of water, which was the only thing
that dared to speak so that I wouldn't be afraid.
(RICHARD *touches her shoulder affectionately.*)

RICHARD   Grandmother!

MARK   Dripping water! What you need is a daily
cloudburst.

GRANDMOTHER (*in a brusque transition.*)   It would
be strange indeed if you didn't get in a blow with
your tail. I always said it: even as a child you
were dim-witted—and just look how you've grown
with age! (RICHARD *picks up his small boat and
begins to smooth it with a file.*) Are you going to
work now?

RICHARD   I would have liked to leave it finished;
but there's not enough time.

GRANDMOTHER   How eagerly you take to work. As
if you'd never done any.

RICHARD   Maybe that's the reason.

MARK   What did you do over there in your land?

RICHARD   I played the Stock Market.

MARK   Aha! (*Short pause.*) And after you played, what did you work at?

RICHARD   The Stock Market isn't a game. It's a market for buying and selling.

MARK   A market?

RICHARD   But not like those here. You buy and sell things. We trade the names of things.

MARK   I don't understand. How could you buy and sell wheat without wheat?

RICHARD   It's very easy. For example . . . (*He takes four glasses from the sideboard and starts placing them in a row on the table.*) You have just sowed a field of wheat that won't be gathered until the next harvest. But since it's necessary to keep on living until then, I will give you credit of a hundred kroner for that wheat. (*He moves the first glass.*) Here is your letter of credit. Do you follow?

MARK   I see. . . .

RICHARD   Now, if when summer comes the harvest is lost, it doesn't matter. You can repay me with a hundred pieces of silver. Isn't that right?

MARK   So it is.

RICHARD   (*taking the second glass.*)   Here are the hundred pieces of silver for the value of the wheat. But since silver is scarce, the Bank withdraws it and puts in its place a piece of paper that says: One Hundred Kroner. (*He takes the third glass.*) Here is the bank note. If, at the time for payment, you don't have the paper at hand, that doesn't matter either: you simply sign an IOU for the value of the bank note. (*He takes the fourth glass.*) Here is the IOU. And here's where the miracle begins. (*Pointing.*) A hundred kroner of credit, a hundred in silver, a hundred in paper, the hundred of the IOU—a total of four hundred kroner on the market and not a single grain of real wheat. (*He dusts off his hands.*) Do you understand now?

MARK (*convinced.*)   Now I do. Two years ago another gentleman passed through here doing the same thing; but that one did it with a top hat, and pigeons flew out of it. Now I'd like for you to explain the trick to me.

RICHARD   There's no trick here, Old Mark. That is . . . I don't know . . .

GRANDMOTHER (*replacing the glasses.*)   So this is the Stock Market? Lord, what people can invent when they have nothing to do.

RICHARD   You don't seem to take it very seriously.

GRANDMOTHER   Lack of habit. I don't know what things are like over there in your world. But here, what little wheat we have is always real. And the hunger, too.

ESTELA *calls out as she comes down the stairway.*

ESTELA   Grandmother . . . ! Grandmother . . . ! Don't you hear it?

GRANDMOTHER   What?

They listen. ESTELA *opens the door, and the clear, insistent tolling of the alarm bell can be heard.*

ESTELA   It's the lighthouse bell. Someone is in danger!

GRANDMOTHER   At sea? Impossible. The fishing boats don't go out until tomorrow.

ESTELA It could be an avalanche. Or a fire. Run and find out, Uncle Mark.

GRANDMOTHER Send him? We'd never find out.

RICHARD I'll go.

GRANDMOTHER You take care of your things; the sun will be setting soon. I'll go with him. (*She exits rapidly with* OLD MARK. ESTELA *listens from the door.*)

RICHARD Let me go with them. I might be needed.

ESTELA (*detaining him and silencing him with a gesture.*) It's ringing more slowly now. . . . It's fading away. . . . If it was a warning, the danger is over now. If it was an accident there's nothing we can do. (*She closes the door.*) The day was too beautiful to end well.

RICHARD Since I've been here I haven't seen a happier one. It seemed a holiday—the harbor white with sails and salt gleaming on the nets. I never saw people so full of joy.

ESTELA It's the first full day of sunshine and they're making their preparations to go to sea. The flight of the petrels tells us that the fish are returning from the warmer oceans. Tomorrow all the boats will go far out. (*She lowers her voice.*) All except one. (*The sun is beginning to go down.*)

RICHARD What do you suppose happened to make them ring the bell?

ESTELA Life is never without danger here. We've heard the bell many times.

RICHARD I want to know what happened before I leave.

ESTELA Does it interest you so much? Two weeks ago those men were nothing to you.

RICHARD Because I didn't know them then. "To suffer another man's pain the first thing that is needed is imagination." The one who said that to me knew what he was talking about. One day we learn that a fisherman is going to die in a village in the North, and we shrug our shoulders. Another day we read that thirty thousand men have fallen on a battlefield, and we continue sipping our coffee calmly because those thirty thousand lives are nothing more than a figure for us. And it's not that our hearts are insensitive; it's because our imaginations are dead.

ESTELA And this is something you did not know before?

RICHARD No. I had to come here to learn a lesson that is so simple: that in the life of one man is the life of all men.

ESTELA (*looking at him with gratitude.*) I like to hear you talk that way. Do you know what I think at times? That you were born here, among us; that then you lived far off for many years, without knowing who you really were—and now you are beginning to recognize your own people again.

RICHARD I wish that were true. To be able to feel that this land is my own and live in it always.

ESTELA Don't let yourself be deceived by the impressions of a few days. You've had two happy weeks of vacation, when the deer are already calling in the alder grove and the nights are white. But you don't know what it's like during a winter of eight months, with ice covering the windows; and those endless nights of eighteen hours, from

the time of the first snow until the song of the
cuckoo.

RICHARD Why couldn't I be expected to endure
what a woman can endure?

ESTELA With me it's different. I've been used to
this life since childhood and I have a faith that
helps me.

RICHARD What are the things you believe in? I'd
like to believe in them too.

ESTELA Actually there aren't many; but I feel them
very deeply. I believe that life—although it may
embitter us at times—is a duty. I believe that all
we need can be found on the earth and in the
sea. I believe that God is benevolent. That is
enough for me.

RICHARD Estela . . . (*He takes her hand across the
table. Evening has come.*)

ESTELA It's time to light the lamp. . . .

RICHARD Will you let me light it?

ESTELA Yes. Thank you. (RICHARD *lights the lamp.
The ship's horn is heard in the distance.* ESTELA
trembles but gains control of herself.) The signal
from the ship. . . . You must go.

RICHARD It's the first call. There's still time.

ESTELA Time for what! (*With anguish.*) Go now,
Richard. I don't know how to say good-bye to
you. What can I say when the minutes are num-
bered?

RICHARD I'm the one who must speak now, Estela;
not you. (*He moves closer to her.*) I came from
far away to tell you something; only one thing
. . . and each time that I was going to speak, a
knot of fear and shame caught the words in my
throat.

ESTELA If it's to be sad, don't say it. It's better to part as we are—friends.

RICHARD I can't keep silent any longer. I need to tell it and for you to hear it. . . . However painful it may be for both of us, you must let me say it now.

ESTELA (*with instinctive fear.*) Then say it.

RICHARD It's about Peter's death. (ESTELA *averts her eyes.*) You told me something the first day: that God did not will his death. Well, you were right, Estela. It was a man who caused it. And that man is here!

ESTELA (*reacting with distress.*) How did you find out? I've accused no one! I can't accuse him! And if anyone else did, I'd say a hundred times that it was a lie! Even though he has destroyed my life, it must be this way. . . . Because my sister and her son stand between us.

RICHARD But whom are you talking about?

ESTELA About Christian!

RICHARD You suspect him?

ESTELA If it were no more than a suspicion! But I know! I recognized his leather jacket from that window. I erased his bootprints myself before dawn. I've bitten my hands to keep silent, night after night, while my soul was crying out inside me. And now you want to undo my work? For the child's sake, Richard, keep silent!

RICHARD Now there is more reason than ever to speak! Knowing what you think, I would be the worst coward of all if I kept silent a moment more. (*He takes her hands.*) Estela . . . ! (*Suddenly there is a pounding on the door and* FRIDA'*s voice calls out in anguish.*)

FRIDA Estela . . . ! Estela . . . !

ESTELA (*startled.*) It's Frida! Don't say anything. I beg you. . . . (FRIDA *enters. She is wearing a shawl and carrying a lantern which she puts down on the way in. She throws herself sobbing into the arms of her sister.*)

FRIDA Estela!

ESTELA Has something happened at your house?

FRIDA Didn't you hear the lighthouse bell? Christian went out in the boat to test the new rudder. When he was passing near the cliffs, he was caught in a squall, and a great wave threw him against a jagged rock that tore into his chest like a claw.

ESTELA Is it grave?

FRIDA I've asked everyone that. But no one answers me, and they all lower their eyes. . . . I know what it means when men are silent like that in the presence of blood.

ESTELA And he . . . he . . . ?

FRIDA He has spoken only one word: your name. You can't let him die like this. Christian is calling for you. He only wants to speak with you! (*She collapses on a chair.*)

ESTELA With me . . . ? (*To* RICHARD.) Will you leave us alone for a moment?

RICHARD Of course. . . . (*He goes upstairs.*)

ESTELA (*waiting until he has left.*) Do you realize what that means, Frida? If Christian thinks that he's dying, and he's calling for me, it can only mean that he wants to confess something to me. (*Leaning over* FRIDA'*s shoulder, with choked voice.*) Am I right?

FRIDA (*hesitates; finally she nods without looking up.*) You are.

ESTELA Did he tell you?

FRIDA He didn't need to. The afternoon I left here blaming you, I was still proud, but the thorn of suspicion was already inside me. From that day I never stopped thinking, and one thought led to another. Then I understood why he would react strangely when I spoke to him and blink his eyes as if waking up from a bad dream; and why his pipe would go out so often between his teeth; and those hundred nights of sleeplessness, when he lay there with his eyes glued to the ceiling. I fought against believing it. But there's no reason for doubt now.

ESTELA Go back to him. Tell him that I already know and that I shall continue to keep silent. But don't force me to hear him say it!

FRIDA You must be the one. Don't you understand that what Christian feels isn't the fear of death? He has defied death time and again on land and sea without trembling. Now he has a deeper fear which only one word can cure. And no one but you can say that word to him. Please don't refuse him now!

ESTELA Frida, I didn't imagine that you loved him so much.

FRIDA Neither did I. I thought that this truth would separate us. And precisely now—when I see him broken and guilty and trembling like a child—now is when I feel that I love him most . . . that I shall love him always and above all things!

ESTELA I'll take him the only strength I can give
him. Come along! (*She throws a shawl over
her shoulders, takes the lantern, and leaves with
FRIDA.*)

FRIDA Thank you, Estela, thank you. . . .

*For a moment there is no one onstage. Then RICH-
ARD comes down the stairs looking toward the door.*

RICHARD (*repeating as in a daze.*) Christian . . .
Christian . . . Can it be possible?

*He starts toward the door as if to follow the two
women. Then the light begins to change, giving an
unreal effect to the scene. The mysterious music of
the first act is heard again.* THE GENTLEMAN IN BLACK
appears on the threshold of the garden door.

GENTLEMAN Good evening, Richard Jordan.

RICHARD You here? Well, you're too late to trick
me again. Now I know the truth. (*He steps toward him resolutely.*) It wasn't I who killed Peter
Anderson. You knew what was going to happen,
and the hour and place in which it would happen. Why did you make me believe that I was
the one who did it?

GENTLEMAN Let's be calm. You're not going to
have any cause for raising your voice!

RICHARD What do you intend to do now? Answer!

GENTLEMAN I've already told you that it was a
kind of experiment. And up to this point it hasn't
turned out at all badly for me.

RICHARD I don't care about your experiments. The
only thing that's clear is that I didn't commit a
murder. It was all your doing.

GENTLEMAN Mine? I'm not the one who determines
life and death. It is . . . The Other One. (*He
points vaguely.*) Even the village children know

this. Only men who have read many books come to forget the simplest things.

RICHARD   Then who killed him?

GENTLEMAN   I thought you already knew. Christian. Only Christian.

RICHARD   And if you yourself admit it, why are you here now? I am free of guilt.

GENTLEMAN   There's where you're wrong. You didn't kill; agreed. But you did will to commit the crime. And for me that is the fact that counts. That day I also told you that the material act didn't matter to me. My only world is the one of desire and intent.

RICHARD   But mine is the one of deeds. And for an evil thought there is no law or court on earth that can punish me.

GENTLEMAN   (*his dignity offended.*) Just a moment! I'm not one of your clever lawyers; I'm a moralist. There are still class distinctions.

RICHARD   Words! How can I be responsible if it was all a lie?

GENTLEMAN   That's what we're going to find out. Your hands did not kill because Christian was one second ahead of you. But it is true that you desired Peter's death—yes or no?

RICHARD   True.

GENTLEMAN   And the money you received in exchange was real. Yes or no?

RICHARD   True.

GENTLEMAN   And the remorse that assailed you afterwards, and which brought you to the brink of confession just a moment ago? And the secret hope that Peter Anderson had been an unworthy man, to justify yourself in your own eyes? And the compulsion that drove you here, as it drives all criminals to the scene of the crime? Wasn't it real? It's amazing how many truths a lie can create.

RICHARD   Now I understand. Was that your experiment?

GENTLEMAN   Only the first part: to measure the distance that the creative power of an idea can take a man. But there remains a second more serious part: payment for the guilt.

RICHARD   I'm ready to pay.

GENTLEMAN   With what? With a bit of breast-beating and some tears of repentance? No, my boy; that's an old-fashioned device, and far too easy.

RICHARD   I'll give up all that you gave me. Take your dirty money with you, every penny of it.

GENTLEMAN   That's still not enough. The money hasn't been of any use to you for some time now.

RICHARD   Then what do you intend to do? What did you come for?

GENTLEMAN   Simply to inform you that your contract continues in effect. (*He takes it from his briefcase.*) Here your intention to commit murder is signed and recorded. When "the hour" arrives, I shall present this statement.

RICHARD   (*thinking a moment.*) What does that contract say?

GENTLEMAN   Just a few words, but clear ones. "Richard Jordan agrees to kill a man . . ."

RICHARD   Bloodlessly.

GENTLEMAN   Bloodlessly.

RICHARD   Very well. The best way to liquidate a contract is to fulfill it. I have promised to kill and I shall kill.

GENTLEMAN *(looking at him in surprise.)* Whom?

RICHARD The very one who signed that paper. Think back to the day you arrived at my office. There you found a coward prepared to commit any kind of crime provided he didn't have to witness it. A comfortable dealer in other men's sweat. A man capable of dumping entire harvests into the sea without giving a thought to the hunger of those who produce them. I have been struggling against that man since I came here; I shall fight against him the rest of my life. And the day when not a trace of what I was remains in my soul, that day Richard Jordan will have killed Richard Jordan. Bloodlessly! (THE DEVIL *lowers his head perplexed.*) Now we are both in the world of intent! You weren't prepared for this, were you?

GENTLEMAN Sincerely, no. The one who signed the contract was so different. . . . Who gave you this new strength? Was it the woman?

RICHARD It was the woman. Until I came to this house I didn't really know what a home could be. Until I met Estela I didn't know what a woman is.

GENTLEMAN I rather feared that. Love. . . . That small detail sometimes slips my mind, and it's what always defeats me.

RICHARD What are you waiting for now?

GENTLEMAN Nothing. . . . Now, anything that I might attempt against you would be wasted effort. Take your contract. A pity . . . It was a nice agreement.

RICHARD You poor devil. I hope this hasn't upset you.

GENTLEMAN *(with a display of elegant melancholy.)* Oh, it's not important. In a profession as difficult as mine, you get used to an occasional failure. But rarely one as complete as this. I came to win your soul, and I unintentionally set you on the road to salvation. It's enough to make one retire on the spot! *(He goes slowly toward the garden door; then he stops for a moment.)* Can I ask you a favor . . . friend to friend?

RICHARD Ask it.

GENTLEMAN Don't tell anyone what has happened between us. It always amuses people to see me look ridiculous; and the more hypocritical souls would even be capable of drawing a moral from all this. Do you promise?

RICHARD I promise.

GENTLEMAN Thank you. Good night, Richard . . . Anderson.

He exits. The light becomes normal again. RICHARD *glances at the contract, crumples it in his fist and throws it on the table when he hears the door open.* ESTELA *returns with the appearance of a person who has made a great exertion.*

RICHARD Is there any hope?

ESTELA Who can say! The jagged rock tore into his breast like a knife. But Christian is stronger than the rock itself. Now he's at peace to await whatever comes: life or death. *(She sits down heavily.)* I never imagined that a single word could have so much power!

RICHARD You forgave him?

ESTELA Yes. It seems so little now, yet it was the beginning of a miracle. And when the words fell from my lips like ripe fruit, it was not only

Christian who was at peace again. I felt myself cleaner, stronger, with all the bonds loosened. (*Again we hear the sound of the ship's horn.* ESTELA *stands up startled.*) The signal again. Why are you still here? Your ship is already preparing to sail!

RICHARD   Where would I go? I have just learned that I've lost all my fortune. I have no country that calls me, nor a single friend who waits for me.

ESTELA   But your life is there! I don't understand.

RICHARD   Listen to me, Estela. I'm no longer the stranger who came to buy peaceful sleep with money. Now I'm a man with no more wealth than his hands, just as he came into the world. One of your people. Let me work at your side.

ESTELA   Here? (*Without daring to believe.*) Don't deceive yourself. Do you truly believe that you could get used to this simple way of life?

RICHARD   There is nothing a man is not capable of doing when there is someone to believe in him with love. Don't you know that?

ESTELA   Yes, I know. This is the strength that a woman can give.

RICHARD   It is the only power that can make all the boats go out to sea and plant roses again in the gardens. (*He reaches out and takes her hands.*) Estela . . . your hands are icy; you're trembling.

ESTELA   It's nothing. The first full days of sun the nights are still cold. We'll light the fire together. (*She notices the contract on the table.*) Is this paper of any value?

RICHARD   No. Not any more.

ESTELA *lights the edge of the paper in the lantern flame and kneels down to start the fire.* RICHARD *leans over her. Three long blasts of the ship's horn are heard. The ship is sailing away.*
Curtain.

After the Civil War of 1936–1939, the publication and production of new plays in Spain was severely limited because of censorship and economic stringencies. By 1949, however, important new plays began appearing, and indeed during the 1950's and 1960's Madrid enjoyed as active a theatre as any in Europe.

This theatre produced several outstanding playwrights who have yet to be given their just recognition in the English-speaking world. Four of these playwrights—with works characteristic of the period's varied trends and aspects—are represented in this anthology. Antonio Buero Vallejo and Alfonso Sastre are the unquestioned leaders among writers of serious drama in Spain; José López Rubio is an acknowledged master of serious comedy as well as a prominent translator and director; and Alejandro Casona is the most important and most successful of the Spanish playwrights who continued their careers in exile after the Civil War.

Taken together, the four plays in this volume introduce the English reader to one of Europe's most vigorous theatres, a theatre that until now has been accessible only to specialists and Spanish readers.